KEELE
UNIVERSITY L

INTERVENTION

*External Involvement
in Civil Wars*

INTERVENTION

*External Involvement
in Civil Wars*

Richard Little

MARTIN ROBERTSON

First published in 1975 by Martin Robertson and Company Ltd., 17 Quick Street, London N1 8HL

ISBN O 85520 104 5

Typeset by Trade Linotype Ltd. Birmingham.
Reproduced, printed by photolithography and bound in Britain at The Pitman Press, Bath.

Contents

To my parents

Acknowledgements

I SHOULD like to thank all my colleagues at the University of Lancaster for their patience during the bouts of antisocial behaviour displayed by me while writing this book. I am particularly grateful to Colin Brown, Al Cohan, Martin Edmonds, Reg Harrison, Bob McKinlay, Peter Nailor and especially Philip Reynolds, who have also read and commented upon various sections. Further afield, I should like to thank Chris Mitchell at City University, London, who has always been a source of encouragement and assistance. I should also like to acknowledge John Burton at University College London, together with Percy Corbett and Carey Joynt at Lehigh University, Pennsylvania, former teachers, to whom I continue to owe an intellectual debt. Finally, I should like to thank Wendy Hopfl, who disrupted her family life to type the manuscript, and Lyn Hunter and Jackie Townson who gave invaluable secretarial assistance at critical junctures.

Introduction

RECENT events like the United States' involvement in Vietnam and the invasion of Czechoslovakia by the Soviet Union have generated widespread discussion and debate. Actions of this kind support the contention that intervention constitutes a major feature of the contemporary international system and that adherence to the nonintervention norm which used to regulate inter-state relations has been steadily eroded since the Second World War. Paradoxically, during a period when the literature in international relations has burgeoned, the extensive interest in specific interventionary situations has not been matched by any general theoretical analysis. In 1964 Rosenau asserted that outside the Marxist literature, the interrelationship between civil strife and international affairs has never been subjected to systematic inquiry.[1] The assertion still remains substantially true.[2]

A possible explanation for the neglect is that the concept of intervention cuts across an established academic boundary. Traditionally, political behaviour has been studied along two dimensions: the first examines activity within the state; the second studies relations between states.[3] Only comparatively recently has the interaction between internal and external politics – providing a third dimension – been considered a separate area of interest.[4] This analysis of international responses to civil wars is designed to contribute to the growing literature on this third dimension.

The failure to examine the concept of intervention along the interstate dimension can also be explained, in part, by the dominating influence of the 'paradigm' formed by the realist school of 'power politics', the assumptions of which are reflected in most research in international politics.[5] As a result, at least two biases are persistently displayed. The first is the penchant for examining 'Great Power' relationships in preference to other forms of international interactions; the second is the tendency to explain international relations in terms of the 'billiard-ball' model, which treats states as autonomous, cohesive actors.[6] The conjunction of these two biases leaves little room for the analysis of interventionary situations. From the power politician's perspective, intervention is just another manifestation of the fact that 'weak' states must submit to the power possessed by 'strong' states. Intervention, therefore, does not warrant special attention; it is encompassed by a general theory of power.

The limitations of this viewpoint become apparent when attention is diverted from the international system. Intervention, like conflict, is a form of behaviour which can be identified in all areas of social activity and it can be conceived as an important integrating concept in the social sciences. Theoretical literature on intervention in other disciplines, however, is also sparse, although there is a growing interest in the problems associated with social intervention.[7] Ironically, while international relations specialists have been disturbed by the increase in the volume of international intervention, sociologists have been troubled by the unwillingness of individuals to engage in interpersonal intervention. Some years ago, for example, a journalist went back to the scene of a murder in New York, where a man had spent half an hour killing a young woman. The event took place in a residential area and the journalist discovered that thirty-eight people had witnessed the murder without making any effort to intervene.[8] Some social scientists were shocked by this information and have subsequently tried to find an explanation for what some analysts take to be a general behavioural phenomenon in contemporary Western society.[9] Reluctance of individuals to intervene in conflict situations is certainly not universal. Two anthropologists, for example, observed in an Indian village they call Namhalli, where the broom symbolizes pollution and filth, that when two women begin attacking each other with brooms, the action indicates high-level conflict and calls for immediate third-party intervention.[10] The divergence in the patterns of behaviour displayed in these two examples cannot be explained within a power framework.

This book was written with the conviction that intervention is an important social concept which deserves more attention than it has so far received. While the study reflects a general interest in intervention and the way in which actors respond when confronted by conflict situations, it focuses specifically on the international response to civil war. When there is a high level of interaction between two states, the decision-makers in one must respond to the emergence of civil war in the other. In this study, the responses of British decision-makers to four civil wars are examined and the attitudes and perceptions of the decision-makers are used to illustrate a series of theoretical propositions about the international response to civil war.

These propositions were derived by a process of retroductive inference. This is the normal mode of inference used in scientific research. Science has not been developed on the basis of either inductive or deductive inference, but rather by a method which involves drawing together both forms of reasoning. The result is known as retroduction and it operates whenever the same body of data is used to derive and test a set of hypotheses. There is a continuous feedback process which links theory and observation. It was on the basis of the constant interaction between hypothesis-building and observed data that Galileo, after thirty-five years, finally managed to achieve a satisfactory explanation of gravitational acceleration.[11]

In an attempt to emulate natural science, many social scientists have employed its formal mode of research; they establish a hypothesis, attempt to test it, and the result, be it positive or negative, is then added to what is believed to be an accumulating body of scientific knowledge. What has not been generally appreciated until recently is that a distinction must be drawn between the way a scientist presents a finding to his colleagues and the process used to achieve that finding.[12] The scientific method is always employed in the presentation of research in order to satisfy the principle of verification, but it may have very little to do with the way in which a finding emerged. In practice, the scientist is interested in reconciling theory with observation. The burden of refutation – an admirable philosophical principle – is normally left to other members of the scientific community.

Although the rigorous techniques used by natural scientists for gathering data were not employed in the research on which this study is based, the same inferential approach was adopted. After deliberating on some of the theoretical and empirical literature concerning intervention in a variety of social situations, I formed a general concept of intervention. This concept eliminated many of the connotations applied to the term in international relations, but it clearly included the situation where a state goes to the assistance of one party in a civil war. A series of propositions were then established to explain the process whereby a state intervenes and then withdraws from civil war. These related propositions can be defined as a model of intervention. On the basis of this model, information about British responses to four civil wars was gathered; it revealed certain deficiencies in the model. In an effort to reconcile the theory and the data, the propositions were reformulated to conform with the information which had been collected. In this book the reformulated model is presented and illustrated by the cases on which the revised propositions were based.

In the process of writing it was difficult not to reflect on the substantial alterations which were being made to the original concept and propositions. The intervention of troops in civil war was conceived at first as a form of deviance in the international system, and the model was built round an explanation of why states deviate from established norms and how they minimize the costs of deviance.

The cases failed to support this aspect of the model; it was found that the decision-makers did not perceive their action as deviant. In fact they stressed the importance of the nonintervention norm. Civil wars were recognized as highly unstable and unpredictable situations, and it was seen that as a consequence military intervention represented an extremely risky and hazardous venture, unlikely to bring any tangible benefits to the intervening state. When decision-makers decided to intervene in civil war, their image of civil war in the target state was taken out of focus. The nature of the conflict was redefined, and the troops were sent into the target state without apparently contravening the nonintervention norm. In the revised model, therefore, instead of the intervention response being viewed as a form of deviance, it is depicted as a result of autistic thinking: a systematic distortion of reality.

The factors which precipitated the transformation of the original model are not discussed when the revised model is presented. This is not unusual; retroductive reasoning is not reflected in the presentation of research findings. This has been a source of concern for some scientists. Bondi, for example, asserts that the form and style which must be adopted in a scientific paper do a 'great deal of violence to any true history of one's thinking'. His solution to this problem is that scientists should come into direct contact with one another, so that they can talk about things which they are 'not allowed' to say in their papers.[13]

This is, no doubt, an admirable sentiment, but it is not very practical. There does seem to be a case for making more explicit the process whereby a set of findings have materialized. But there are considerable difficulties associated with any attempt to present a 'true history of one's thinking'. Retracing steps is often easier said than done and the result may not necessarily be illuminating. Moreover the process may simply confuse the reader. Attempts to explain the theory of relativity, for example, are often rendered unintelligible if the explanation is fitted into its historical context.[14]

Despite these problems, it was felt that some attempt should be made in this book to explain the way in which the concept of intervention and the model of the interventionary situation were modified after the empirical investigation had been carried out. In order to avoid confusion, discussion about the delimitation of the concept is restricted to the first chapter, and the analysis of the model's transformation is reserved for the concluding chapter. Between these two chapters, making up the body of the text, is an elaboration of the model of the international response to civil war.

CHAPTER 1

A General Concept of Intervention

INTERVENTION is a ubiquitous social phenomenon. Actions varying from the donation of foreign aid to the use of military force are described as intervention in the international system, while intervention in the domestic system extends from financial support for private industry to measures introducing wage restraint. At the individual level social workers intervene in family relationships, policemen intervene in brawls and parents intervene in the lives of their children. The use of the word is prodigious even when it is restricted to political relationships, and it has been calculated that it is one of the terms most frequently employed by political commentators.[1]

The pervasive character of intervention places it in the same category as conflict, its diversity challenging social scientists who wish to identify order in the social world. They assume that conflict exhibits general patterns in all areas of social interaction, but assert that only if a general theory is formed can behaviour in different areas be compared.[2] The emergence of general systems theory and its application to the social sciences encourages this type of thinking, which also reflects a desire to invalidate the empiricist's claim that observation is the first task to be undertaken in social science.

Unlike conflict, intervention has never generated much research at the theoretical level. This study was intended to help fill the gap – examining a series of interventions in the international system by using a concept which could form the basis for a general theory of intervention. Disciplines often develop specific concepts which cannot be extended to other areas; this reduces the possibility of identifying isomorphic relationships. An attempt is made here to formulate an interdisciplinary concept of intervention. As will be explained, the attempt fails; a more limited concept is accepted and the utility of the study for developing a general theory is consequently reduced.

THE PARADOX OF CONCEPTUALIZATION

Once all the connotations associated with intervention have been taken into account, it is apparent that the word itself denotes very little. Like many important terms used very frequently, we find on closer inspection that it possesses no accepted technical meaning. Words like 'power', 'personality', 'communication' and 'conflict' fall into the same category. A definition of 'intervention' wide enough to take in all the meanings attached to the word will be masked by imprecision.

On occasions it is argued that a concept is so basic to an area of knowledge that it can be defined only in terms of itself. Biologists, for example, have stipulated that it is neither necessary nor possible to define the notion of 'cell', which underlies most biological research; they can work with the concept and, furthermore, explicate the nature of other concepts, like 'tissue' and 'bone', on the basis of the undefined notion. By analogy, it is argued that progress can be made in linguistics by assuming that the concept 'sentence' is understood.[3]

No such assumption can be made in the case of intervention. The absence of a definition does not imply that there is a professional understanding of the concept. Quite the contrary. It is just a word, not a concept, and some means has to be found of moving from the word to a concept. The transition is a complex methodological procedure which inevitably confronts the 'paradox of conceptualization'. The paradox asserts that while a theory cannot be formed without a concept, by the same token a concept cannot be formed without a theory. So it is necessary to have an understanding of the concept before it is formed.[4] The paradox denies the possibilities of forming a concept on an inductive basis. Because there are so many connotations to the word 'intervention', this position is accepted: an examination of all forms of behaviour identified as intervention will not help to elucidate a concept. Certain *a priori* assumptions have to be made and many connotations associated with the word must be eliminated if a clearly defined concept is to emerge.

One way of circumventing, although not of solving the paradox, is to accept a definition which has already been formulated. In international relations a systematic attempt has been made to form a definition: intervention is identified with a type of behaviour which 'constitutes a sharp break with the then-existing forms *and* whenever it is directed at changing or preserving the structure of the political authority in the target society'.[5] The formulation is designed to exclude activity like the donation of foreign aid (an important consideration because intervention is often extended to cover most foreign policy activity) and to eliminate the need to examine the motives for intervention.

On·both counts the definition is unsatisfactory. Behaviour such as the donation of foreign aid does fall within the boundary of this definition and the need to examine motivation is not eliminated. For example Marshall Plan Aid supplied by the United States to Europe after the Second World War constituted a sharp break with the existing pattern of behaviour, but whether it aimed at preserving the political authority structures of the European states can be verified only by examining the motives of the American decision-makers. From this perspective, the definition remains too broad, and since it is established in the context of the international system, the definition also fails to provide the basis from which a general theory can emerge. It cannot be used to examine behaviour in other areas. So from this perspective the definition is too narrow.

Despite the failure of this definition to resolve the problem of concept formation, an examination of other discussions about intervention in the international system is instructive. Two broad approaches can be identified. In the first, Morgenthau argues: 'From the time of the ancient Greeks to this day, some states have found it advantageous to intervene in the affairs of other states on behalf of their own interests and against the latter's will.'[6] This interpretation reflects Morgenthau's view of international politics; intervention is defined as a conflict relationship between two states and analysed in terms of power, with one state exercising control over the other.

Another exponent of the 'realist' school of politics – Thucydides – provides a second and very different approach to the analysis of intervention. He argues that during the Peloponnesian War, when instability prevailed throughout the Hellenic World, there were

> . . . rival parties in every state – democratic leaders trying to bring in the Athenians, and oligarchs trying to bring in the Spartans. In peace-time there would have been no excuse and no desire for calling them in, but in time of war, when each party could always count upon an alliance which would do harm to its opponents and at the same time strengthen its own position, it became a natural thing for anyone who wanted a change of government to call in help from outside.[7]

This model of intervention is more complex; it establishes four distinct parties and explains the intervention in terms of violence going on in the bipolar international system. But if the conditions of either bipolarity or violence are removed, then the explanation offered by Thucydides can no longer operate.

These are two very different conceptions of intervention. Morgenthau identifies a 'push-theory', which concentrates on the motivation of the intervening actor when explaining intervention; Thucydides identifies a 'pull-theory', which refers the intervention response back to actors operating in the target state. Despite the potential for controversy centred on these two divergent theories, there has been little research carried out on inter-

vention in international relations. This is all the more surprising because
during the 1950s and 1960s intervention became an increasingly prominent
feature of the international system.

Three main factors have been used to explain this increasing intervention: the proliferation of nation states, most of which were not considered
to be capable of maintaining their own independence; the existence of a
sharp ideological cleavage between the two 'super-powers', which precipitated attempts to gain support from new states; and, finally, the production
of nuclear weapons, which eliminated the possibility of war between the two
major actors and encouraged them to employ subversive tactics.
Traditional distinctions between international and domestic politics – which
justified the emergence of international politics as an independent discipline – began to break down in the face of these developments. The state-
centric model used in the analysis of the subject cannot contain such
changes, for it is premised on the assumption that states are independent,
antonomous actors. For the same reason, the model cannot be successfully
used in an analysis of intervention.

Morgenthau, who has done much to propagate the utility and efficacy
of the state-centric model, can define intervention only in terms of dyadic
interaction between two states, accepting that it is a form of behaviour
which extends beyond the normal diplomatic pattern of exchange. Behaviourally oriented writers have attempted a more radical accomodation to
developments in the contemporary international system, with the idea of
'penetration', which postulates that state boundaries are no longer imper-
meable. It is contrasted with the billiard-ball or state-centric model and is
designed to encompass behaviour which the traditional model fails to
embrace.[8]

Superficially it provides a fresh orientation, but it has not succeeded in
generating any new interest in concepts like intervention, which are
incompatible with the billiard-ball model. On reflection, the failure is not
surprising because penetration provides only an extension to the state-
centric conception of the international system. If anything it concentrates
attention on 'Great Power' behaviour; penetration stresses that the 'Great
Powers' can control the domestic politics of weak states, which is hardly a
new idea. During the 1970s criticism has been levelled against the concept.
It is argued that the ability of the 'Great Powers' to penetrate the domestic
political system of other states has been considerably over-estimated and
the potential which did exist has diminished.[9]

The model established by Thucydides circumvents the power assumptions made by Morgenthau and provides a link between inter- and intra-
state politics. Thucydides shows that intervention can be defined as a
response to a stimulus and provides an interesting basis for developing a
theory of intervention. But in the form he presents, it is restricted in its
application to a bipolar international system in which the two international

denoting knowledge gained independent of experience

actors are linked to two intra-state actors. His conception of intervention can be retained and generalized if the number of actors is reduced to three. On an *a priori* basis it is stipulated that the triad forms the most useful structure with which to examine intervention in all areas of social activity. In a triad two actors, by conflict or cooperation, create a stimulus to which a response from a third actor can be partial or impartial. So four distinct situations, all associated by connotation with the word 'intervention', are contained by the triad.

In the first an actor responds impartially to cooperative interaction between two other actors. A father, for example, may intervene when he observes that his daughter is becoming friendly with a boy of whom he disapproves. The stimulus is clearly cooperative and the response can be considered impartial since it will not be desired by either the boy or the girl. In the second situation a stimulus created by conflict between two actors precipitates an impartial response. This may take the form of a physical interposition by a third person in the case of violent conflict between two individuals, while in a communal conflict, armed force may be employed in order to separate two groups. When force is not used, the form of an impartial response changes and the third party is often described as an arbitrator or mediator. His task is to find a mutually acceptable solution to the conflict. In some instances an arbitrator favours one side to the conflict, but he can still be considered impartial if the parties agree initially to accept his decision.

Intervention takes on a very different appearance when the third party displays partiality by forming an alliance or commitment with one of the actors creating the stimulus. In the third situation, where the stimulus is provided by cooperative interaction, such a commitment may be a source of conflict. If, for example, an actor establishes a preferential trading agreement with one of two traditional trading partners, the response may have a disturbing effect on the established pattern of interaction. In the fourth situation conflict between two actors forms the stimulus and a commitment by the third actor to one side of the conflict forms the response. The United States entry into the First World War is often described as intervention.

Despite the common structure, the behavioural patterns and attitudes of the three actors in these four cases are quite distinct. To establish a relationship between the orientation of the mediator and the state which joins a war, or between the competitive trading state and the irate father, necessitates working at a high level of abstraction. General theory is useful if it can isolate isomorphic relationships, but at this stage there does not seem to be any real theoretical advantage to be gained from searching for a link between such different forms of behaviour. It was considered preferable to concentrate on one of the four situations. For reasons which relate to a later refinement of the concept, it was decided to focus attention on the fourth situation, where an actor responds partially to a stimulus created by two conflicting actors.

Even in this delimited form, the concept can still describe three distinct behavioural patterns. The first involves three actors which are similarly constituted – such as three individuals or three firms. The nature of the situation changes in the second case, where the third party is distinguished from the other two in terms of status – a parent may assist a child who is fighting a friend, a government may help to finance one of two competing firms, or an international organization may support one state involved in a dispute. In a third situation which can be discerned, an actor is divided – by civil war in a state, two factions in a trade union, or divorce in a family – and a second actor is confronted by the possibility that the existing dyadic pattern of interaction can no longer be maintained. In that event a triadic relationship must be established.

In an analysis of activity in the international system the need to make a distinction along these lines has long been recognized, although not in this precise formulation. For fifty years, Lord John Russell, an important British Secretary of State for Foreign Affairs, argued that intervention 'has been wholly perverted from its original meaning by the application of the term intervention not merely to interference in domestic disorders and disputes of a foreign state, but to interference to prevent one foreign state from crushing by arms any other state'.[10] The quotation illustrates that while the importance of the triad has been acknowledged in the analysis of international relations, there is a preference to restrict the term intervention to foreign involvement in domestic politics and, because of the predominant state-centric view of the world, intervention is thereby defined as a two-party conflict.

If the concept of intervention is restricted to the third behavioural pattern – where one actor goes to the assistance of a unit contained within a divided or bifurcated actor – then it is possible to integrate the dyadic and triadic conceptions of intervention. Confronted by a *bifurcated actor*, a second actor will have to modify the established dyadic pattern of interaction to take account of the bifurcation. The actor can either form a relationship with both units – a response defined as nonintervention; or establish a commitment with one side of the bifurcated actor – a response defined as intervention. It is this conception which is used to characterize an interventionary situation in this study. With the implementation of an intervention response or a nonintervention response, an interventionary situation is established; dyadic interaction becomes triadic. It is also stipulated that the emergence of an interventionary situation, involving three actors instead of two, constitutes a system change. The intervention stimulus precipitates change rather than transformation of the system because it is assumed that at this stage it is possible for the original dyadic pattern of interaction to be restored. System change persists through a phase which is terminated when either the split within the bifurcated actor is institutionalized or a new dyadic pattern of interaction is initiated. At this level of abstraction it may appear that transformation occurs when two distinct actors emerge from the bifurcated actor, while a re-established dyadic pattern of interaction denotes a restoration of the original system. But when the level of abstraction is lowered, and the nature of the actors and their interactions is specified, such an assertion cannot be made; it is difficult to establish a conception of transformation which can be applied in different areas of social activity.

When bifurcation occurs in a marriage, for example, and there is a threat of separation between husband and wife, another couple may attempt to play an impartial role or they may intervene. In either event, if there is a reconciliation, the original dyadic pattern of interaction can still be re-established. If divorce occurs, then independent relationships can be established with the two new actors, and the system is transformed. But in the cases of both reconciliation and divorce, during the period of system change, the relationships with the third party may become so acrimonious, either because of the intervention response or the nonintervention response, that a future relationship with either member of the bifurcated actor cannot be maintained. In this event, the original system is not transformed but dissolved.

A similar analysis cannot be sustained when the interventionary situation involves states operating in the international system. At this level, the context of the interventionary situation has a critical effect on whether system restoration or transformation occurs. In the first instance, if a bifurcated state is reintegrated, it does not necessarily mean that the original situation is restored; a new regime may emerge from the conflict with a radically different ideological orientation, and the former pattern of dyadic interaction may be replaced by a completely different pattern. The original system is not restored; it is transformed. A new pattern of interaction may develop in the case of individual relationships, but this is a second-order, rather than a first-order consequence of the interventionary situation.[11] The idea of system dissolution is also precluded in international politics; states cannot avoid some minimal level of contact with each other in the international system. Even the denial of recognition for a prolonged period is a difficult policy to sustain.

Some fundamental problems are therefore encountered in an attempt to establish a clearly defined concept of an interventionary situation which can apply in all areas of social interaction. The concept which emerges here is tailored to an application at the level of the international system. It cannot be applied in all areas and this reduces its usefulness in the task of developing a general theory. However, this analysis suggests that it is not possible to move towards a general theory until more is known about specific types of behaviour. For the purpose of this study, it is stipulated

bifurcated
— forking into two branches

that: *An interventionary situation exists when an actor responds to an intervention stimulus. The stimulus emerges when conflict develops between the units in a bifurcated actor, creating a potential for system transformation. Maintaining a relationship with one side of a bifurcated actor constitutes an intervention response; maintaining a relationship with both sides of a bifurcated actor constitutes a nonintervention response.* On the basis of this formulation it is possible to proceed with an analysis of the interventionary situation at the level of the international system.

THE INTERVENTIONARY SITUATION IN THE INTERNATIONAL SYSTEM

Bifurcation, conflict and the potential for system transformation are the three conditions necessary to describe an intervention stimulus. The bifurcation of a state occurs when there are two authority structures operating within a single political system. Sometimes this represents a constitutional arrangement, for example, the complex relationship which existed in Great Britain with Northern Ireland, before the suspension of the Stormont Government. Often, however, the two authorities are competing for power, as in the case of the National Liberation Front and the Saigon Government in the Vietnam War.

Between these two extremes, there is the ambiguous situation which exists when an election occurs within a state. On the one hand there is a single authority structure and an election determines which party should occupy it. On the other hand elections can heighten divisions within a society and sharpen areas of conflict; they can undermine political stability and may be followed by a coup or civil war.

When bifurcation represents a mutually acceptable distribution of power within a state, then destructive conflict is unlikely to arise unless developments reduce the acceptability of the established power distribution. When the distribution is unacceptable, an element of conflict is structured into the situation and this is as true for an election as for a civil war. Both contain the potential for system transformation. The emergence of a new actor has been represented as a form of system transformation, and a regime change which alters the existing pattern of interactions with other states in the system can have the same effect. The transfer of power to the Bolshevik Government in 1917 illustrates internal changes which had major ramifications for the international system. Regime change as the result of elections, for example Chile in 1970, can also precipitate system transformation.

The existence of an intervention stimulus requires an external actor to modify its relationship with the bifurcated actor. An election requires adjustment to existing behaviour to accommodate for a possible regime change. Following the announcement of the 1970 General Election in Britain, for example, the Soviet Union was criticized when the incumbent Prime Minister was invited to visit Moscow after the election. While it is not difficult for an external actor to modify its behaviour so as to remain uninvolved in an election, it is argued that no external actor can remain uninvolved in a civil war because inaction provides tacit support for the stronger party.[12] In this study it is stipulated that a policy of nonintervention is not synonymous with inaction, for it requires a commitment to be made to both parties.

There is a wide variety of intervention responses which operate in the international system. They can be classified as coercive, involving the use of military force; utilitarian, such as the application of economic sanctions; or identitive, for example, spreading propaganda.[13] An alternative classification, related to military intervention into civil wars, identifies three stages: first, the provision of material and financial assistance; second, a limited participation in military operations; and finally, the stage where the intervening force becomes the dominant element in the war effort.[14] Both these classifications suggest the possibility of building an escalation ladder. Eight possible steps are established.

On the bottom step, there is verbal intervention response. Words are relatively cheap and decision-makers generally restrict intervention responses to this level. But de Gaulle's fracas with the Canadian Government following his comments on the Quebec Liberation Movement in 1969 illustrates the importance which can be attached to verbal support. A major problem with such a response is that the audience may infer more than is implied. Hungarians involved in the 1956 uprising, for example, were convinced that they would receive assistance from the United States on the basis of broadcasts over Radio Free Europe. No commitment of this sort was ever made – although states do tend to encourage ambiguity in this area. In 1970, for example, while the Secretary of State informed a conference of American ambassadors to Africa in Kinshasa that the United States would identify with the 'unfinished business' of winning political freedom for black populations living under white minority rule, the President issued a statement on foreign policy indicating that there was going to be support for the South African regime.

The second level of response relates to *de jure* recognition. If certain governments deny recognition to a regime in a bifurcated state, then there can be major ramifications for the stability of the regime. After Chief Jonathan of Lesotho suspended the constitution when he lost the election in 1970, there was a threat that he might go to South Africa for military support if the British Government failed to recognize the new regime, because of the encouragement which opposition groups would derive from the British position. Decision-makers take the issue of recognition very seriously and it can lead to internal friction. When the republican regime took control in the Yemen in 1962, for example, the Foreign Office in Britain favoured recognition but there was opposition from the Colonial Office and the War Office, and the regime was not recognized.[15]

The donation of foreign aid provides the third step on the ladder. Economic support for a non-legitimized regime may precipitate internal conflict, but the action only constitutes an intervention response when decision-makers perceive the possible emergence of the intervention stimulus. As the communist threat in Latin America waned during the 1960s, for example, so did the American interest in aid donation. It is claimed that Kennedy used to say that Castro was the 'true father of the Alliance for Progress'. This perception of a possible intervention stimulus is also important if the supply of arms is to be defined as an intervention response. On this fourth step, arms supply forms a clear intervention response if the policy is introduced when a stimulus already exists, as in the case of the Nigerian Civil War, but the policy still constitutes an intervention response if there is an intention to prevent the development of internal military conflict. This was the reason for American aid to Thailand during the Vietnam War.

Only a limited number of countries can operate on the fifth step of the intervention response ladder. It emerges when a government permits its territory to be used as a sanctuary area – an essential concept in guerrilla warfare theory. When Zambia was used as a sanctuary area by guerrilla movements operating in Rhodesia after the Unilateral Declaration of Independence it gave rise to threats of military retaliation. But it is not always clear just how much control a government has on this issue; the Lebanese Government, for example, persistently disclaims responsibility for the Palestinian guerrilla movements operating against Israel.

The final three steps on the intervention response ladder all involve direct military assistance. Of least significance is the threat to send volunteers into a situation. During the French and British invasion of Egypt in 1956, an offer to send thousands of communist volunteers was made to Egypt, but this step seems to reflect propaganda rather than policy. Much more significant are external military manoeuvres which can take place on land, sea or air. In 1968, military manoeuvres on the borders of Czechoslovakia preceded the occupation. On a smaller scale, Equatorial Guinea declared a state of emergency in 1969 when the Spanish Government sent a gunboat to Bata, an action which was perceived as an intervention response.

Finally there is direct military involvement; it represents the last step on the intervention response ladder. It is often characterized by escalation, as the French involvement in Chad illustrates. In September 1968, the French Government sent a garrison of 1000 men to Chad for the purpose of 'logistic support' against a group of 'rebels'. By April 1969 they were reinforced by several hundred paratroopers and 350 military advisers. A further 650 troops were sent the same year and by 1970 there were 2500 French troops in Chad. It was 1971 before they were removed.

Although the order in which these responses are arranged may be questioned, decision-makers are conscious that responses can be represented on a scale or escalation ladder and that there are critical threshold points. It was for this reason that American decision-makers were very anxious that the personnel in Vietnam before 1962 should be called 'advisers' although it was known that they were involved in tasks which could not be called advisory. Similar distinctions were developed during the build-up to the 1970 invasion of Laos. It is also now clear that during the Korean War the Chinese issued 'signals' indicating that there was a threshold to American action, the crossing of which they would not tolerate.[16] These signals were unintentionally ignored. To prevent a similar occurrence during the Vietnam War, the United States deliberately established thresholds as a means of providing signals to the North Vietnamese and the Chinese. The inauguration and the cessation of bombing were used for this purpose. Psychologists have closely examined the relationship between signals and thresholds but there has been little research on this area in international relations.[17]

Despite this absence of research in the area of signals and thresholds, it is possible to envisage what might be called an 'intervention field', with different types of intervention stimuli displayed on one axis and the range of responses on the other. It is impossible to give a detailed analysis of the field but there is a very clear threshold point defined by both axes; it occurs when a civil war creates the stimulus and the response takes the form of military involvement. Although this represents only a small segment of the intervention field, issues which are present at all earlier thresholds become critical at this particular point. For this reason, and because it is not possible to examine all the threshold points which exist along the two axes, the subsequent analysis is restricted to this segment of the field. Since most major issues concerning an intervention stimulus and response are accentuated at this threshold, the analysis may well have direct relevance for the analysis of other thresholds.

THE RESEARCH DESIGN

If the continuing debate on methodology in international relations is sometimes misguided in its focus of attack, it does illuminate the strengths and weaknesses of the available approaches to the discipline. The decision to concentrate on military intervention into civil wars precipitates the need for a research strategy which will reflect the qualities of whichever approach is selected. One important approach recommends the use of aggregate data. The information in L. F. Richardson's *The Statistics of Deadly Quarrels* can be used to draw up a list of military interventions into civil wars during a 125-year period, but in doing so, certain critical questions about the definition of the stimulus and the response are side-stepped (see Appendix 2).

Critics of the behavioural approach to political science have justifiably argued that there has been a failure in the past to pay sufficient attention to the actor's definition of the situation.[18] This study is centred on the definition and, as a consequence, an aggregate approach is not employed.[19] In the case of an interventionary situation, there are three actors to con-sider, but the critical definition rests with the actor which implements the intervention response. Partly because of the ease of access to source material, but, more important, because Richardson's statistics indicate that Britain played a part in over half of the interventions during the period surveyed, this book concentrates on the British definition of the interven-tionary situation.

A detailed analysis of all the cases of interventionary situations is not undertaken; instead two criteria are adopted to select a limited number of cases. The first stipulates the need to have each of the four possible types of interventionary situation in which an actor can be involved represented by an individual case. The types of interventionary situation are: 1) a *unilateral intervention response*, where the actor implements an unaided intervention response; 2) a *collective intervention response*, where the actor implements an intervention response in conjunction with other actors; 3) a *unilateral nonintervention response*, where the actor implements a non-intervention response in the face of an intervention response introduced by another actor; 4) a *collective nonintervention response*, where all actors implement a nonintervention response.

The second criterion stipulates that the cases must be selected from different points in time. Only in this way is it possible to start the evalua-tion of two opposed views on the use of historical data in international relations theory. The first reflects the relativist position adopted by the school of historical sociology, which argues that current theorizing pays too much attention to the contemporary period: it is claimed that an analysis of historical data will demonstrate that this tendency is misleading because every concept used has a different meaning depending upon con-texts of time and space.[20] The other view argues that there are certain processes which will always be presented in international relations and that if the appropriate level of analysis is identified, the use of historical data will reveal the nature of these processes.[21]

These two criteria are reflected in the choice of the four cases which are examined in this book; each type of interventionary situation is represented and the cases are dispersed over a wide time-span. The Portuguese Civil War, in which the British alone pursued an intervention response, provides the stimulus for the case of a unilateral intervention response (1826–8); the Russian Civil War, in which the British pursued an intervention response in conjunction with France, Japan and the United States, provides the stimulus for the case of a collective intervention response (1917–20); the Spanish Civil War, in which the British nonintervention response was confronted by an intervention response initiated by Germany and Italy, provides the stimulus for the case of a unilateral nonintervention response (1936–9); and the American Civil War, in which the British with others pursued a nonintervention response, provides the stimulus for the case of a collective nonintervention response (1861–5).

The information gathered on the four cases does not reflect the use of quantitative or rigorous data-collection techniques. But a model of an interventionary situation established before the research began did dictate the areas of information selected. It was an intuitive model (although the intuition was to some extent informed by earlier research on the Egyptian intervention into the Yemen and European intervention into Latin America during the nineteenth century). The information collected showed that the propositions which made up the model were inaccurate.

It is a revised version of the model, based on the information about the cases which is presented in the chapters which follow; the propositions are illustrated by the relevant section from each case. This eliminates the possibility of a continuous narrative account, but this disadvantage is offset by the advantage of being able to examine the cases on a comparative basis. (In Appendix 1, a short description of each case can be found.)

The revised model hinges on the idea that decision-makers are influenced by their perception of norms in the decentralized international system. Decision-makers are aware of a norm which proscribes military intervention into civil wars (Chapter 2). This affects their reaction to foreign civil wars. When a *nonintervention* response is implemented, the decision-makers define the intervention stimulus as a civil war; when an *intervention* response is implemented, some information described the situation as a civil war, but its credibility is down-graded as the intervention response is initiated (Chapter 3). Before the intervention response, the situation is also defined in some information received by the decision-makers as an international conflict. This information is brought into focus during the decision to intervene. In the case of unilateral nonintervention, the British decision-makers oscillate between two divergent images of the situation. So, the acceptance of an unambiguous image of a civil war only exists in the case of collective nonintervention (Chapter 4). In all interventionary situations, there is an active attempt by decision-makers to get other actors in the international system to accept the image which they eventually employ (Chapter 5).

Almost all Cabinet members support both the intervention and nonintervention responses which are implemented, but the nature of the consensus is different in each case (Chapter 6). The divergences have a significant impact on subsequent decision-making. They precipitate post-decision rationalization among some Cabinet members. Only in the case of the collective nonintervention response is there no element of rationalization (Chapter 7). A psychological commitment to a response builds up among those decision-makers who experience the need to rationalize the initial decision. This creates an important division among Cabinet members (Chapter 8). Decision-makers who are not engaged in a process of continuous rationalization eventually redefine the situation which precipitated the emergence of the intervention stimulus. A consensus forms around this group and a dyadic pattern of interaction with the bifurcated actor is restored (Chapter 9).

In the final chapter, the model described in this book is compared with the model used to gather the original information. There is a discussion of why the cases did not conform with some of the initial premises and there is an assessment of how the new propositions would fare if used in an analysis of the contemporary international system, where it is often claimed that the norm of nonintervention, so important in the explication of the model, is no longer accepted.

CHAPTER 2

The Nonintervention Norm

INTERNATIONAL actors have always expressed concern about the propensity displayed by states for intervening in one another's domestic affairs – a persistent feature of the international system. When states do intervene, attention is drawn to the norm which proscribes intervention in the domestic jurisdiction of a target state. The existence of the norm is widely acknowledged. In the Covenant of the League of Nations and the Charter of the United Nations, it is accepted that while the organizations have the right to regulate inter-state behaviour, intra-state behaviour is inviolable. The Charter contains an element of ambiguity because it allows the organization to intervene in those domestic situations which threaten international peace and security; but the obligation of the state, as opposed to the international institution, to refrain from intervention is reasserted in a General Assembly Resolution which declares that intervention is inadmissible and that there is a duty to protect the independence and sovereignty of all states.[1] The Resolution is accepted almost unanimously by members of the international system, yet deviations from the nonintervention norm continue to occur.

These deviations present both the realist and idealist schools of thought in international relations with an analytical problem, since both approaches identify the state as an autonomous, cohesive and rational actor. Intervention undermines this conception, for it presupposes that one of the states is no longer independent or sovereign; it is consequently treated as a special condition in the context of the international system. The two schools offer very different explanations of intervention; and they reflect conflicting assessments about the role which norms play in the international system. The conflict is the product of two divergent philosophical perspectives and before stipulating the way in which the nonintervention norm is analysed in this study, it is necessary to examine these existing perspectives in order to assess the utility of a normative approach to the study of international relations.

15

Two perspectives on the interventionary situation

A realist view of the international system can be traced back to Thucydides, who argues that behind all the reasons given for the outbreak of the Peloponnesian War lies the unalterable factor of power. The belief that international relations are synonymous with power politics has persisted ever since. The international system is depicted as anarchic and devoid of rules which can guide decision-makers. Machiavelli relates state behaviour to the animal kingdom: an essentially anomic world where behaviour is governed by force and deception; the Prince must be a fox to recognize traps and a lion to frighten the wolves. Such an analogy is not necessary for Hobbes, who argues that while the pernicious aspects of human nature can be controlled within a state, under the guidance of a strong leader, the absence of a sovereign authority in the international system requires the state to be in a continuous 'posture of war', thus creating a permanent state of insecurity among all actors in the international system.

From this perspective, a sharp distinction must be drawn between human activity in the domestic system and in the international system. Order in the domestic system is ensured because of an established framework of rules which regulate behaviour within the state; this has been considered a defining characteristic of the political system. It is argued that a similar structure of norms cannot be observed to influence the behaviour of states; for this reason, and also because of the absence of an authoritative institution which can enforce norms and influence the allocation of values and resources, it is not possible to consider the existence of an international political system. The normative order of the state system is contrasted with the anarchy which prevails in the international system, and this view encourages references to the unorganized and irresponsible nature of international behaviour.

But the belief that the absence of a normative order precludes the possibility of some kind of order in the international system is strongly contested by the realist school of 'power politics' in international relations, which maintains that power and not the existence of rules is central to the analysis of order in the international system. In its most clearly defined form, 'power politics' asserts that states can only expect to survive if they engage in a constant struggle for power, and this feature of state behaviour is consequently the dominant characteristic of the international system.

The state is thus depicted as an actor pursuing its own self-interest in an amoral society without regard for the interests of other states and owing allegiance to no authority. In a system made up of such actors, order is derived from a balance of power in which the nature of the balance reflects the existing distribution of power. If two actors are disproportionately

more powerful than the other actors, then order within the system will be maintained on the basis of a bipolar structure of power. When a rough equality of power exists among the actors, then a more complex alliance system will emerge and the balance of power is defined by the shifting distribution of power among the actors. Far from denying the existence of order in the international system, the analysis of power politics reflects a preoccupation with the concept.

The system of order maintained by a balance of power includes the possibility of war, and if there is a threat to the continued existence of one party, a third party will go to its assistance in order to maintain the balance. In this way instability within the international system is minimized by the balance of power. But the balance of power is not equipped to contend with instability within the state; such instability undermines the power of that state and creates an area of uncertainty in the international system. According to the realist, if the unstable state falls within the sphere of influence of a hegemonic state, which perceives that the uncertainty is undermining security or stability within its sphere, then the hegemonic state will intervene. Other states may also contemplate intervention if they perceive that their power position will be enhanced by exploiting the area of uncertainty. From this perspective, therefore, states do not intervene for ideological, sentimental, moral or other non-power reasons.

On occasions a state miscalculates and its power position will deteriorate as a result of the intervention, but this does not invalidate the power orientation of the original decision. By the same token, if an actor fails to intervene in a situation and retrospectively it can be shown that such a policy would have been advantageous, this apparent rectitude cannot be attributed to an acceptance of the nonintervention norm; states do make reference to the norm but only as a diplomatic device. In the absence of primary documentation, these arguments are irrefutable because of their tautological formulation. This, no doubt, partially explains the attraction of the realist approach and, on the basis of its assumptions, diametrically opposed interpretations of the same event can be sustained.[2]

A very different perspective on the nature of relations within the international system has been put forward in the idealist school of thought. Here it is argued that states operate in the context of an international society which presupposes the existence of international norms and where states do accept limitations on their independence and sovereignty by operating within the constraints created by these norms. In order to sustain and justify this perspective, the idealists adopt a very different line of argument from the realists. The initial starting point is the same; the state is conceived as an independent, cohesive, autonomous actor operating in the international system. It is also accepted that there is no authoritative institution in the international system. States nevertheless do observe norms, it is asserted, and so they must voluntarily limit their own freedom of action. This restraint does not arise from altruism, according to the idealists, because it is also argued that states are rational, self-interested actors. The limits to a state's freedom of action exist because decision-makers conform to Locke's conception of man; the conception is grounded in the belief that the dominant principle of human nature is reason and, in consequence, individuals will subordinate their actions to establish rules.

The purpose of international norms, therefore, is to assist in the development and maintenance of an ordered international society; a goal which is generally accepted by most states. They abide by the norms to promote this order. One of the cardinal rules which underlies the conception of an international society is the nonintervention norm. It is on the basis of this norm that the sovereignty and independence of states are maintained. The norm imposes an important series of rights and obligations on states. It means, for example, that if a citizen goes to another state and violates the law he can expect to be fairly tried by the laws of that land. Only if these laws are not fairly operated can he anticipate that his own state may provide some sort of assistance. Without a conception of international society, a basic principle of this kind cannot function.

Internal instability within a state immediately threatens the fabric of international society. If the sovereignty and independence of a state begins to break down, then other states can no longer rely on it to fulfil its obligations to international society. In the first instance, the nonintervention norm acts as a palliative measure, cordoning off the unstable state from the rest of international society, providing the state with the opportunity to resolve its problems, and discouraging other states from internationalizing the problem. But the effects of domestic instability may still 'spill over' and destabilize the international system. When this happens, some form of change in established behaviour patterns may have to be sanctioned. 'Spill-over' becomes almost inevitable when domestic instability develops into civil war. At that point, the nonintervention norm is superseded by a metanorm of nonintervention which permits actors in the international system to acknowledge the existence of a second authority structure in the target state.

The analysis of norms in international relations

For reasons associated with the historical development of the discipline, these rival perspectives on the study of international relations – idealism and realism – have never entered into direct competition. After the First World War, when international relations was first established as an independent area of study, the idealist approach came to dominate in the English-speaking countries; most teaching and research was carried out in the areas of international law and institutions. The total failure of this approach to anticipate or explain the outbreak of the Second World War and the subsequent rivalry between the United States and the Soviet Union gave substance to the realist charge that idealism reflects utopian ideas and, moreover, that its prescriptions fail to take account of the essential elements which dictate the nature of behaviour in the international system. In 1939 when E. H. Carr produced his seminal work *The Twenty Years' Crisis*, he maintained that it was written to counteract a twenty years' total neglect of the factor of power. The realist framework seemed better suited to analyse the events of this period and, as a consequence, the discipline came to be directed by the realist approach. Its influence has remained pervasive, and realist assumptions are firmly embedded in most recent behavioural literature.

If the element of power was neglected during the period before the Second World War, there has been a comparable neglect of the normative factor in the subsequent period. The study of norms has been relegated to the field of international law. Until recently, this has meant that the analysis of norms has been severely retarded. International lawyers have been unwilling to break away from the conception of law reflected in the domestic legal system. Here, law is identified with a body of rules which are authoritatively established and enforced. Since there is no similar authority in the international system which can carry out these functions, the reality or existence of international law is often questioned, even by international lawyers themselves. There is a tendency to consider that the normative order in the international system is at an inchoate stage of development.

The weaknesses of this approach are starting to become apparent as some international lawyers have begun to adopt a more behavioural orientation to their research. Much of this research reflects a sociological perspective. In particular, international lawyers acknowledge the importance of the distinction between institutional and noninstitutional norms. Institutional norms are imposed from above and are maintained by the threat and employment of punishments. Noninstitutional norms, mores and folkways, as Sumner called them, are generated within any informal group. Sociologists assert that norms can emerge as the result of interaction within the group itself, without the assistance of a superior authority, and are maintained by the group on the basis of punishments and rewards. The norms allow the individuals in the group to stabilize and structure their relationships. Research in this area gives some support to the idealists' assertion that individuals experience a need to operate in an ordered environment. Social psychologists have also demonstrated that individuals display a similar need to structure and stabilize their perceptions at the cognitive level.[3]

Reflecting this differentiation between institutional and noninstitutional norms, international lawyers now distinguish between vertical and horizontal legal systems. A vertical legal system exists when a hierarchical arrangement of norms is enforced by an institutional hierarchy, while a horizontal legal system exists when there are formally equal participants in the system which implement the norms on the basis of self-help and restraint. Using this formulation, therefore, it becomes possible to speak of a legal order in the decentralized international system.[4]

Two further developments have occurred in the study of international law which have helped to promote the study of norms in international relations. First, there has been a movement away from the belief that international law carries a connotation of universality. It is accepted that the international system may exhibit various forms of public order. This idea is also reflected in the international relations literature which has identified the existence of subordinate state systems, such as Africa and South East Asia, where regional rules form. The second development stems from the argument that the existence of law can be observed in the behaviour which flows from the policy-making process. If this argument is accepted then the existence of law can be traced by a systematic examination of the behaviour of all relevant states on a particular issue. The critics of this approach consider such a procedure debases the conception of law and argue that if law is reduced either to a particular type of decision in the policy-making process, or to a behavioural regularity, the legal conceptions of compliance and violation lose all meaning.

There is merit in both of these approaches which suggests that norms should be defined both as prescribed rules which guide decision-makers in the process of policy formulation and as behaviour patterns which develop in any policy-making process. The distinction needs to be drawn between prescriptive and behavioural norms. A prescriptive norm describes a form of behaviour, or standard, which is authoritatively, or by consensus, recommended. When a doctor advocates that cigarettes should not be smoked, exercise should be taken regularly, and alcohol consumption kept to a minimum, he is describing a form of behaviour which he believes ought to be followed. In practice, neither he nor his patients may observe the prescribed norms.

Behavioural norms describe actions which are habitually followed, and just as prescriptive norms may not be reflected in behavioural patterns, behavioural norms may not reflect prescribed norms. If a small boy forgets to shut a door, no matter how often he is told to close it when he leaves the room, this represents a behavioural norm, a recurring piece of behaviour which becomes routinized although it is not prescribed. There is, therefore, no necessary relationship between prescriptive and behavioural norms, although a link often exists. When two Englishmen meet for the first time it is prescribed that they should shake hands; generally this behaviour is observed.

The process by which norms are formulated and implemented in the social system is still far from being understood, although it is recognized that there is a complex relationship between institutional and noninstitutional norms; they overlap and are mutually interdependent. If institutional norms run counter to noninstitutional norms, for example, they are unlikely to be successfully implemented. This happened during the period of Prohibition in the United States, when the norm prescribed at the institutional level was undermined by the behavioural norm which disregarded the prescription. A direct comparison between the way in which norms operate in the social and international systems is, therefore, unlikely to be very helpful because the absence of institutional norms in the international system eliminates the possibility of such an interplay between these two types of norms.

As an alternative, it is suggested that there is a direct isomorphic relationship between the way in which norms function in the international system and among certain 'primitive' tribes, the relationship arising from the decentralized nature of the systems.[5] In such horizontal systems, prescriptive norms emerge when a *consensus* develops among the actors on the desirability of a particular way of dealing with a situation; behavioural norms develop when a particular pattern of behaviour becomes *routinized* over time. The processes of consensus and routinization are therefore basic to the formation of norms in decentralized systems. The two processes are interrelated and supplement each other; one acts as a catalyst for the other. Consensus on a prescribed norm may precede the evolution of a behavioural norm, or the advantages observed in a routinized behavioural norm may consolidate a consensus on a prescribed norm.

Both consensus and routinization reflect the existence of *reciprocity* within the international system. Normative order requires an element of reciprocity to survive and decision-makers are conscious of the need to ensure that they and other actors observe reciprocal agreements.[6] The significance of this argument is clearly understood by British decision-makers, who recognize that they should aim not 'to seek out for exceptions to the great general principles, but to observe that course of conduct which we wished to be observed with respect to us, under similar circumstances, and that, too, which was consistent with the doctrines which must be held as governing the practice under international law'.[7]

Conscious efforts are made to ensure that decision-makers in other states accept this point of view. Decision-makers believe that they operate on the basis of defined rules. They endeavour to ensure that other actors operate on the basis of the same rules. For this reason, the British refused to negotiate with the Bolsheviks. A Foreign Office official noted in 1918 that the British could not reach an agreement with the Bolsheviks 'now or in the future' because 'they are fanatics who are not bound by any ordinary rules'.[8] It was on these grounds that the possibility of negotiation was resisted in the Cabinet. Lloyd George, the Prime Minister, disagreed; but then he believed that Lenin, and the other Russian leaders, would respect their word.[9] Even when the British came to terms with the idea of reaching an agreement with the Bolsheviks, it was specifically stated by the Cabinet that there was 'no question of entering into peace negotiations with the Bolsheviks until they had demonstrated . . . their intention not to interfere, by propaganda or otherwise, in the affairs of their neighbours'.[10]

Whenever there is a change of regime in a state, other actors will attempt to ensure that the new regime accepts the existing international order. During the turmoil in Mexico, at the time of the American Civil War, the British Government maintained that 'if they could see in Mexico a Government acceptable to the people of that country, which would maintain order at home and act with good faith in its relations to other nations, HMG would not care what form that Government assumed nor who was the ostensible ruler'.[11] Similarly, during the French Revolution, the British issued a declaration which stipulated that 'some legitimate and stable government should be established, founded on the acknowledged principles of universal justice, and capable of maintaining with other Powers the accustomed relations of union and peace'.[12]

Reciprocity, however, has not been consistently applied in the international system. Palmerston, one of the chief architects of British foreign policy during the nineteenth century, explained in the defence of his China policy that the principle could not be universally extended.

> It invariably happens that when a highly civilized race comes into contact with a half-civilized race, you will find that they act upon different rules of conduct. The highly civilized one expects good faith, justice, the fulfilment of engagements, honour and an absence from wrong-doing. The half-civilized race, on the other hand, are in habit totally different.[13]

The cynicism, no doubt, accurately reflects the image which Palmerston had of the international system.

Despite decision-makers' claims that their actions are based on established rules and principles, this aspect of international relations is often neglected. Most writers concentrate on elements of disorder in international systems. There are many studies of the conflict and tension which occur between states, few on the peaceful interactions. This emphasis tells as much about the sociology of knowledge as it does about the international system. The vast majority of interactions between states are non-violent, and they appear to reflect established norms. So far, very little research has been done to explain the nature and character of these interactions. If more work is done in this area, the significance of norms may become more apparent.

THE NORM OF NONINTERVENTION

Recently, social psychologists have become interested in the reluctance of third parties to go to the assistance of an individual being attacked, or take any action which might ameliorate the situation. They argue that the inaction contravenes a clear humanitarian norm about helping the victim. One experiment attempts to explain the failure to help in terms of a diffusion of responsibility: the willingness to help decreases with the number of people available.[14] However, instead of examining the triadic relationship defined by the observer, the attacker, and the attacked, the experiment examines a dyadic relationship between an observer and a subject who is feigning illness. The experiment consequently excludes any possible consideration of a nonintervention norm as defined in this study; only the humanitarian norm is open to question. But in an interventionary situation it could be that the desire to help is suppressed through fear of becoming involved. There does seem to be a powerful norm of this kind which operates in an interventionary situation at the individual level. The existence of the norm is reflected in such adages as 'they who in quarrels interpose will often get a bloody nose' and 'If you would keep out of strife, step not in twixt man and wife'. Both of these sayings were cited by Palmerston in support of his conviction that there should be no intervention into the American Civil War.[15]

There is a nonintervention norm which operates at the international and the inter-personal level, but Palmerston fails to take account of the meta-norm of nonintervention which comes into operation when internal conflict begins to 'spill over' into the international system in a way which cannot be identified at the interpersonal level. While international lawyers insist that intervention is in principle contrary to international law, they also argue that when civil wars occur, actors in the international system are within their rights 'in declaring themselves neutral in the struggle, and since there can be no neutrals unless there are two belligerents, such a declaration is equivalent to a recognition of the belligerency of both parties'.[16]

Such a move obviously represents a serious blow to the incumbent government. Whenever a government is faced by a serious disruption, it is placed in an extremely delicate position: the more stringent are the measures applied against the rebels, the more likely are the rebels to receive some kind of formal recognition from other actors in the international system. At the same time, recognition is not an easy action for external actors to take, for if the rebellion is crushed, the incumbent government is unlikely to forget this unfriendly action. They might well agree with Talleyrand that nonintervention is a diplomatic word which means much the same as intervention.

International lawyers do not accept this position, and argue that a civil war must be distinguished from a rebellion. They assert that rebellion is a domestic affair with which other states have no concern, but that as the level of the conflict rises, this attitude of detachment can no longer be fairly demanded of them. Before an external state can take purposive action, however, two conditions must be satisfied: firstly the conflict must have reached the dimensions of a war, which means that the insurgent government must have control over its own territory; and secondly, the war must have developed in such a way that other states simply cannot stand aside from it. This happens when the troops of one party cross onto the territory of another state, or if shipping is affected by the course of the war.[17] Only when these conditions are fulfilled is an actor permitted to transcend the boundary of dyadic interaction and establish a triadic relationship. There is, therefore, a *nonintervention norm* which covers dyadic interaction between states and a *metanorm of nonintervention* which precipitates system change by introducing a third actor into the situation, thereby forming a triadic interaction system.

Both the norm and the metanorm can be identified as nonintervention because each reflects a common motive: to permit the unstable actor to settle its own affairs without external interference. The nonintervention norm continues to function after the implementation of the metanorm. Whether or not the metanorm is brought into play depends upon the nature of the situation. Under any circumstance, however, it is stipulated that:

> *Proposition 1: There is a prescriptive norm in the international system which proscribes military intervention into civil wars and a behavioural norm which reflects the prescription.*

The cases of interventionary situations examined in this study can now be used to substantiate the existence of the prescriptive norm which is accepted by decision-makers (although it will be found that there is no clear distinction between the norm and the metanorm of nonintervention). But the cases cannot demonstrate the existence of a behavioural norm. To do this, further use will be made of Richardson's data in order to show that intervention does not represent a behavioural regularity in the international system.

NONINTERVENTION AND THE UNILATERAL INTERVENTION RESPONSE

In the House of Commons debate which sanctioned the sending of British troops to Portugal in 1826, references to the norm of nonintervention were clear and explicit. One minister, Brougham, insisted that if the Portuguese who were coming over the border were taking part in a civil war, 'we should be found to adhere to the salutary political maxim of not interfering in the internal concerns of other countries'. He added: 'It was indispensable to the peace of the world and the general liberties of mankind that such a maxim should be acted upon as the rule of our foreign policy.'[18] The same point was made by the Foreign Secretary, Canning: 'I have already stated, and I now repeat, that it never has been the wish or pretension of the British Government to interfere in the internal concerns of the Portuguese nation. Questions of that kind the Portuguese nation must settle among themselves.'[19]

Temperley, in his exhaustive study of Canning's foreign policy, has concluded: 'The true policy of England had always been that of non-interference with regard to the internal affairs of other countries from the days of Walpole', and that Canning believed: 'Any attempts at forcible interference with their internal affairs, unless in the case of direct peril to the nation which intervened, were dangerous and opposed to international law.'[20]

Throughout the period that the British troops were stationed in Portugal, the British continually reiterated the importance of the nonintervention norm. Six months after the troops arrived, Dudley, who was to become the next Foreign Secretary, suspected 'in the Portuguese Constitutionalists a disposition to consider our doctrine of non-interference, merely as an ostensible and *parliamentary* principle, intended only to cover designs of a contrary nature'.[21] He insisted that this was not the case. The decision to withdraw the troops was also made in the name of nonintervention when it was argued that 'our practice and principle have invariably been non-interference and neutrality; and that any other course on this occasion (besides withdrawal) would not only have been unjust, but would inevitably have involved us in war'.[22]

NONINTERVENTION AND THE COLLECTIVE INTERVENTION RESPONSE

The same insistence on the inviolability of the nonintervention norm is found during the British involvement in the Russian Civil War. In a House of Commons debate, Lloyd George, the Prime Minister, referred to 'the fundamental principle of all foreign policy in this country – a very sound principle – that you should never interfere in the internal affairs of other countries'. He elaborated on the principle. 'Whether Russia is Menshevik or Bolshevik, whether it is revolutionary or reactionary and whether it follows one set of men or another, that is a matter for the Russian people themselves.'[23]

Despite the decision to send troops to Russia after the Bolsheviks took control, the British decision-makers continued to insist both in public and in private that they were adhering to the norm of nonintervention. The Under Secretary for Foreign Affairs, Robert Cecil, maintained in a Parliamentary Debate: 'I think the Honourable Member opposite has a kind of idea that we have, as it were, some personal or political quarrel with the Bolsheviks . . . I assure the Honourable Member he is entirely mistaken. In our view the domestic policy of Russia is a matter for Russia alone. Whatever Government the Russians desire to have, the Russians ought to have, and it is not for us to interfere in any way in that matter.'[24]

Balfour, the Foreign Secretary, made the same point at a meeting of the British Empire Delegation in 1919, the year after the first troops had been sent, when he insisted that Britain had 'always explicitly stated that we did not wish to intervene in Russian domestic affairs, and that we must not be regarded as champions of this or that party'.[25] A Foreign Office official minuted the previous year, before troops were actually sent, 'Whatever form intervention takes, it is generally agreed that it must be founded on non-interference in the internal affairs of Russia.'[26]

When Lockhart, the British agent in Russia after the Bolsheviks took control, sent reports to England which questioned the aim of suppressing Bolshevism, Balfour expressed considerable concern. He noted on one of the despatches, 'I have constantly impressed on Mr. Lockhart that it is not our desire to interfere in Russian internal affairs. He appears to be very unsuccessful in conveying this view to the Bolshevik Government.'[27] In a despatch to Lockhart, Balfour noted, 'your observation about the "suppression of Bolshevism" is not understood'.[28] Since Lockhart had undertaken the mission to Russia on the understanding that 'our two main objects are (1) the defeat of German militarism, and (2) the suppression of Bolshevism'[29] it is not surprising that he had difficulty explaining the nature of British policy to the Bolsheviks.

NONINTERVENTION AND THE COLLECTIVE NONINTERVENTION RESPONSE

Britain's policy towards the American Civil War was shaped by the norm of nonintervention. When the conflict broke out, the Admiralty gave instructions that the navy should 'abstain from any measures or demonstration likely to give umbrage to any party in the United States, or bear the appearance of partizanship on either side'.[30] Similarly, Lyons, the ambassador in Washington, was instructed not to give any comment on the situation, in case this could be construed as intervention.[31] Decision-makers in London felt the need to deny, even among themselves, any intention of intervention. When Palmerston wrote to a colleague stressing the need to resist Gladstone's demands to reduce the size of the navy, he related this to the danger of conflict with the United States, but he found it necessary to add that this was not for the purpose of interfering in the American quarrel.[32]

When the conflict broke out, Palmerston maintained that 'our best and true policy seems to me to go on as we have begun and to keep quite clear of the conflict between North and South'.[33] He felt that any interference would be an infringement of the sovereignty of the United States: an element which underlies the norm of nonintervention. A direct reference to the norm occurred in the instructions sent to Lord Lyons, when he went to take up his post in Washington, where it was stated, 'nothing but imperative necessity could induce HMG under any circumstances to depart from their general principle of abstaining from all interference in the affairs of other states'.[34] But Russell was relating the general principle on that occasion to the civil war which was going on in Mexico; a situation where the British eventually sent troops.

NONINTERVENTION AND THE UNILATERAL NONINTERVENTION RESPONSE

When Lord Cranborne, an Under Secretary of State, defended Britain's policy towards the Spanish Civil War, he included a reference from the 1820 White Paper written by Castlereagh, which established nonintervention as a basic tenet of British foreign policy.[35] From the early stages of the conflict, Britain's policy was based on this norm. When the French put forward the idea of a joint agreement among the Great Powers which would be designed to prevent arms reaching either side in the civil war, British officials adopted a very cautious attitude. Mounsey, a Foreign Office official, argued that 'our main object should, I think, be to be completely impartial and free to pursue the policy of nonintervention in Spain'.[36] Two weeks later, when the French proposals were being treated very seriously because of the extent of the assistance which was being received by Franco, the perception of the situation altered, but the importance of the norm is still apparent. Mounsey wrote to Cadogan, another Foreign Office official, 'There are several possible courses. That of assistance to the rebels only must of course be ruled out as contrary to all our principles of correctness and justice.'[37]

The British were not alone in their attitude. The United States sent specific instructions to their embassy in Spain stipulating that 'in conformity with its well established principle of noninterference in the internal affairs of other countries, either in time of peace or in the event of civil strife, this government will, of course, scrupulously refrain from any interference whatsoever in the unfortunate Spanish situation'.[38] The large number of states which adhered to the nonintervention agreement suggests that most states were anxious to be associated with the norm of nonintervention. When the Polish Government sent a note agreeing to cooperate, they stated they were willing 'since it was a cardinal principle of Polish foreign policy to refrain from interference in the internal affairs of other states'.[39]

Both the German and the Italian Government gave their firm support to the principle. When the German head of the European section of the Political Department saw the Portuguese Minister, shortly after the war broke out in Spain, he informed him that the German Government strictly believed in the principle of nonintervention in internal Spanish events.[40] And when the French raised the issue of a nonintervention agreement, the German and Italian Governments maintained that since their countries naturally did not interfere in Spanish internal politics, it was quite unnecessary for them to make a formal declaration of neutrality.[41]

THE BEHAVIOURAL NORM OF INTERVENTION

The case studies indicate that decision-makers are aware of the prescriptive norm of nonintervention. But some decision-makers deny that the prescription has any effect on behaviour. In 1830, for example, after Britain finally withdrew troops from Portugal, a move which Wellington defended in the name of nonintervention, Palmerston strongly contested whether this was the motive of the policy and maintained that 'their alleged principle of neutrality and noninterference, has only been a cloak under cover of which they have given effectual assistance to that party which they secretly favoured'.[42] Lamb, the British ambassador in Portugal at the time of the withdrawal, went even further:

> As to all political doctrines, I hold them but as arguments by which statesmen justify the course of action which interest or necessity calls upon them to take; never as the motive by which that course is decided. Take the non-interference doctrine, for instance; it was invented by Lord Londonderry when the country would not sanction the length to which the Holy Alliance wished to go . . . This non-interference doctrine, which has never been fairly in operation in the whole history of Europe has subsequently been slackened or tightened according to the temper and circumstances of the country.[43]

Wellington, the Prime Minister, and a staunch defender of the nonintervention norm, was furious, and a colleague indicated that 'The Duke was desirous of recalling Lamb for his offensive letters.'[44] In addition, he was anxious to have the letters removed from the Foreign Office files because of their controversial nature.[45] A certain scepticism about the extent to which the norm affected behaviour can also be found in Lord Salisbury's survey of British foreign policy since the Treaty of Vienna, when he suggests that 'All failures that have taken place have arisen from one cause: the practice of foreign intervention in domestic quarrels.'[46]

Theorists in international relations have dealt cautiously with this issue. Parsons defines norms as 'patterns of desirable behavior which implement values in a variety of contexts' and he acknowledges the existence of international behavioural norms.[47] There is some agreement that nonintervention does represent a behavioural norm; Modelski, for example, argues that there is a reluctance of states to become involved in internal conflicts and that this reflects 'prevalent values in the international system'.[48] Using the figures found in Richardson's *The Statistics of Deadly Quarrels*, some support can be found for this position. The figures indicate that during the 150 years which he examined, there were 129 civil wars and 45 occasions when the civil war precipitated an intervention. The ratio between intervention and civil wars is 45:129, which means that there is a probability of 0·35 that a civil war will precipitate an intervention. But in order to establish the extent to which the figures indicate the existence of a behavioural norm, it is necessary to compare the number of interventions which occur, with the possible number of interventions which could take place. This can be expressed in the formula

$$\frac{A_1 \, R_1}{(A - 1) \, R}$$

where A = the number of states in the system; A_1 = the number of states which intervene; R = the number of civil wars; and R_1 = the number of civil wars when intervention occurs.

Using Richardson's figures as a very rough guide, and assuming that on average, during the period under consideration, there were 50 states in the system, and that, on average, an intervention response will involve three states, then:

$$\text{intervention ratio} = \frac{3 \times 45}{49 \times 129} = \frac{135}{6321} = \frac{1}{48}$$

This means that the probability that a state will activate an intervention response when confronted by an intervention stimulus is ·02. In practice, the distribution of interventions is likely to be skewed, but this is an attribute of any deviation. Although the figures are very rough, they do indicate that nonintervention represents a behavioural norm. (See Appendix 2.)

THE RATIONALE FOR THE NONINTERVENTION NORM

The distinction which has been drawn between the norm and the metanorm of nonintervention indicates that civil war is perceived by decision-makers to be an idiosyncratic condition in the international system which warrants special attention: civil wars can pose a threat to international stability. Despite this potential for generating international instability, the metanorm of nonintervention is still framed in a way which minimizes external involvement in domestic jurisdiction. Under special circumstances, intervention is condoned by international actors, but not prescribed. The absence of a metanorm which specifies a need for intervention rather than nonintervention when 'spill-over' occurs can be explained by the conventional wisdom which has accumulated about civil war over time.

In the first place, it is believed that intervention into civil wars is dangerous because of their intensity. In 1825 the Spanish Government requested Canning to return a group of political prisoners, who had escaped to Britain from the civil conflict in Spain; he refused. In an explanation of his position, Canning observed: 'in the fierceness of civil contest, the thirst for vengeance and the rigour of proscription rage on one side and the other, with a violence unknown in the struggles of open war.'[49] This perception was endorsed by Bright, the nineteenth century radical, in a debate on the possibility of an American civil war. He suggested that since the Americans were 'more extensively educated probably than the population of any other country in the world' it might be possible to solve the problems 'without those extensive cruelties which almost always accompany a civil war'.[50] His hopes were not fulfilled and, later, Palmerston observed that compared to the American situation, the German Thirty Years War was a 'joke'.[51]

Secondly, it is believed that intervention into civil wars will prove to be counter-productive. Wellington, who was particularly opposed to any form of intervention, argued: 'Experience has shown that during revolutions the minds of men are influenced by motives of party and faction, and that which is most repugnant to their feelings *is the formal organized interference of foreign powers*, and that the effect is to weaken and endanger the party in whose favour it is exerted.'[52] Pitt put forward the same argument and maintained that the invasion of France by Prussia and Austria during the French Revolution would tend to consolidate the power of the Jacobins and delay the re-establishment of order.[53]

Finally, there is the knowledge that civil wars precipitate unstable and uncertain conditions. This is often a function of the way in which a civil war is structured. Russell, Foreign Secretary during the American Civil War, stressed that the war posed particular problems because 'no side is sufficiently strong to outweigh the other side'.[54] The sources of information which exist during civil wars also give rise to uncertainty. On a despatch which reported on the large volume of support which Franco had engineered during the Spanish Civil War, one official noted: 'This is interesting, but it is impossible to put any faith in the numerous reports to the effect that the majority of the Spanish population are behind the government of one side or the other. We have only today received a readable report from Mr. Haymans in which he expressed the view that General Franco had very little support with the populace.'[55] Canning expressed the same view when confronted by a civil war in Spain more than a hundred years earlier. 'Let it be considered, moreover, that Spain is at present a divided nation; that we know not how to estimate the comparative strength of the Royalists and Constitutionalists.'[56]

This body of conventional wisdom about the nature of civil war represents part of the 'immense store of information concerning the nature of problems, their possible solutions, and approaches to these solutions', which accumulates over time and can be found in any society.[57] Norms and metanorms are derived from information of this sort and through the medium of norms, decision-makers can gain access to and take advantage of past experience. Because of the perceived link between norms and experience, when confronted by situations characterized by a high level of uncertainty decision-makers often search for a norm which can be used to guide policy. The norm can help to define and structure the situation and thereby render it less unpredictable. Norms possess the capacity for uncertainty absorption.[58] Once a norm is applied to a situation, it can absorb some of the uncertainty which the decision-maker otherwise experiences.

Operating on the basis of an established norm represents a safe policy for a decision-maker. By implementing a policy on this basis, the decision-maker displays an interest in 'satisficing' rather than 'optimizing' his policy options.[59] In other words, the decision-maker prefers to minimize risk and potential gains. Given the beliefs about the nature of civil wars, for example, an intervention response must be seen as a high risk policy. If 'rationality' is defined in terms of minimizing losses, rather than maximizing gains, then it can be seen that nonintervention is the 'rational' response for decision-makers confronted by an intervention stimulus.

Very often, however, decision-makers do not have any vested interest in a situation yet they still have to make some kind of response. Under these circumstances there is an even greater incentive to minimize potential costs and reduce uncertainty. During the Spanish Civil War, for example, legal advisers to the British Government were anxious to have both parties in the conflict granted belligerent status: the advantage

... would be that we should have adopted a perfectly definite position and should apply sufficiently defined rules; at present we suffer in dealing with the daily problems which arise from the absence of such a position and of definite principles to apply... These rules, which would be applied impartially to both sides, would be based on the rules of neutrality, which in this respect are sufficiently definite.[60]

For political reasons, belligerent status was never granted, but until the final victory by Franco, there was constant pressure to move to this position and permit a clear application of the rules associated with the law of neutrality. Because of the ambiguity created by the intervention of Germany and Italy, as well as the Soviet Union, the decision-makers preferred to restrict their policy to the norm, rather than the metanorm, of nonintervention. But the failure to implement the metanorm did not undermine the adherence to the general principle of nonintervention.

This chapter has shown that decision-makers do acknowledge nonintervention as a prescriptive norm in the international system and that the norm reflects past experience, which demonstrates the dangers of becoming involved in civil wars. Nonintervention, therefore, represents a policy which is designed to minimize potential costs and reduce uncertainty. It can be defined as a 'rational' response to civil war. From this perspective, there is nothing problematical about nonintervention, there is a clear rationale for such a response; it is intervention, not nonintervention, which requires explanation. At first sight, it could be suggested that when intervention occurs, decision-makers are operating on the basis of a different strategy, attempting to optimize their gains rather than minimize their losses and thereby deliberately implementing a high risk policy. The cases examined here, however, do not support this explanation. The strategy remains unchanged. Subsequent chapters offer an alternative explanation which depends upon the initial failure of the decision-makers to identify their policy as an intervention response. As a consequence, in all the cases examined the decision-makers verbally adhere to the nonintervention norm throughout the interventionary situations.

CHAPTER 3
Definition of the Intervention Stimulus

THE nonintervention norm is not a moral or ethical principle, but a practical rule designed to discourage states from becoming involved in unstable and ambiguous situations. States may derive positive benefits from an intervention response, but the norm indicates that there are high risks associated with such a policy and that there is a correspondingly high probability that the situation will fail to yield tangible results. The realist interpretation of intervention indicates that when the effects of intervention are deleterious, miscalculation must have occurred. But the cases examined suggest that this view is over-simplified; the importance of nonintervention and the dangers associated with intervention are, if anything, stressed more forcefully in those cases where the intervention response is introduced. In this chapter it is argued that the reiteration of the nonintervention norm by decision-makers engaged in intervention does not denote deception or hypocrisy, as the realists might assert; instead it is demonstrated that in these cases, the decision-makers fail to identify the intervention stimulus and do not define their behaviour as an intervention response.

For the purpose of this analysis, an intervention stimulus is characterized as a conflict between the units of a bifurcated actor which carries the potential for system transformation. The specification of these three components, however, does not make it self-evident when an intervention stimulus has emerged. Situations do not define themselves. They encompass a body of information which may be complex, competing and ambiguous. The information has to be evaluated, ordered and classified and this involves sifting, filtering and simplifying the information which is available. This process can have a considerable effect on the way in which a situation is finally defined. The definition of a situation, therefore, poses problems for the analyst which are not dissimilar from those of the actor whose behaviour is being examined. Actors can fail to agree on the definition of a situation; so can analysts. In this chapter it is argued that the definitions of an intervention stimulus employed by the actor and the analyst can also be asymmetrical.

This asymmetry is not accidental. It constitutes an important factor in the explanation of the intervention response. Often the emergence of asymmetrical definitions can be attributed to a failure by the actor to receive or process critical information which is available, retrospectively, to the analyst. But in the cases examined in this study, the information used by the analyst to define the emergence of an intervention stimulus was available and was considered by the actor. Only after deliberation did the actor exclude this information when defining the situation. The resulting asymmetry raises an important epistemological issue about the relative status of the definitions used by the actor and the analyst. The issue is particularly relevant because use is made of the asymmetrical definitions in the proposition employed in this chapter. Before stating the proposition, the components used by the actor and the analyst to define an intervention stimulus are examined and the epistemological problem which is posed by the emergence of asymmetrical definitions of the same situation is discussed.

THE COMPONENTS OF AN INTERVENTIONARY SITUATION

Decision-makers assert that civil wars are not scaled-down versions of inter-state wars; they possess different characteristics and pose different problems for actors in the international system. During an inter-state war, actors desiring to remain uninvolved declare a position of neutrality and accept the rights and obligations associated with this position – the rules of neutrality delineate an impartial course between the two clearly demarcated sides to the conflict. But in civil conflict, as a legal adviser to the Foreign Office has argued, it is necessary to decide if two parties have formed, before making the additional assumption that a state of war exists:

> When hostilities break out between two separate countries this question does not arise, because it is evident from the start that two separate parties exist. So long, therefore, as one of the two countries considers itself to be at war there is unquestionably a war with all the legal consequences thereof. The essential difference between this case and that of a civil dispute is that in the latter you start not with two, but only one party. What is going on is simply a riot, revolt, revolution, civil dispute, or what you will. It may, and indeed usually does, start with a mere local outbreak or insurrection, perhaps not more than a local disorder. Nobody would pretend at that point that there was a war or that there were two parties. There is only one party, the State itself, represented by its legitimate government.
> Given that, as the affair grows more serious, a second party may come into existence, it still remains the fact that unless and until it does, there cannot be a war, for it takes two to make a war.[1]

The assumption contained in this analysis – that bifurcation is an adjunct to conflict – is not correct; bifurcation may precede conflict. But in which-

ever order the components emerge, the shift from dyadic to triadic interaction is difficult because it necessitates transcending the boundary which
defines inter-state relations and involves a 'step-level function'. The 'step'
occurs when a 'variable has no appreciable effect on others until its value
has increased or decreased by some minimal increment'.[2] In a situation of
domestic instability, it is acknowledged that the 'step' occurs when conflict
within a target state can no longer be defined in terms of a 'riot' or a
'rebellion' and must be considered as a 'civil war'. Once this 'step' is
crossed, decision-makers recognize that they may have to extend the existing pattern of interaction to include a third party. It is stipulated that this
development precipitates system change and that the change contains the
potential for system transformation.

The discussion of system transformation in international relations is
normally conducted at the macro-level of analysis. For example, it is
frequently stipulated that the Peace of Westphalia in 1648 brought about
a system transformation because that point marked the genesis of the
modern European state system. Changes of this sort occur very rarely and
decision-makers may not even be aware of these macro-developments.
Retrospectively, the signing of the Treaty of Rome in 1957 may be seen
as initiating a system transformation, but at the moment there is no consensus among actors or integration specialists on the current state of
European integration. On a day-to-day basis, decision-makers are
unaffected by the thought that the international system may be undergoing a slow transformation at this macro-level. But they often have a very
clear conception of system transformation at the micro-level and they are
concerned with basic changes which they can perceive to be taking place.
Notions of change and transformation, therefore, are relative concepts,
varying with the time-scale and perspective which is employed.

The international system is in a constant state of flux and decision-
makers are continuously having to cope with perceived changes in the
system; only a small proportion of these will transform the system. Permanent changes in alliance systems, for example, are a rare occurrence,
as Liska has pointed out.[3] Jervis has also argued that decision-makers are
reluctant to admit the possibility of basic change and he draws attention
to the number of occasions when decision-makers ask each other to make
declarations about their intentions and assume that the declarations are
valid. He suggests: 'It may be that statesmen do not like to think of the
possibility of basic change in the system or the possibility that others are
expecting such change.'[4] If this analysis is correct, civil war becomes an
unusual event because it is defined in terms of a system change, and presupposes the possibility of system transformation. In this study, system
change and transformation are defined at the micro-level. Instead of relating the concepts to the international system, they are confined to the
dyadic interaction system which operates between two states. A noninter-

vention response precipitates system change in the dyad by incorporating a new actor into the system. Such a development contains a potential for system transformation either by the emergence of a new state, or a new regime which refuses to operate within the norms which governed the original dyadic interaction system.

By defining a situation as interventionary and implementing a nonintervention response, an actor precipitates system change and moves away from the stability associated with the established dyadic interaction system. The definition of an intervention stimulus, therefore, represents an important step which is not undertaken lightly or unnecessarily. Nor is it easily undertaken.

Decision-makers may not agree that the facts indicate the need for such a definition; they may accept the same body of information but disagree on the symbolic significance of various facts. To some extent, it is a matter of judgement when the facts indicate that a 'rebellion' has become a 'civil war'. There is also no guarantee that the actor and the analyst will coincide in their judgement on this issue. When a discrepancy arises, some assessment has to be made about the validity of the two definitions: this raises an epistemological problem which must now be broached.

THE ANALYSIS OF REALITY

It is generally accepted that 'reality' is never described simply on the basis of observation; perception is, consciously or unconsciously, conditioned by initial assumptions. This proposition holds true for descriptions by natural and social scientists. Only if it is assumed, for example, that the earth rotates, can it be asserted that the daily revolution of all celestial bodies around the earth is simply an apparent motion: an illusion based upon an incorrect definition of the situation. The idea that the earth rotates is now part of conventional wisdom, but for thousands of years the illusion was accepted as a reality. Before making any observation, therefore, the natural scientist must make certain *a priori* assumptions about reality. Once a basic set of assumptions has been established – they are normally embedded in an accepted paradigm – the analyst does not question the veracity of the observations which he uses to describe that aspect of reality under examination.

One of the two major modes of research in social science has attempted to emulate this approach adopted by natural scientists. It was clearly articulated by the behaviourists in psychology before the First World War. The behaviourist observes and records overt behaviour without any attempt to discover what the individual perceives, or what he intends, when performing a given action. The object of an investigation is to examine the relationship between an observable stimulus and an observable response. Explanations are restricted to observed behaviour and all subjective factors are ignored. In such research, it is the analyst's definition of the situation which is employed.

Much important research in all areas of social science has been conducted on this basis. But it is apparent that research of this kind cannot ignore an important distinction between social and physical behaviour: social behaviour, unlike physical behaviour, is affected by cognition. When a physicist describes the behaviour of a falling object, there is no consideration given to the reaction of the object to the situation, nor is it necessary to consider the object's motive. An individual, unlike a stone, may be conscious of and have a reason for falling, but this will in no way affect the validity of the law of gravitational acceleration which describes his descent. But if an individual throws himself off a cliff, in order to commit suicide, then the action is invested with meaning. There is a symbolic content to the action and if the concept is deprived of this content it becomes meaningless.

The behaviourist may wish to eschew an analysis of the subjective factors which precipitate suicide, but because the concept has an intrinsic meaning – the symbolic significance invested in the action by the individual – at some point in the investigation the analyst must infer how the actor defined the situation which engaged the behaviour. If official statistics on suicide are employed, then responsibility for identifying the actor's definition of the situation is left to the coroner who records the cause of death. Almost all research of this kind incorporates the subjective element by inference.

A second mode of research in social science makes an overt attempt to examine this subjective element. At the beginning of the 1950s, when the conception of the behavioural sciences first emerged, it was asserted that any theory of behaviour must take account of intra-personal phenomena like attitudes, beliefs, values, motives and perceptions. It was felt that the early behaviourists were mistaken when they suggested that the subjective element could not be encompassed by the scientific method. The value of both approaches is now appreciated, but the difference is apparent: in the first, an actor's behaviour is defined in terms of the analyst's definition of the situation, whereas in the second, there is a deliberate attempt to specify the actor's own definition of the situation.

At the individual level, much research has been conducted on the subjective element of human behaviour. But in international relations, where the interactions between states emerge from complex decision-making processes, there is considerable reluctance to employ an approach which involves the subjective element. Most of the major quantitative research relies on the observable actions which state-actors direct at each other. Such behaviour is identified and classified according to criteria established by the analyst. Quantitative research which does examine intra-personal factors tends to concentrate on the analysis of key decision-makers. The public statements of John Foster Dulles, for example, have been subjected to content analysis to establish the nature of his belief system. It is assumed that Dulles played the key role in determining the course of American foreign policy during the Eisenhower administration and that public pronouncements provide an adequate basis from which to infer the characteristics of the man's belief system. Both assumptions can be challenged. The research concludes that Dulles operated on the basis of a 'closed' belief system and that all information was received and interpreted in a way which preserved the hostile image of the Soviet Union contained by the belief system. This conclusion assumes that the analyst has access to a definition of the situation which is more accurate than the definition employed by Dulles.[5]

Given the complexities of the international system, it is not surprising to find that some of the most interesting work which examines image-formation does not use quantitative techniques.[6] This literature is not extensive and most of it fails to make a formal distinction between the actor and analyst's definition of the situation. Attention has been drawn to this omission by Harold and Margaret Sprout, who assert that a distinction must be made between the *psycho-milieu*, which represents the perceived image of the actor, and the *operational milieu*, which represents the perceived image of the analyst. They argue further that because there is no such being as the omniscient observer, the operational milieu must be used to represent the environment in which the actor operates. The importance of the distinction can be illustrated by many examples drawn from all levels of social interaction. The Sprouts cite the man walking down a dark street whose psycho-milieu does not include the open manhole which exists in the operational milieu. This lack of knowledge increases the possibility of an accident because the man's ignorance precludes the possibility of his taking precautionary action. At the international level, the American commanders at Pearl Harbour in December 1941 did not consider the possibility of a Japanese invasion. Their psycho-milieu did not include a factor which any retrospective analysis would place in the operational milieu.[7]

When the argument is stated in these terms, with the actor failing to recognize the existence of something which the analyst knows to be present in the environment, the distinction between the psycho-milieu and the operational milieu is easily drawn and the value of using the operational milieu as a description of the actor's environment can be demonstrated. But the issue becomes more problematical when it is viewed from the angle that – in the words of Thomas – 'If men define situations as real they are real in their consequences.' The idea contained in this dictum finds powerful expression in the self-fulfilling prophecy. If, for example, an individual enters a new situation with the belief that he is not going to find any friends, then according to the self-fulfilling prophecy, his subsequent behaviour generated by this belief may have the effect of confirming the belief. The interaction between the individual and his environment has the effect of changing the environment to the point where it is congruent with the individual's conception of it. But how can the analyst be sure that this is what has happened? It could be that the individual's perception was correct and the appearance of a self-fulfilling prophecy is created because the operational milieu identified by the analyst did not accurately reflect the 'reality' of the actor's environment.

This is not an artificial problem. The debate among 'Cold War' historians, for example, depends to some extent upon different assessments of whether the United States decision-makers were confronted by a real Soviet threat, or whether their reaction to this perceived threat precipitated actions which confirmed the nature of the threat. It could be argued that if all the documents were available this debate could be finally resolved. However, this is unlikely. More probable is that there would be a discussion of what constitutes a threat. It may well be that it is the nature of a threat, rather than the facts, which is in dispute. When arguments of this sort arise, it can be seen that the use of the operational milieu to define an actor's environment raises an epistemological question. No answer can be given. Only by self-consciously making the distinction and observing the nature of the interaction can progress be made. If this is not done, then, as the Sprouts observe, there can be 'no end to the epistemological and conceptual confusion that bedevils discussion of both the psychological and nonpsychological aspects of man-milieu relationships'.[8]

On these grounds it is stipulated that when the three components of the interventionary situation coalesce in the operational milieu, then at that point the interventionary situation exists in the actor's environment, irrespective of whether it is defined as such in the actor's psycho-milieu. As indicated earlier, an actor may well perceive the existence of a conflict without defining it in terms of bifurcation; however, it is unlikely, given the existence of internal conflict, that the actor will fail to consider the possibility that bifurcation may occur.

In practice, it is impossible to make a sharp distinction between what an actor wants to happen in the future and how he defines the current situation. It has to be accepted that there is a 'complex interweaving of affective and cognitive processes. What a person wants and likes influences what he sees; what he sees influences what he wants and likes.'[9] When information is complex and ambiguous, it is clear that there will be wide scope for this interactive process to operate. Because of the existence of this process, there is a very real possibility that an actor will fail to identify an actual or potential interventionary situation which is defined in the operational milieu. The cases studied support the utility of distinguishing between the operational milieu – which is regarded here as the environment in which the actor operates – and the psycho-milieu. It is stipulated that:

Proposition 2: In an interventionary situation, the operational milieu and the psycho-milieu of an actor will converge when a nonintervention response is implemented and diverge when an intervention response is implemented.

The implication of the proposition is clear. It means that when a nonintervention response is implemented, this event will be acknowledged in both the psycho-milieu and the operational milieu. Although this development marks system change, the response is in accord with the established rules. But when the intervention response is implemented, the actor is denying that system change has occurred and continues to operate in the context of the dyadic pattern of interaction. It is only in the operational milieu that the actor's behaviour is defined in terms of system change and can be identified as an intervention response which deviates from the accepted rules. An analysis of the cases allows this distinction to be drawn more clearly.

THE DEFINITION OF THE AMERICAN CIVIL WAR

The perception by British decision-makers of bifurcation and potential system transformation preceded the outbreak of the American Civil War. Russell, the Foreign Secretary, noted at the beginning of 1861 that he did not see 'how the United States can be cobbled together by any compromise'. There was no suggestion that conflict must ensue as a consequence. He went on: 'The best thing *now* would be that the right to secede should be acknowledged and that there should be separation . . . But above all I hope no force will be used.'[10]

It was not envisaged that such a change would alter the existing power balance. The Southern States were not considered likely to offer a threat to Great Britain, partially because of the bias towards Great Britain which was perceived to exist in the Southern States, but also because it was asserted that 'the new Republic will never rise to eminence as a great power on the earth'.[11] Separation and the resulting system transformation were, nevertheless, seen as a source of instability, because 'sooner or later it seems impossible that they should not quarrel and fight, whether there remains two great republics, or one large one and a number of small independent states'.[12]

Other aspects of the instability created by the potential system transformation gave the British decision-makers cause for concern. They reflected the British preoccupation with the defence of Canada. Before the outbreak of conflict, the British were aware of the American Secretary of State's speeches which indicated his determination to acquire Canada if the United

States lost the South.[13] The threats were taken very seriously. Lyons, the British ambassador in Washington, stated: 'I myself consider the danger to be sufficiently imminent to render it only a matter of prudence to put Canada into a state of defence.'[14] Palmerston supported this view:

> The Federal Government have been rousing the military spirit of the people, and have been telling them that their national dignity and power and position among the nations of the earth will be greatly damaged by the separation of the Southern States.
> The Northern States may find that it is beyond their power to reunite the broken federal link and they may think of indemnifying themselves in the North for what they have irrevocably lost in the South.[15]

Lyons went further. He did not regard a 'sudden declaration of war against us by the United States as an event altogether impossible at any moment'.[16] The disturbed state of affairs in the United States caused the British to send reinforcements to both the West Indies and Canada.[17] System transformation as the result of bifurcation seemed imminent and the British decision-makers conceived of the consequence in terms of an aggressive reaction from the Northern States.

The British conviction that the bifurcation of the United States was likely to lead to a system transformation preceded the outbreak of conflict by several months. The potential for bifurcation was acknowledged by January 1861, three months before the attack on Fort Sumter provided the indication that President Lincoln was determined to use force.[18] Within a month, Russell asserted that the situation in the United States 'cannot be designated otherwise than a civil war'; at the same time, the British Government felt 'they cannot question the right of the Southern States to claim to be recognized as a belligerent'.[19] By granting the Southern States belligerent status, the British decision-makers initiated system change. The 'step-level function' occurred on the initiation of conflict; it was not felt necessary to gauge its scale and intensity.

Dallas, the United States ambassador in London, complained to Russell that the British had acted precipitously. He compared the short period of time taken by Britain to accord the Southern States with belligerent status, with the time which elapsed before classifying the Greeks as belligerents in their struggle with the Turks. Russell contended that the United States was of greater importance and required more speedy attention.[20] A very different answer was given in the House of Commons, when defending the same decision. There, he reverted to the 'sound maxim of policy enumerated by Mr. Canning, that the question of belligerent rights is one not of principle but of fact'.[21]

It was not the initiation of conflict which provided the critical 'fact' encouraging the British decision-makers to transcend the boundary of dyadic interaction, but the introduction of a Northern blockade of the Southern ports. Ever since the perception of bifurcation had emerged, it was this factor which caused concern. In February Russell wrote to Lyons: 'Above all things, endeavour to prevent a blockade of the Southern coast. It would produce misery, discord and enmity incalculable.'[22] From this point it was appreciated that it was a blockade which would permit the 'step-level function' to occur. Up to the outbreak of conflict, Lyons was doing all he could 'to make the Government here aware of the disastrous effect of their blockading the Southern ports or attempting to interfere in Southern commerce'.[23] He indicated that such a move might leave foreign states with little choice but to recognize the Southern confederacy, since the alternative was to tolerate an interruption of their shipping.[24]

On the day Fort Sumter was attacked, Lyons indicated that the naval preparations 'look painfully like a blockade';[25] a proclamation announcing the blockade followed a week later. Within a month, Russell informed Lyons that the Law Officers expressed the opinion that Britain must consider the civil war in the United States as a regular war.[26] The following year the United States Supreme Court endorsed this judgement, stating that the President's Proclamation of 19 April 1861 was itself 'official and conclusive evidence to the court that a state of war existed'.[27] The British definition of the situation, therefore, appears to have been accurate and there was a close correspondence between the operational and psycho-milieus. It is also apparent that the norm associated with this definition of the situation was implemented.

THE DEFINITION OF THE SPANISH CIVIL WAR

News of an attempted army coup in Spain was received on 17 July 1936; it was soon apparent that the coup was symptomatic of more significant developments. Less than a week later, the Foreign Office had circulated a memorandum to all the governments of the Dominions. Admitting a short-age of information, it stated, 'there seems however to be little doubt that fighting is widespread, and that the issue of the struggle between rebel military forces and Government forces is still uncertain'.[28] The following month, reports describing the firm control by the army in northern Spain were accepted. A Foreign Office official minuted, 'This predicts a long drawn-out conflict.'[29]

The consequences of this development were still uncertain. Pollock noted in mid-August that the army leaders had no 'real popular support worth anything at all. Nor after a month of civil war is there any sign of a leader who is the least likely to capture the public mind.'[30] This acceptance of the conflict as a civil war indicates that the perception of bifurcation quickly followed the initial outbreak of conflict. It was also feared that the bifurcation could give rise to system transformation. Eden, the Foreign

Secretary, maintained in the League of Nations that an objective of British policy was to preserve the territorial integrity of Spain.[31] The following year, a Foreign Office official continued to insist: 'The maintenance of the integrity of Spain is certainly a British interest in the present circumstances, because if Spain were to disintegrate, the separate parts might very well fall under the control of one or other foreign country.'[32]

System transformation was not restricted to images of disintegration. It was believed that Franco could hold North Africa for an 'indefinite period' and the Republican offer to revise the *status quo* in North Africa in favour of Britain was regarded as 'very impertinent'.[33] As early as October 1936, the Cabinet had to consider the possibility of a Fascist victory and Eden observed: 'As the insurgents seem to be getting the upper hand there would seem to be some danger that the civil war might end with a Government in power somewhat resentful of our attitude.'[34] Profound consequences seemed likely to follow a Fascist victory. It was observed: 'We can hardly avoid the supposition that Italy will regard disturbances in Spain not only as a struggle between Fascism and Communism but also and primarily as a field in which she might find herself able to strengthen her own influence and to weaken Britain's sea power in the Western Mediterranean.'[35] The possibility of system transformation arising from the civil war in Spain, therefore, was an important consideration arising from the system change.

The defining characteristics of an intervention stimulus were quickly recognized by British decision-makers and there was no significant disparity between the operational and psycho-milieus. But in this instance the nonintervention response which was implemented did not completely correspond with the behaviour prescribed by the metanorm. This created a source of endless confusion and difficulty for the British decision-makers. The nature of the response prescribed by the metanorm when a situation is defined in terms of an intervention stimulus was known and advocated. Lord Cranborne, a key decision-maker, contended that

> A nation torn by revolution presents no immediate menace to any other power. While conditions remained chaotic, we had no reason for anxiety. That phase of the Spanish conflict is however now over. It has ceased to be a revolution. It has become a civil war. There are two Spanish Governments each with its own internal administration and its own foreign policy.[36]

The logic of this analysis, as Cranborne pointed out, dictated that Britain should pursue a policy of neutrality. Despite constant discussion, Britain never did grant belligerent rights to either party. They operated on the basis of the nonintervention norm.

No move was made when it was first appreciated that an intervention stimulus had emerged. When the Portuguese Government pressed for action, Seymour, a head of the Western Department in the Foreign Office, indicated that recognition of the civil war 'would no doubt come to the front, unless there is a rapid change in the situation'. But it was stressed that for Portugal to take such a step at this stage would be 'entirely premature and strongly to be deprecated'.[37] In mid-October, the Cabinet decided that they would recognize the insurgents as belligerents when they had captured Madrid.[38] A dramatic event of this kind would justify the 'step-level function' involved in the process of recognition.

The fall of Madrid failed to materialize at this time, and in the meantime, the German and Italian Governments announced on November 18 that they were granting General Franco's Government *de jure* status. They were not treating the conflict in Spain as a civil war, but accepting that a change of government had occurred. The move caused Eden, Britain's Foreign Secretary, to rethink the existing policy. He decided to delay granting belligerent status, because it would leave the Government open to the charge that Britain was following in the wake of the dictators' policy. For some Foreign Office officials, this argument did not over-ride a need to overcome the existing anomalous situation, where decision-makers accepted the existence of civil war in Spain but publicly refused to acknowledge the fact.

Internal contradictions inevitably flowed from this position. Shortly after the military insurrection began, for example, the Republican Government indicated that they were going to introduce a blockade; Shuckburgh argued that Britain could only deny the legality of the blockade if it was ineffective, and an effective blockade would amount to a recognition by the Republican Government of the 'belligerency' of the insurgents.[39] A direct parallel was being drawn with the American Civil War and it was accepted in the Foreign Office that this did provide the leading precedent.[40] But not all officials agreed with this interpretation. While it was admitted that by accepting the legality of the blockade the insurgents would be raised to belligerent status, it was not agreed that an 'effective' blockade was thereby legal.[41] After further discussion within the Foreign Office, it was decided that the legality of the blockade could only be established after the insurgents had been conferred with belligerent status. However, British merchant ships were informed that they would not be protected if they entered a Spanish port after being warned away by Spanish warships.[42]

Nevertheless, the decision marked a reversal of the precedent laid down during the American Civil War, rejecting the event which had been used to precipitate the 'step-level function' which demarcated the boundary between dyadic and triadic interaction. The advantage of transcending the boundary of the dyadic interaction system after the introduction of a blockade is that responsibility for introducing the blockade rests with the incumbent government in the target state. Responsibility for the system change is therefore shared. A high level of ambiguity followed this failure to take advantage of the blockade, and in September, when the Republican Government appealed to the British sense of fair play on the grounds that an arms embargo the British had introduced affected the incumbent government and not the insurgents, Shuckburgh was forced to comment: 'It is difficult to think of an answer to this appeal, except that the political consequences of giving the legal government the facilities to which it is undoubtedly entitled would have been far too great to have been risked.'[43]

The ambiguity was eventually resolved by an acceptance of the fact that decisions could be based on one of two distinct systems. First, there was the dyadic interaction system reflecting a normal relationship between two states; second, there was a nonintervention interaction system reflecting a triadic relationship between two states, when one is bifurcated. The two systems were superimposed and decisions were related to one of the two systems. When defending the decision to impose an arms embargo, Sir Herbert Malkin, the senior legal adviser to the Foreign Office, insisted that it was important not to confuse civil war with the suppression of a rebellion. He designated the Spanish conflict as a civil war, and, consequently, 'no policy is legitimate which does not involve treating both parties alike'.[44] The policy was based on the nonintervention system.

When British insurance firms contacted the Foreign Office about policies which covered 'loss or damage in a war', they wanted to know if there was, in fact, a war going on in Spain. Fitzmaurice, a Government legal expert, advised that while the belligerent status of the insurgents had not been recognized, 'we do not regard this as being necessarily conclusive on the question whether a state of war exists within the meaning of state of war as used in particular documents'. He went on:

> The existence of a state of war is a question of fact. The express recognition of it by according the status of belligerents to the contending parties is a question of policy not of law. Recognition would not have the effect of creating war when none existed ... we are not asked to say whether the struggle is or is not a war but whether we so regard it or not. The fact of the matter is that we so regard it for some purposes and not for others. For instance, we regard it as war for the purposes of the Foreign Enlistment Act, but not for the purpose of allowing the contending parties to exercise belligerent rights at sea.[45]

The dyadic interaction system was, therefore, always employed whenever the question of belligerent status was raised. Firm denials were always issued when it was suggested that the refusal to recognize a civil war was inconsistent with the norms associated with the situation. Malkin asserted that in matters like recognition:

> The practice of nations is more important than the opinion of writers, however logical their arguments may be, and I do not think that there is anything in the precedents which can be regarded as establishing this thesis. The precedents are not numerous and it is not always clear exactly what occurred; but the most that can be said is that in a fair number of cases during the nineteenth century where the necessary conditions were

fulfilled the states concerned acted in a manner which involved the recognition of belligerency. This falls a long way short of establishing the proposition that they were bound to do so.[46]

Accepting this argument, the fact remains that the Foreign Office acted contrary to their preferred pattern of behaviour. They failed to press the insurgents' claim for belligerent status when the blockade was introduced in deference to the Admiralty, who were anxious that the parties should not be allowed to exercise belligerent rights at sea. Foreign Office officials expressed some irritation when they discovered at the beginning of November 1936 that the First Lord of the Admiralty now wished to give belligerent status to the parties when Madrid fell. Mounsey commented: 'The *volte face* on the part of the Admiralty is most disconcerting. It was on their behalf that we have been endeavouring up to now to avoid the necessity of according the Spanish naval authority belligerent rights at sea; and their change of view may seriously affect our whole attitude in the Spanish problem.' Vansittart, the Permanent Under Secretary, added: 'This is odd and may be rather tiresome.'[47]

And so it proved. Once the two systems were superimposed, it appeared impossible to find an alternative to the blockade on which to establish a 'step-level function' which would stabilize a nonintervention system. A decision was always delayed. Beckett observed much later in the conflict:

> If the British scheme for offering belligerent rights at some time in the future does come into operation, it would seem likely (unless the conflict takes a very different course from that which it appears likely to follow) that it will constitute the crowning illogicality of the whole treatment of the Spanish Civil War. The step of according belligerent rights is to take place at that moment when the war seems likely to end by the defeat of one side.[48]

THE DEFINITION OF THE PORTUGUESE CIVIL WAR

From the moment that news of Pedro's constitution for Portugal reached Europe, together with his decision to renounce the crown in favour of his daughter, British decision-makers felt that the potential for an interventionary situation had been created. Canning believed that if Metternich were to allow Miguel, Pedro's younger son, to leave Vienna at that moment, with the prospect of his arrival in Portugal, 'The consequences of such a step could be nothing but civil war.'[49] This prognostication was based on an assessment of the instability inherent within the Portuguese political system. Before the arrival of the constitution, A Court, Britain's ambassador in Lisbon, forecast that the government would fall as soon as the Ultras took control of Spain.[50] The lack of stability was a reflection of a fundamental cleavage within Portuguese society.

A Court also believed that it was impossible to prevent Miguel's return to Portugal for any length of time, but with his return 'an explosion would be inevitable, if some guarantee were not given for the liberty of the nation'. On the other hand: 'His long protracted exclusion from any share in the government might have the same result, though the movers of the disorder would in that case be different.'[51] Bifurcation was a feature of the Portuguese political system and the changes proposed by the new constitution served to accentuate the existing divisions. When A Court was informed of the nature of the provisions, he indicated that if Miguel returned at that moment 'he would probably assume complete control within a week without a shot being fired'. But he felt a need to qualify this assessment by adding that the liberals were determined to 'hang on' to the rights received under the constitution.[52]

Canning was convinced that if the constitution was not enacted, there would be a dispute with Pedro. 'The consequences of such a dispute are all too plain: civil war and foreign intervention.'[53] Despite Canning's concern, the official ceremony accepting the constitution passed peacefully at the beginning of August, although the absence of the Russian, Austrian, Prussian and Spanish ambassadors was noted.[54]

As the months passed, the polarization became more sharply defined. In September, A Court informed Canning: 'The principal question is no longer the constitutional question. The whole country is gradually splitting into Miguelite and anti-Miguelite.'[55] Canning requested him to impress on all parties in Portugal that in the event of a civil war, Great Britain would take no part.[56] The image which Canning was forming of a civil war in Portugal was reinforced by despatches from other sources. Granville informed him that Damas, the French Foreign Minister, had come to the conclusion that it was almost impossible 'to devise a mode of conduct which could preserve the kingdom from the evils of a civil war', although Villele, the French Premier, was less certain about the inevitability of this event.[57]

In conjunction with this clear image of a potential civil war in Portugal, an alternative image of the future developments in Portugal was formed. In mid-July, the Portuguese Government asked A Court if Britain would offer support in the event of an attack by Spain.[58] The answer was quite clear. Britain was committed by a series of ancient treaties to defend Portugal in the event of an external attack. Canning confirmed that 'we will fulfil the engagements of our treaties if the *casus foederis* should unhappily arise, but we will do nothing to hasten and everything in our power to avert it'. But it was clear that British decision-makers would determine when the *casus foederis* occurred. 'We will not send a military force to Portugal for any other purpose than to repel or avenge external aggression; in a case so clearly a *casus foederis* as to be stated to Parliament; and our Army will even in such a case, take no part in the internal dissension of the kingdom.'[59]

The prospect of a war between Spain and Portugal was perceived to be very real. It carried with it the potential for major system transformation. In May, A Court observed that there was no doubt about the Spanish hostility and that there were some in Spain who wished to absorb Portugal.[60] For Canning, the possibility of system transformation extended to the level of the international system. He believed:

> These are not ordinary times. Neither Portugal nor Spain is in an ordinary state. A war begun between Portugal and Spain would not only spread over Europe, but it would, from the cause in which it would originate, from the circumstances under which it would be carried on, become in a very short time a war of the most tremendous character, a war of extreme political principles committing not only nation against nation, but party against party throughout the different nations of the world.[61]

Given this perspective, any conflict on the Peninsula was likely to have important ramifications.

Because of the interdependence of the political systems in Spain and Portugal, it was difficult to envisage conflict being contained in either state. This was clearly appreciated by Lamb, the British ambassador in Madrid, who stated that revolution in Portugal would spread to Spain, and the Spanish Government would be 'pressed' to support the Apostolical party in Portugal.[62] The governments of both countries operated in environments over which they had little control and they had no guarantee that the directives which they issued to subordinates outside of their immediate control would be observed.[63]

A distinction between the two images formed by Canning cannot be maintained if the interdependence of the two political systems in Spain and Portugal is accepted. Canning insisted that Britain would not become involved in a civil war in Portugal but would send troops in the event of an external attack. This distinction was rigidly maintained. Yet all the information which Canning received indicated that the distinction was meaningless. Civil war in Portugal would engage Spain just as conflict within Spain would engage Portugal. It was not possible to envisage a civil war in Portugal which was confined within the Portuguese borders. The decision-makers, however, attempted to operate on the basis of two different definitions of the situation without ever questioning the interrelationship. A Court asked for a clarification of Britain's obligation to defend Portugal against an external attack, and his instructions in the event of a civil war, but no clarification of his instructions if the civil war was precipitated across the Spanish border.[64] The answer to this despatch was reflected in the instructions which A Court gave to the Portuguese Foreign Minister in November when it was accepted that the *casus foederis* only operated when Spanish troops invaded Portugal.[65]

When the Portuguese Government accepted Pedro's constitution, insur-rections broke out in Tras os Montes and Minho. The soldiers who revolted

proclaimed Miguel as king. Although the government successfully controlled these disturbances, thousands of Portuguese crossed the border into
Spain and formed a military force to support the absolutist cause in
Portugal.[66] Shortly afterwards, the Portuguese soldiers re-entered Portugal
and a major conflict developed.

Observers in Portugal were forced into defining the situation in terms of
one of the two images which had already been developed. Within two weeks
of insisting to the Portuguese Foreign Minister that the *casus foederis* could
only be activated in the event of an invasion by the Spanish troops, A
Court now agreed with the Portuguese Government:

> ... that if an invasion of this country take place by troops whose deser-
> tion has been provoked by Spain, who have been trained and exercised
> in Spain, who have been fed by Spain and paid by Spain, it matters not
> whether the troops are Portuguese or Spanish to make it a hostile aggres-
> sion by Spain, and consequently a *casus foederis*.[67]

Beresford, who had been sent out by the British Government to reorganize
the Portuguese army, was aware of the choice and asked: 'Will these
troops coming in be considered as an invading army? ... allowing these
troops to muster and indeed to give them arms and ammunition, is
clearly an act of hostility on the part of Spain as great I think as if her
own troops had accompanied them.'[68] However, after two days reflection
he preferred to define the situation as a civil war.

> I cannot say how you in England will consider the entrance into Portugal
> of these Portuguese troops a cause to induce you to take part against
> them and their adherents in Portugal, or if you will consider them in
> Portugal as the two parties fighting for superiority. But until we know
> here how you feel there on this point, as *de facto,* it is a civil war.[69]

It was A Court's definition of the situation which Canning chose to
accept. On 8 December, he wrote to Liverpool, the Prime Minister, and
argued, 'whether the rebels backed by Spain get on into Portugal, or are,
in this instance, driven back, it is plainly manifest that nothing but a direct
and unequivocal demonstration on the part of this country can save that
from revolution by foreign intrigue assisting domestic treason'.[70] He
defined the situation even more clearly in Parliament:

> If you do not go forth on this occasion to the aid of Portugal, Portugal
> will be trampled down to your irretrievable disgrace: and then will come
> war in the train of national degradation. If under circumstances like
> this, you wait till Spain has matured her secret machinations into open
> hostility, you will in a little while have the sort of war required by the
> pacifactors – and who shall know where that war will end?[71]

He argued that if it was suggested events in Portugal were:

> ... nothing of an external attack, nothing of foreign hostility, in such a
> system of aggression – such pretence would perhaps be only ridiculous;

if they did not acquire a much more serious character from being employed as an excuse for infidelity to ancient friendship, and as a pretext for getting rid of the stipulation of treaties.[72]

Canning accepted both the nonintervention norm and a norm which dictated the faithful execution of treaties. In terms of the operational milieu which existed, it was not possible to satisfy the two norms simultaneously. Civil war and external aggression were inextricably combined. Given the situation, one of the norms had to be sacrificed. By defining the situation as external aggression when conflict was initiated, troops had to be sent if the norm requiring the observation of treaties was to be satisfied. This was the policy which was pursued. If the situation had been defined as a civil war, then the norm dictating nonintervention must have taken precedence. Canning did, therefore, manage to operate within the ambit of both norms, but it was at the expense of the definition of the situation. There was a divergence between the operational and psycho-milieus. In the next chapter, those factors which determined the image used to define the situation will be examined.

THE DEFINITION OF THE RUSSIAN CIVIL WAR

Before the Bolsheviks took control in Russia and the war between Germany and Russia was terminated, the possibility of a civil war in Russia was considered.[73] The possibility was taken seriously and the Foreign Office informed Buchanan, the British ambassador in Russia: 'HMG feel strongly the disaster to the cause of the allies and to the future of democracy which will result from civil war in Russia.' He was requested to attempt to bring the various factions together.[74] A more clearly defined image of bifurcation emerged in a report written at the end of 1917 by Young, a British official in Russia. 'Northern Russia is more or less in the hands of the Bolsheviks, Southern Russia is more or less controlled by the opponents of the Bolsheviks.' He went on to suggest that the position of the anti-Bolsheviks was more secure. 'Northern Russia can be starved out by Southern Russia. Southern Russia on the other hand receives practically nothing from Northern Russia which it could not do without.'[75]

Lloyd George projected a similar image of bifurcation when he drew an analogy with Greece.

We did not abandon our friends, but put ourselves in a better position to help our friends. In Greece you had two communities led by the King and by Venizelos. The King was our enemy and Venizelos our friend. What did we do? We recognized both, but we utilized our position at Athens to protect Venizelos.[76]

The fragmentation which had gone on in Russia during the course of the war with Germany and after the demise of the Czar made this a difficult image to sustain. For many decision-makers, an image of anarchy within Russia prevailed. Buchanan observed in mid-December 1917: 'The Russians are quite incapable of rescuing their country from existing anarchy or of carrying out the work of reconstruction without foreign assistance.'[77] Sometimes the source of the anarchy was attributed to the Bolsheviks as a prelude to requesting the Germans to restore order;[78] on other occasions it was seen to be inherent in the situation. 'What with the growing influence of the anarchists and the struggle that is pending over the constitution, the ground is being prepared for that complete state of anarchy which will be but the precursor of monarchy.'[79] Milner felt that there was an advantage to be gained from this situation; the important factor was to prevent an authority structure forming in Southern Russia which would establish favourable trade terms with Germany. 'Civil war, or even the mere continuance of chaos and disorder would be an advantage to us from this point of view.'[80]

Finally, there was a potential image of a united Russia with which a normal dyadic interaction system could be established. There was a strong incentive to activate this image because of the role which Russia was playing in the war with Germany. After the first revolution, Buchanan was instructed to throw all his influence 'into the scale against any administration which is not resolved to fight to a finish'.[81] When the Bolsheviks established a government and sued for peace, Buchanan informed Trotsky that this constituted a violation of the agreement signed by Russia with the Allies at the beginning of the war.[82] The ability of the Bolshevik Government to negotiate with Germany indicated the existence of a dyadic interaction system and that they should be accorded *de facto* recognition. Buchanan's advice, at this time, pointed in this direction:

> The situation here is now so degenerate that we must reconsider our attitude and apply some new and exceptional treatment to the disease from which this country is suffering... I am of the opinion the only safe course left to us is to give Russia leave of absence from her word and tell her people that realizing how worn out they are by war and disorganization inseparable from great revolution we leave it to them to decide whether they will purchase peace on Germany's terms or fight on with the allies.[83]

If this advice had been accepted, it would have been appropriate to define the Bolshevik Government as a *de facto* government within a bifurcated state. Instead, the British attempted to implement the reverse of this policy. Buchanan was advised that it was to be the policy of the British Government: (1) to support any responsible body in Russia willing to oppose actively the Maximalist movement; (2) within reason to give money freely to such bodies as were prepared to help the allied cause.[84] It was the anarchy image which had been used to define the situation. In terms of this image, there was nothing resembling a government in Russia; the Bolsheviks were a movement sponsored by the Germans; it was the absence of a formulated government which prevented the Russians from continuing the war with the Germans.

The decision ran directly counter to all the advice being forwarded by Buchanan. At the beginning of December, he stated categorically: 'I am afraid the position in Russia is not at all understood at home. No Russian, Cossack or otherwise, will fight unless compelled to by foreign forces.'[85] When he received a memorandum from the Cabinet indicating that if a Southern bloc could be formed consisting of the Caucasus, the Cossacks, the Ukrainians, and the Roumanians, it would be possible to create a 'reasonably stable government',[86] he cabled back that he thought the plan 'fantastically unlikely'.[87] He also questioned the general instructions which he had been sent. 'To ask us to intrigue with the Cossacks while we are in the power of the rebel government is merely to get our throats cut to no purpose.'[88]

Other officials in Russia had the same reaction. Barclay, in Jassy, who was instructed to finance the anti-Bolsheviks in the Ukraine, observed: 'I should fail in my duty if I conceal from you my opinion that all our efforts in this direction, however generously financed they may be, are nothing but a forlorn hope.'[89] Officials in London soon came to share this opinion. Cecil noted: 'We have been trying not very successfully to get in touch with our organizations in Southern Russia. The Russians seem determined not to fight with anyone except one another. Even that they do in a half-hearted way.'[90]

There appears to have been a wide disparity between the operational and psycho-milieus of the decision-makers when they initially defined the situation. A modification of the policy followed almost immediately. On 9 December, Balfour, the Foreign Secretary, was arguing against 'an open breach with this crazy system'.[91] It was agreed with the French that both countries should remain in communication with the Bolsheviks for as long as possible, but that 'support should be given to the anti-Bolshevik elements in Southern Russia who wished to continue the war with Germany, even if the ultimate result might be to render the Bolsheviks antagonistic'.[92]

French agents, however, continued to be encouraged to support organizations which were to fight both the Germans and the Bolsheviks. Cecil commented: 'I wish the French would not talk about fighting the Maximalists. We have neither business nor intention of doing so. Our sole object at present should be to strengthen Southern Russia so as to prevent its supplies falling into the hands of the Germans.'[93] But in terms of the operational environment, the conflict was with the Bolsheviks and not the Germans. Support given to Southern Russia contributed to the civil war, despite Cecil's disclaimer. Confusion about the motive behind the support for Southern Russia persisted. Four months later, a Foreign Office official minuted: 'Our object in assisting the Ursuri Cossacks was to enable them to consolidate their position with a view eventually to attacking the Bolsheviks at Habervorsk. If, however, there is any serious hope of a rapprochement between the Allies and the Bolsheviks, it seems undesirable that we should continue to assist the opponents of the latter.'[94]

The confusion was never resolved. And as the result of backing any group which claimed to be anti-Bolshevik, two years later British decision-makers were providing support to all the independence movements within Russia together with those leaders who favoured a united Russia. Curzon referred to the situation as a 'Frankenstein'.[95] Throughout this period, importance continued to be attributed to the nonintervention norm. It was possible to do this by continuing to define the situation in terms of an anarchical system where there was no *de facto* government. But the decision to send troops into Russia was made in the context of the dyadic interaction system. This system was based upon a definition of the situation in which the Bolshevik Government was treated as the *de facto* government. The factors which permitted the superimposition of these two divergent definitions of the situation will be examined in the next chapter.

AMBIGUITY AND DEFINITION

The four case studies provide some confirmation for the second proposition. In the two cases where the sharp divergence between the operational and psycho-milieus occurs there appears to be a higher level of ambiguity contained within the situation, and before the definition of the situation was precipitated alternative images of the situation did seem to exist. Holsti has attributed the capacity of decision-makers to formulate a definition of the situation which diverges from the operational milieu to a closed belief system.[96] It appears from the case studies examined here that a divergence can be more easily explained by reference to the nature of the situation which is being defined.

The process can be compared to rumour formation, where 'the basic unit of analysis becomes the *ambiguous situation* and the central problem is to ascertain how working orientations toward it develop'.[97] Allport and Postman summarized their findings in terms of three concepts: '*leveling* designates the tendency of accounts to become shorter, more concise, and more easily grasped; *sharpening*, the tendency toward selective perception, retention, and the reporting of a limited number of details; and *assimilation*, the tendency of reports to become more coherent and consistent with the presuppositions and interests of the subjects.'[98]

When situations give rise to complex and ambiguous information, decision-makers seem to formulate a series of divergent images which can be potentially employed to define the situation. Each image represents a considerable simplification of the operational environment. When a response is implemented, only one of the images is used to define the situation and, as a consequence, the situation is defined on the basis of an image which diverges in some important aspects from the operational environment. In the next chapter, there will be a discussion of the factors which influence the image used to define the interventionary situation.

CHAPTER 4
Definition of the Response

ALTHOUGH states often interact in the international system at the multilateral level, most international behaviour is bilateral and norms defined as international are designed to guide bilateral interaction. By adhering to these norms, states develop stable relationships which persist over time and these can be defined by dyadic interaction systems. Systemic behaviour can be identified when actors evolve a set of formal or informal rules which guide their decisions. When behaviour is routinized or rule-governed, a boundary can be located which circumscribes this behaviour and defines the system. Because each dyadic interaction system is idiosyncratic in some respects, the exact location of the boundary will vary in each case, but through a process of socialization, actors in any social system can learn and readily identify systemic and extra-systemic behaviour. There are occasions when established norms are broken and an actor operates outside the system, but most of the time actors prefer to operate within the systemic boundary, accepting the constraints on behaviour imposed by the norms, in order to maintain a stable environment.

The analysis of behavioural systems, therefore, cannot be restricted to an investigation of the way in which the actors behave within the system; the cognitive element must also be examined. It is the factor of cognition which distinguishes social and mechanical systems. To ignore cognition is to ignore a key attribute of the social system. In this chapter it is argued that the boundary of the dyadic interaction system is defined by the participating actors. Under conditions of stability, boundary definition presents no problem; behaviour is routinized and does not endanger the established boundary. However, when an element of instability is introduced into the system and the actors have to cope with uncertainty, boundary definition becomes of critical importance.

Instability within the state is regulated in the international system by the nonintervention norm, which stipulates that international actors must refrain from interfering in each other's domestic jurisdiction. The essential characteristics of all international dyadic interaction systems – the cohesion of the component actors – is dependent upon this norm. But certain events can render any norm inappropriate as a means of maintaining stability. To accommodate such events, any stable system possesses metanorms which take precedence over the established norms on these occasions. System change is precipitated in the interest of maintaining stability within a framework which will permit the restoration of the original point of equilibrium. The nonintervention norm is covered by a metanorm; it specifies that civil wars constitute a form of subsystemic conflict which necessitates system change. The established point of equilibrium in the dyadic intervention system cannot contain the resulting instability and the metanorm identifies a new point of equilibrium which embraces the two units in the bifurcated actor.[1]

When a system operates on the basis of an equilibrium perceived to be stable, actors pay little attention to the delineation of the boundary which describes the system. Behaviour tends to be routinized and by definition such behaviour falls within the established boundary of the system. However, when a system becomes unstable, actors become preoccupied with the restoration of stability, either by reasserting the established equilibrium or by precipitating system change and introducing a new point of equilibrium. Both possibilities are discussed in this chapter and it is shown that decision-makers do become acutely conscious about the location of the system boundary under such circumstances. Before stating the proposition on which this chapter is based, the relationship which exists between system change and transformation and the location of a boundary to a system will be clarified at a theoretical level.

SYSTEM BOUNDARIES AND SYSTEM CHANGE

All systems display the property of boundary maintenance. In the case of a mechanical system, like a car or a central heating unit, the boundary of the system can generally be located by defining the physical structure of the system's components. For some social scientists, biological systems can be identified in the same way, and it is maintained that 'the task of distinguishing the organism from its environment is rather easy; the parameters of the environment stop at the organism's skin'.[2] This reflects the kind of over-simplification which a social scientist would be quick to point out if it was stated that: the boundary of a school system is rather easy to observe; it extends to the perimeter of the school property. Natural and social scientists, when operating in their own spheres, however, recognize that boundary definition presents problems. The difference between natural and social systems relates not to the observability of the boundary but rather to the capacity of actors to change the location of the boundary by modifying their conception of the system. For some people, the boundary of a school system does only extend as far as the physical limits of the school; this influences their behaviour, which in turn affects where a social scientist defines the boundary of a school system.

Although social behaviour is influenced by the location of physical boundaries, it is not normally useful to employ boundaries of this sort when identifying a social system. It is on the basis of behavioural interaction that these systems can be defined. Deutsch examines systems in terms of communication patterns and suggests that boundaries occur where there are 'marked discontinuities in the frequency of transactions and marked discontinuities in the frequency of responses'.[3] When a child leaves home, he may continue to rely on his parents for money or affection, and the resulting transactions ensure that the child remains part of the family system. If these transactions terminate, then the child is excluded from the system. Actors are conscious of operating in a system and they can identify behaviour as systemic or extra-systemic. Their behaviour is constrained by the knowledge of where the boundary of the system is located.

An actor's definition of the situation is, therefore, an important component of a social system. This is true even in role-defined systems. Individuals who adopt roles know the rules which define their respective roles; the system forms as soon as the roles are occupied, even when there has been no previous interaction between the individuals playing the roles. But the exact location of the boundary will be determined by personality and situational factors; customers and waiters, for example, often attempt to locate the boundary in a position which favours their own role.

The more imprecise the norms associated with a system, the more flexible becomes the location of the boundary. But any stable interaction system must allow for some flexibility, reflected in the 'equilibrium oscillations' displayed by a system.[4] The oscillations denote the presence of feedback in the system. In a theatre, for example, there can be constant feedback between audience and actor and the relationship can undergo substantial changes during the course of a performance, all within the limits of an accepted boundary. The relationship can range from the audience and an actor being cold and unresponsive, to where an actor is obviously responding to an audience's enthusiasm. But there are limits to how far a boundary can be extended in any system and this circumscribes the kind of responses open to the actors. The nature of these limits varies considerably from milieu to milieu: what is permissible for an audience watching a Victorian melodrama, for example, is certainly not permissible for an audience watching a Shakespearean tragedy.

Because rules are mutually accepted by actors in a dyadic interaction system, an attempt to change the rules unilaterally by one actor will prove disconcerting to the other. An audience in the theatre, for example, can become very hostile if the actors do not 'act' but attempt to converse with the audience. No doubt a string quartet would also be disconcerted if the audience audibly displayed their enthusiasm during the course of a performance as generally happens in a jazz concert. At the international level, the United States reacted in a hostile fashion when the Soviet Union placed missiles on Cuba. The Soviet action contravened the informal rule which gives each 'super-power' hegemonic rights in their respective spheres of influence. The United States was caught off-guard on this occasion because the action deviated from the accepted code of conduct. Deviation from the established rules creates uncertainty and actors will generally attempt to reassert the original rule as soon as possible after a deviation has occurred. If this attempt fails, and a new pattern of behaviour emerges, then the development marks a system transformation. For example, if a waiter is invited to join some customers at a table, and does so, generally the management will find this an unsatisfactory arrangement. However, if custom increases as a consequence, the behaviour may be institutionalized, denoting a transformation of the system.

System change and transformation can come about in one of two ways. First the change may reflect a *diachronic* pattern of exchange, where the actors mutually agree to change or transform a system. For example, if the wardrobe staff go on strike in a theatre, actors and audience may agree to allow a performance to proceed without the use of costumes. This constitutes a system change, because the original situation will be restored as soon as the strike is settled. But there can be a mutual agreement to transform a system. Most of the British colonies established their independence on this basis. Secondly one actor in the system may undergo a fundamental and unilateral change over which other actors have no control, but to which they will have to adjust unilaterally. This is termed *synchronic* adjustment. For example, if a state places a large tariff on all imported goods, then other states will have to adjust synchronically.[5] Normally, change within an actor does not affect the system in which it interacts. It is possible for an actor to undergo substantial internal change without disrupting or destabilizing the system itself to any great extent.[6] Subsystemic disruption only impinges upon the system when it affects the ability of the actor to operate within the boundary of the system. A state, for example, can undergo considerable turmoil without causing any disruption to its external relations, but at some point the disruption will affect the ability of the state to operate in the international system. When this point is reached, it may be necessary to modify the existing boundary of the system.

The nonintervention norm is premised on the assumption that a clear distinction can be drawn between domestic and international politics. Its accompanying metanorm sustains this distinction, but indicates that the boundary of the nonintervention system must be redrawn in the event of civil war, changing the point of equilibrium in the system to include a third actor. The nonintervention norm stipulates that an incumbent government must be given every opportunity to settle any disorder which may occur within the state up to the point where the subsystemic conflict constitutes an intervention stimulus: then the metanorm stipulates that a second state must adjust synchronically and establish contact with both units in the bifurcated state. Only the nonbifurcated actor can shift the point of equilibrium in this way. But once the system change has been accomplished synchronically, then the actual delineation of the boundary which describes the system change will often be established on a diachronic basis, with the nonbifurcated actor attempting to delineate the boundary in a way which will minimize any antagonism caused by the system change.

In none of the cases examined did the nonbifurcated actor feel entitled to deviate from the nonintervention norm on the grounds of extenuating circumstances. Decision-makers, however, are aware that no norm is universally applicable and that all norms are subject to a metanorm which permits a particular norm to be disregarded if its implementation is likely to precipitate conflict or lead to international instability. It would be generally accepted that

> There occur, from time to time, cases in which the ordinary rules established by the Law of Nations cannot be observed without promoting the continuance of wars, desolating in their character, threatening a wide extension, and dangerous to the balance of power. For instance, there is no more confirmed rule than that of leaving every sovereign the unrestricted power of putting down rebellion in his own territory.[7]

Lord John Russell, who put forward this argument, went on to cite several instances where the European states felt that it was necessary to modify the rule. This metanorm was not employed in the cases of intervention responses examined here. It was not the norm but perception which was modified.

It is stipulated in this chapter then that the definition of the stimulus is dictated by the nature of the response which is implemented. It is proposed that:

Proposition 3: When an actor implements an intervention response, the interventionary situation is defined in terms of systemic conflict; when an actor implements a nonintervention response, the interventionary situation is defined in terms of subsystemic conflict.

This proposition represents an unusual formulation. Behaviourists distinguish sharply between the stimulus and the response: a stimulus (the cause) is considered to precipitate a response (the effect). It is insisted that cause precedes effect. If the effect precedes the cause, then the explanation becomes teleological and traditionally the scientific method dictates that teleological explanations are invalid. With the infusion of systems thinking into the behavioural sciences, however, it is now acknowledged that if behaviour can be defined in terms of a system, then the linear relationship postulated in causal explanation breaks down. If a feedback loop is included in the analysis, it can be seen that how an actor decides to behave will affect the way in which a situation is defined; because of the feedback

loop, the nature of a response will have an important effect on the perception of the stimulus.[8] The analysis of the cases which follow illustrates that
the nature of a stimulus perceived by an actor is determined by the kind of
system which an actor identifies, and the location of the system boundary
is determined by the response which is implemented.

BOUNDARY FORMATION AND THE COLLECTIVE NONINTERVENTION RESPONSE

Before the outbreak of conflict in the United States, British decision-makers
already possessed an image of bifurcation. Contingency plans were discussed concerning the synchronic adjustment of the boundary of the interaction system which had to be made once conflict occurred. The French
were also concerned with the problem, and the French ambassador in
Washington wrote a paper in which he argued that the Southern States
ought to be recognized before conflict was initiated in order to avoid giving
the impression that the act was unfriendly. Lyons believed that such a move
would not be given a friendly interpretation and he advised that the
boundary must not be altered until absolutely necessary. But he did
recognize a critical point in this process. To avoid delay, he even suggested
that the local consuls should be empowered to grant recognition when this
critical point was reached.[9]

The introduction of the blockade, when conflict was initiated, made it
relatively easy for the British decision-makers to introduce system change
by conferring belligerent status on the Southern States. Because of the
synchronic nature of the change, the Northern decision-makers had no
alternative to accepting the alteration in the boundary implemented by the
British. But once the change had taken place, the diachronic pattern of
exchange returned, and the Northern States were in a position to affect
the definition of the new boundary. The principal concern of the Northern
States was to prevent system transformation. In its most extreme form,
Lyons indicated that the Northern States were prepared to declare war on
any party which recognized the Southern States.

Behaviour which reflected system change rather than transformation,
and the boundary which separated the two, was established by mutual
interaction. Adams indicated that he would be forced to break off diplomatic relations with Britain if there was contact with the Confederate agents
in England.[10] Russell only saw them in an unofficial capacity.[11] Lyons
insisted that the British Government would find it necessary 'to make the
Cabinet of Washington clearly understand that the British *must* and *will*
hold unofficial communications with the Southern Government on matters
concerning the interests of their subjects'.[12] The boundary did eventually
distinguish between official and unofficial contact.

BOUNDARY FORMATION AND THE UNILATERAL NONINTERVENTION RESPONSE

While boundaries which established the triadic structure of a nonintervention system were formulated and maintained with comparative ease during the civil war in the United States, the formulation and maintenance of boundaries remained a persistent problem throughout the civil war in Spain. To a great extent, this reflected the failure in the early stages of the conflict to acknowledge the existence of the triad, which can be accounted for by a combination of circumstances. The failure of Madrid to fall, for example, removed the event which was to provide the 'step-level function'. In addition, the French refused to regard the event in this light, intending to withdraw their *chargé d'affaires* if the city was captured, without giving any form of recognition to the insurgents. Eden attempted to modify French policy[13] but it was his attitude which changed when the German and the Italian Governments accorded Franco's Government *de jure* status.

When Franco announced his intention to blockade Barcelona, Eden argued: 'He could not do this without exercising belligerent rights, and by granting them we should be held to be taking a preliminary, indispensable step to his acting and thus helping his cause.' It was further suggested that Franco's cause was failing at that moment and Britain's recognition would lead to even more assistance being given by the Germans and Italians.[14]

Once this position was established, then it appeared that any attempt to change the existing boundary would lead to system transformation rather than system change. There did not seem to be any way in which the intermediate stage could be defined. When the War Office requested the Foreign Office for approval to send a military attaché to Franco, Eden expressed considerable concern and asked if the issue could be held over for a week or two.[15] After reconsideration, the Foreign Office accepted the need for the military attaché, but Eden continued to worry in case the action would extend the existing boundary. He eventually agreed to have an assistant military attaché sent from Paris at intervals.[16]

A similar problem arose some weeks later when a memorandum was sent to Eden in which it was argued that British commercial and military interests were suffering because of the failure to establish direct contacts with the Franco Government. It was specifically argued that the appointment of agents 'on an informal basis does not mean that HMG considers that the present situation justifies recognizing General Franco's administration as the Government of Spain'.[17] The Cabinet accepted this argument, reflecting a change in the perception of what constituted boundary-breaking behaviour. It was agreed that an attempt should be made to establish an agent with General Franco but that this should not be on a reciprocal basis.[18] The absence of reciprocity now provided the critical demarcation line.

The offer was refused and the subsequent negotiations were conducted in the context of diachronic exchange. Eventually, the British agreed to modify the boundary, and Eden announced: 'I propose that we should inform General Franco that we are prepared to accept an agent of his in London in exchange for the establishment of a British agent at Salamanca.'[19] In the course of the negotiations, the British decided that the boundary could be extended to incorporate the reciprocal arrangement without extending recognition to the Franco regime. The failure to give Franco any formal *de facto* recognition was a source of considerable irritation to some Foreign Office officials. One claimed 'ever since September 1936, by our whole course of action we have admitted and could not deny that there was a war and that Franco was a party'.[20] The failure to resolve this problem provides a measure of the difficulty associated with altering established boundaries.

During the civil war in Spain, the boundary which distinguished action of the private citizens for which the government was responsible also came under constant discussion. Initially, there was a conscious effort by the Foreign Office to dissociate the Government from action which could be attributed to a private citizen. They refused to comment when the Air Ministry asked for an opinion on a private company which was known to be supplying aeroplanes to the insurgent government, beyond the fact that while they disapproved, the government had no authority to interfere with the transaction. Malkin added: 'It seems rather a pity that any question of "approving" the transaction has been raised.'[21] It was decided as a matter of policy not to give advice to firms which were approached by the insurgents. Mounsey argued: 'If we once begin giving advice or putting pressure on any of these people, we shall get ourselves into very deep water.'[22]

It is impracticable for governments to assume responsibility for a wide range of activities undertaken by private citizens, but some areas must be considered. In the course of defining the boundary of a nonintervention system, the Italian Government insisted on a provision which precluded public subscriptions for either side in the civil war. A Foreign Office official noted: 'If the Italians make a condition about public subscriptions a *sine qua non* it doesn't look very hopeful.'[23] The Home Office was quick to point out to Eden that it was 'not aware of any provision of English law under which it could be a criminal offence for a person in England to invite a subscription to a fund to either party in the present Spanish conflict'.[24] An Act of Parliament was, therefore, required in order to enforce an international agreement to this effect in England. The Home Office, responsible for the enforcement of such a provision, was not anxious to see the boundary which defined governmental responsibility extended in this way.

For British decision-makers, the action of private citizens only affected the boundary of the nonintervention system when they volunteered for either side in a civil war. Traditionally, this had delineated the point when the individual could intervene, and the law prohibited him from doing so. During the Carlist Wars in the 1830s this law had been rescinded and 8000 British mercenaries had been recruited following a special arrangement with the government;[25] this had blurred the boundary and caused confusion. In 1860, Palmerston used the Italian conflict to clarify the situation. He suggested that 'the best course to take when any fresh application is made to enforce the Foreign Enlistment Act against excursionists for Italy, would be to submit the papers to the Law Officers of the Crown and do whatever they may advise'.[26] A further attempt to clarify the issue was made in 1870 when a new Foreign Enlistment Act was passed. When the Italian Government attempted to equate the Italian troops who were volunteering to fight for the insurgent government with the British citizens who were volunteering to fight for the incumbent government, decision-makers referred back to the 1870 Act.[27]

This caused some confusion because Sir John Simon, for the Home Office, argued that the Act could be interpreted to mean that volunteers were permitted to fight for the incumbent, but not the insurgent, government. The Foreign Office were sure that those who framed the Act must have been aware that

> HMG have normally adopted an attitude of neutrality in civil wars and have often issued proclamations of neutrality in such cases; yet a situation in which it was an offence without licence from the crown to enlist on one side in a civil war, while it was no offence to enlist on the other, would clearly cut across the ordinary obligation of neutrality under international law.[28]

The Foreign Office asked the Attorney General for clarification and he accepted their interpretation, that it would be illegal for a British citizen to participate on either side of a civil war.[29]

Given the confusion which existed among officials on this issue, it was felt necessary to make a public declaration on the matter, thus clarifying the boundary. Even this proved controversial. One Foreign Office official, Roberts, doubted 'whether we should take any steps here in advance of other countries and I think we should consider further the question of the appropriate moment for the issue of a warning'.[30] When officials in Madrid asked what attitude they should adopt towards the volunteers, Fitzmaurice, a legal adviser, argued that in the light of the ruling on the Foreign Enlistment Act, no assistance should be given to them; since the ruling had never been made public, other officials felt that this judgement was too severe.[31]

Shortly afterwards, the ruling was made public. Republican supporters considered it biased in favour of the insurgents, and issued strong criticism. Since the insurgent government had never received any form of recognition, it was not possible to defend the action with reference to the norm of nonintervention, though it was this norm which had dictated the ruling. Officials were very sensitive on this point. Shuckburgh simply affirmed the legality of the action and argued: 'Nor is the supply of volunteers by Germany and Italy any reason why we should permit similar movements contrary to the law. It is absurd to interpret our action as "support for the rebels".'[32] British decision-makers, continuing to work on the assumption that he had received recognition, warned Franco that Britain would react very strongly if her volunteers were not treated according to the dictates of international law.[33]

As the conflict progressed, the British decision-makers became increasingly concerned to ensure that Britain's behaviour was circumscribed by the boundary of the nonintervention system. This is reflected in the attitude to 'humanitarianism', which was initially distinguished from intervention. Offers of humanitarian assistance were turned down by both sides, at first, and it was decided to reserve humanitarian efforts until the proposals became 'practical and acceptable'; before then, they would give 'countenance but no support to the various private British charitable organizations which have been doing some excellent work on a small scale in Spain'. Mounsey felt that this policy had undergone a change which made it difficult to offer advice.

> The apparent change of policy occurred most markedly when it was decided that British foodships should be forcibly escorted to Bilbao waters at a time when Bilbao was on the verge of surrender through lack of food. Having been prevented from starving Bilbao into terms by one act, Franco resorted to bombing it into fear . . . HMG then permitted the navy to evacuate the civil population.

He concluded that 'the increasing emphasis which HMG are evidently now laying upon what was hitherto their subsidiary humanitarian policy' was 'at the direct expense of the policy of non-intervention'.[34]

The absence of any divergence between the operational and psychomilieus forced the decision-makers to conform their behaviour patterns to the nonintervention system dictated by the accepted definition of the situation. Although it was maintained that some decisions were based on the dyadic, and some on the triadic interaction system, it was impossible to sustain this position. Behaviour overwhelmingly reflected the nonintervention system. The increasing anomaly of the situation, where behaviour diverged from the stipulated definition of the situation, helps to explain why the boundary between recognition and non-recognition moved in such a marked fashion during the course of the conflict.

BOUNDARY FORMATION AND THE UNILATERAL INTERVENTION RESPONSE

Portugal seemed to pose an intractable problem. Near the end of October 1826, Canning wrote to his ambassador in Paris: 'The war between Spain and Portugal, or rather by Spain and Portugal, is actually begun.' As a consequence, this brought 'the question of *casus foederis* home to us in a manner we cannot escape'.[35] Four days later he observed to his ambassador in Lisbon: 'The *casus foederis* has not occurred, and our wish and our duty ... is rather to prevent its occurrence than to anticipate it by a single hour.'[36] Neither statement accurately reflected the way that Canning perceived the situation. The first was written in an attempt to convince the French that the situation in Portugal was viewed in a serious light; the second, to deter the thought that British involvement was inevitable.

During October, the Portuguese had made two requests for British auxiliary troops to be sent to Lisbon. Canning sensed that these were to ensure internal security within Portugal. On this he commented:

> It is possible that it may be so; but there is no certainty, on the other hand, that the presence of the British army in Portugal might not create dangers within, and promote aggression from without. If there be a party in Portugal not hostile to the new order of things, what more plausible pretext could be afforded to the opposition of such a party, than that a foreign army had been brought into the country to force a constitution upon the people? ... The arrival of the British army in Portugal would be a signal for increased activity [of the fanatical party in Spain] and would furnish many topics to inflame the passions of the Spanish nation.[37]

The use of the army could only serve to exacerbate the problem which the British wished to resolve. When Liverpool laid down possible lines of policy, in the event of an attack on Portugal, the use of troops was not even mentioned.[38]

The danger of becoming involved in a civil war had long been recognized. Castlereagh argued in 1820: 'Our engagements were never intended to apply to combatting revolutionary movements inside Portugal itself.'[39] As soon as the first signs of bifurcation were perceived in 1826, the boundaries of an incipient nonintervention system began to be established. A series of incidents threatened to violate the boundaries of this system and they were all resolved in favour of nonintervention. The constitution which Don Pedro granted widened the existing cleavages within the Portuguese political system. It was brought to Portugal by Charles Stuart, the British ambassador in Brazil, causing the British Government some embarrassment.

It was argued that he performed this task in his capacity as a private citizen, while simultaneously playing the role of ambassador. Shortly after Stuart arrived in Portugal, Canning requested his recall, in order to elimi-

nate the difficulties created by this dual role. Canning noted that although
A Court might be able to observe a clearly marked distinction, 'it is not
to be supposed that such a line of demarcation can have been visible at a
distance or that the nations of Europe... would consent to overlook
altogether Sir Charles Stuart's British character and to presume his conduct and character to be entirely independent of the British Government'.[40]

The implications of a nonintervention system were spelled out to the
Portuguese Government. A Court informed them that if he saw 'any
symptoms of a disposition to go beyond what had been legally established
or to excite sedition and revolt' he would withdraw the British fleet from
the Tagus.[41] The fleet had been sent to Portugal in 1823; the Portuguese
Government had requested troops, a request which was firmly refused.
Canning agreed to send the fleet in order to give some satisfaction to the
Portuguese while allowing Britain to retain mobility and freedom of
action.[42] As the situation in Portugal deteriorated, the presence of the
fleet was a source of concern for Canning, and he required A Court to
threaten the Portuguese Government that Britain would be 'the first to
shrink away from any sort of connection with those who confounded those
blessings [of civil and religious liberty] with revolution and anarchy'.[43]
Canning sent explicit instructions that there could be no question of Britain
participating in a civil war.[44]

In October 1826, all Portuguese troops were required to leave Lisbon in
order to subdue insurrections in other parts of the country. The Government requested A Court to permit troops to land to protect the King. At
first, A Court refused, but later relented and agreed that a guard could be
landed 'every day for the *sole service* of the Palace'. He did not believe
that there was any concern for the royal family, and he defined the request
as 'merely a pretext, and the moral effect is the object aimed at'. But he
argued that since the action was taken 'without the risk of committing
ourselves beyond our profession I cannot think that HMG will disapprove
of my having afforded this last assistance to what I fear is a sinking
cause'.[45] Canning condoned the assistance but decided to reduce the size
of the fleet. The Portuguese were to be told: 'The present aspect of affairs
in Portugal is so very satisfactory and the chances of a foreign aggression
appear to be so diminished... that His Britannic Majesty's Government
think it advisable to seize this opportunity of reducing the amount of the
British force stationed in the Tagus.'[46] Before the order could be implemented, the decision to send troops had been made.

Failure to implement the nonintervention system, and the perception
of the conflict at the systemic level, allowing the defence system to come
into operation, reflected a predisposition among British decision-makers
which was in evidence before the situation was finally defined in terms of
external aggression. The possibility of defining the conflict at the subsystemic level had always existed. Granville, looking at the situation from

a French perspective, noted in August that if the Spaniards continued to take Portuguese deserters, while the Portuguese gave refuge to Spanish deserters, 'this will soon end up with civil war in both countries'.[47] Canning recognized the implication of this argument and expressed it in strong terms; it was 'against *unprovoked* aggression only that HMG is bound to defend Portugal. And if it be true, as Y.E. justly observes, that Spain may resort to other modes of aggression than open attack, it is no less true, on the other hand, that Portugal without doing any hostile *act* may be guilty of a hostile provocation.' Prophesying a revolution in Spain, he felt, would constitute just such an act.[48]

During these months, there were numerous examples of provocation on either side of the border. But while a favourable interpretation was always placed on the Portuguese motivation, Spanish actions and intentions were condemned. In September, A Court indicated that although the desertion into Spain from the Portuguese army had stopped, Spainsh troops continued to come over the border into Portugal. He commented on how difficult it was for the Portuguese to control such action.[49] Later in the month, after a complaint from the Spaniards that there had been incursions into Spain by Portuguese troops, the Portuguese explained to A Court that this was a retaliation for the foray into Portugal. It was carried out 'without the knowledge of the Portuguese authorities', and A Court added, 'It really does appear to me to be impossible not to admit the spirit of conciliation, the prudence, and the moderation which have marked all measures of the Portuguese Government.'[50]

By October, A Court had to admit that there were elements within the Portuguese Government wanting to pursue measures which would cause an 'explosion in Spain'.[51] Four days later, he reported about a club that had been formed to raise recruits from among the Spanish refugees and that the Minister of War was involved. The Portuguese Government assured him that the situation would be rectified. But later that month, Spanish officers were allowed to arrive in Lisbon and their intention was to link up with the Spanish deserters in Portugal. Again, the government agreed to take steps to control the officers.[52] When the situation was defined at the systemic level, Canning argued that the Portuguese Government had exercised great restraint and the conflict could not be attributed to them. 'The forbearance of that Government has been superhuman.'[53] Blame was always attached to the Spanish. 'It is obvious', Canning noted, 'that the intention of the Spanish Government (or rather the party which governs that Government) is to place Spain in an attitude towards Portugal which may excite disquietudes and encourage disaffection in the latter kingdom without committing Spain in actual hostility.'[54] A similar bias is apparent in A Court's perception of the situation. 'Desertions from this country have been provoked and encouraged by Spanish emissaries, whereas the desertions from Spain have been discouraged in every possible manner. Offers of desertion have been made upon almost every point along the frontier, and it is with great difficulty that a much more considerable number of troops are prevented from coming over. The Portuguese Government is irreproachable upon this head.'[55]

The source of this predisposition seems to relate to the continued presence of the French troops in Spain, which, after three years, Canning considered 'unendurable'.[56] Granville and Lamb indicated that while the French were anxious to end this expensive venture, the Spanish Government felt the presence of the troops ensured their security and were unwilling to see the French depart.[57] Lamb was convinced that there was no adequate reason for their continued stay.[58] Serious discussions about the departure of the French troops began at the beginning of June[59] but by mid-June, the French were expressing concern about the possible effects of the Portuguese constitution on the tranquillity of Spain.[60] The question of withdrawing the troops was postponed[61] and the French ambassador in Madrid supported the decision to move Spanish troops to the Portuguese border.[62]

When the decision was taken to send troops to Portugal, the presence of the French troops in Spain had become a preoccupation with Canning, to the point that Wellington had to remind him that the British troops were not being sent to Portugal 'because the French troops are in Spain'.[63] In fact, this was the context in which Canning's decision was made. On previous occasions, when Wellington had wanted troops to be sent to Portugal, Canning had always opposed the decision on the grounds that it would involve an interference in the domestic affairs of the country.[64] On this occasion, Canning insisted that if Britain had not sent troops, there would have been a movement to the 'frontier of Portugal with a *reinforced* French army in Spain'.[65] The subsytemic aspects of the action were ignored; the perception of the situation was focused at the systemic level and it was in this context that the situation was defined.

In the debate upon the decision to send troops, Bright reminded the House that the 'assailants were exiles who had taken refuge in Spain. The country was divided; and if England were to side with either party, she would be taking part in a civil war.'[66] Outside of Parliament, it was also commented that there was a distinct possibility 'of all being settled before our troops can get out, and then we shall be in rather a puzzling position'.[67] As far as Wellington was concerned, this problem was immediately resolved by resort to the subsystemic definition of the situation and he noted, when drawing up the instructions for the troops, that he was sure that A Court 'will not allow them to be landed even upon the requisition of the regent to involve them in a hopeless revolutionary contest at the very moment of their disembarkation'.[68] Once the decision to send the troops had been made and the situation defined at the systemic level, it was possible to allow the alternative definitions of the situation to come back into focus.

BOUNDARY FORMATION AND THE COLLECTIVE INTERVENTION RESPONSE

When the Bolsheviks withdrew Russia from the war with Germany, the event constituted system transformation for many British decision-makers. The event was perceived to eliminate the Eastern front, thereby allowing the Germans to concentrate their forces on the Western front. The military felt that drastic measures should be taken to remedy the situation; it was stipulated by the War Office that if troops were not sent to Russia immediately, 'we shall have no chance of being ultimately victorious and shall incur serious risk of defeat in the meantime'.[69] Decision-makers in the United States found it difficult to accept this interpretation of events. House wrote to President Wilson, 'It is a panicky document in the main and neither Reading nor I agree to the statement that a decision is not possible on the Western front without an Eastern front as well.'[70] Lloyd George had also 'lost interest in Russia as a working factor in the success of the allies'[71] and was not anxious to see troops sent to Russia. Advocates of the policy, like Cecil, recognized this fact and complained that if the Prime Minister 'attached the same importance to Allied intervention in Siberia that you do to the increase of American troops in France, I feel that the whole treatment of the question would have been different'.[72]

Considerable support for the need to send troops came from other sources, however. The British representative in Odessa argued that because the Russians were incapable of organizing themselves, the organization must be done by an outside power. 'If the Allies do not make up their minds to help Russia actively to restore order, then I am of the opinion that Germany will establish a hold on this country such as it will be impossible to remove.'[73] Greene, the ambassador in Tokyo, put forward a similar policy. 'Owing to the present conditions, it is inadvisable for the Allies to continue a policy of non-intervention in Russia. The present situation is a second revolution organized by Germany and is vitally dangerous to the Allies.'[74]

Arguments of this sort, stressing the instability of the situation, all operated at the systemic level, although they reflected the image of anarchy within Russia. They contrasted sharply with the information which was sent by other British representatives in Russia. Lindley, who saw most of the telegrams which Trotsky sent from Brest Litovsk, insisted that they 'show conclusively that Trotsky did everything possible to thwart and make difficulties for the Germans. There can be no question of his honesty in this matter.'[75] Lockhart argued 'we cannot do more than delay and hamper as far as possible German economic penetration in Russia and towards that end the Bolshevists are more likely to help us than any other group'.[76]

Foreign Office officials were unable to assimilate this information within

the image of anarchy. In the same way, any attempt to establish an image
of a bifurcated system within Russia, divided between the Bolsheviks and
the anti-Bolsheviks, was undermined by information sent from Russia. The
Bolshevik side of the image was clear enough, but despite the support given
to the anti-Bolsheviks, information from Russia denied their existence as
a cohesive force. A War Office official commented, 'we have backed every
anti-Bolshevik movement and every one has collapsed. Every man on the
spot considers that we are backing the wrong horses – in practice all our
horses have been scratched and I venture to say that we have much to
gain and nothing to lose by frankly acknowledging the fact.'[77] The Bolsheviks existed as a cohesive government; the anarchy image was more
appropriate when applied to the anti-Bolsheviks. By mid-February, some
Foreign Office officials felt that Britain must come to terms with the
Bolsheviks. It was suggested that Britain should trade commodities required
by the Russians in return for the war material at Archangel and Vladivostok, which it was felt the Russians no longer needed. 'At the same
time we should do all we can to mediate between the Bolsheviks, the
Rumanians and the Cossacks, undertaking not to intervene further if the
safety of the latter is assured.'[78]

There was a strong predisposition against accepting the policy implication arising from this analysis, which was that the Bolshevik Government
should be given *de facto* recognition. When Buchanan suggested that Britain
should establish unofficial relations with the Bolsheviks, Foreign Office
officials, writing minutes on the suggestion, were unanimously opposed.[79]
Cabinet members rejected a suggestion to give the Bolsheviks *de facto*
recognition;[80] and when Balfour wrote to the United States on the issue, he
commented that the Bolsheviks had neither *de facto* nor *de jure* claim to
the government of Russia. He indicated that their claim was no better than
that of the autonomous bodies of South East Russia.[81]

As a consequence, the British considered the question of sending troops
to Russia in the context of a nonintervention system. The Foreign Office
wrote to Lockhart and indicated that the boundaries of this system would
have to be established before detailed plans for sending troops to Russia
could be framed. 'The main conditions of a political character with regard
to such assistance are that the Allies should bind themselves to evacuate
all Russian territory at the end of the war, and that while they are in
Russia, they should take no part in the political or economic controversies
which divide that country. The whole object should be to free Russian soil
from the enemy and restore its independence.'[82] Further efforts to define
the location of the boundary were made when the question was raised of
Russians coming to Britain to 'reawaken the conscience of Russia' and
bring Russia back into 'union with the Allies'. Balfour observed: 'I suppose
it would take the form of an interference in Russian internal affairs and
would probably produce trouble.'[83]

As the situation developed, and the perceived importance of sending the troops increased, it proved impossible to restrict the analysis of policy to this definition of the situation. A second image had to be superimposed. In essence, this depicted a dyadic interaction system. It was indicated that the only way that troops could successfully be introduced into Russia was with the consent of the Bolshevik Government, treating them as the effective government of Russia. Lockhart expressed this view in emphatic terms. 'Intervention can only be successful if it obtains the consent of the Bolshevik Government. If it is forced, we are risking a disaster the magnitude of which must not be underrated.'[84] Decision-makers in London eventually accepted this position but were able to avoid the need to recognize the Bolsheviks by retaining a modified image of bifurcation in which the anti-Bolsheviks were envisaged as a potential force for the future. The interrelationship between these two images was demonstrated clearly in a telegram to Jordan, in Peking, which spelled out British policy towards Russia.

> The intervention of an allied army from Vladivostok is an essential part of this policy. Its main object is the liberation of Russia from foreign control and exploitation and we hope it will result in a rapid national revival .... Whatever may be the truth as regards the honesty of the Bolshevists, they represent at the moment the *de facto* Government of Russia with whom it is impossible not to reckon, and intervention taken in defiance of them might involve the risk of throwing them directly into the army of Germany. Accordingly our efforts have been directed to obtaining an invitation to the Allies to come to the military assistance of the Russians. To achieve this end it is necessary for the Allies to avoid taking sides with Russian political parties or giving any pretext for the charge that their intervention will aim at supporting a counter-revolution. On the other hand, it is important not to alienate the non-Bolshevist elements who may ultimately regain power, and we do not propose to give any formal recognition to the present regime.[85]

The position also had to be explained to the French, who had a very different conception of how the 'intervention' should take place.

> The French Government apparently think that we should launch intervention in league with the Siberian Provisional Government. But this is not at all in accordance with our view, which is to steer clear of all entanglements with Russian parties. Should we not make this clear to the French Government or they may go ahead on their own account and we may be working at cross purposes.[86]

A letter was sent within the week. The boundary of the nonintervention system, therefore, excluded any collaborative ventures. These boundaries, however, reflected synchronic exchange; they did not emerge as the result of mutual adjustment between the parties within the system. Nor did they accurately reflect existing behaviour patterns, since assistance was being given at this time to anti-Bolshevik groups. The assistance was all being given for the purpose of fighting the Germans, and by defining the action at the systemic level, it was possible to ignore the subsystemic ramifications.

Bolshevik approval for the intervention of troops was not easy to acquire. The Foreign Office claimed to find the reluctance difficult to explain, in light of the inability of the Bolsheviks to check the German violations of the Treaty of Brest Litovsk. 'If the Moscow Government are, as they seem to be utterly powerless to resist these successive outrages, is it not time that they gave us to understand that they are prepared to accept our assistance? If they still refuse to do so, what explanation can be given for their conduct?'[87] Lockhart explained:

> It is clear to everyone, and to no-one more clearly than the Bolsheviks themselves, that in accepting intervention they sign their own death warrant. On the other hand, they have still more to fear from the Germans with whom they can hardly hope to come to terms. They are therefore straining every effort to put off taking any decision until as late a date as possible.[88]

An initial step towards making a decision seemed to have been made by Trotsky at the beginning of April. Lockhart reported: 'Allied officers saw Trotsky today and after long and violent discussion, certain conditions were defined which the Allied Governments should examine before there can be any agreement on Allied intervention into Siberia.'[89]

The Foreign Office inferred from this that Trotsky had come to 'share the conclusion that everyone else had reached some time ago: that the Russians could not defend themselves against the Germans'.[90] Some days later, Trotsky indicated to Lockhart that 'help would be most desirable' and he invited the allied governments to 'submit to him at earliest opportunity a full and proper statement of help which they could furnish and of guarantees they are prepared to give. If conditions are friendly he considers a conclusion of agreement both necessary and desirable.' Cecil noted that 'Trotsky's present answer can, possibly by a slight stretch, be construed as an invitation for allied assistance. It offers a sufficient basis on which to found a scheme for a joint Anglo-Japanese-American intervention.'[91]

Lockhart was requested to find out if Trotsky would welcome assistance to defend the Murmansk coast.[92] He discussed it with the head of the Finnish social movement who claimed that Lenin would 'look through his fingers' at any action which the British took at Murmansk to assist the Finns.[93] Shortly afterwards, Lockhart informed London: 'I fear in view of the change in German policy towards the Bolsheviks, the latter now only wish to remain neutral and avoid fighting at any price.' He went on to suggest that the 'most serious menace to their neutrality is Murmansk'.[94] The previous week, the War Cabinet had ordered a small expeditionary force to be sent to Northern Russia.[95] It marked the beginning of the intervention into Russia. Approval from the *de facto* government had been given, as far as the decision-makers in London were concerned. There was no attempt to revise the decision. The absence of concern about Bolshevik opinion after this point will be examined in subsequent chapters.

IMAGES, STABILITY AND BOUNDARIES

The cases illustrate the importance of distinguishing between the actor's and the analyst's definition of the situation when the relationship between a stimulus and a response in a behavioural system is being identified. In the operational milieu, the stimulus in all four cases arises from subsystemic conflict: civil strife within the target state. But only with the introduction of a nonintervention response is this image sustained in the psycho-milieu of the nonbifurcated actor; the response precipitates the formation of a nonintervention system in which the boundary of the system is determined by the metanorm of nonintervention. But while the boundary of the system is clearly drawn in the case of the collective nonintervention response, a certain amount of confusion exists when the unilateral nonintervention response is implemented. The decision-makers move between two points of equilibrium, one based on the norm and the other on the metanorm of nonintervention. The tendency to oscillate between two points of equilibrium can demonstrate ultrastability, but in this instance, it reflects continuing instability arising from the exigencies created by the intervention responses implemented by other international actors.

When an intervention response is introduced, the nonbifurcated actor perceives that the source of conflict extends beyond the established dyadic interaction system. The stimulus is identified at the systemic level and the actor defines the response in the context of a defence system, brought into operation to contend with an external threat. In such a system, it is the norm, not the metanorm of nonintervention which is implemented. This norm is contained by the boundary of the established dyadic interaction system and the question of boundary redefinition is not raised. On the other hand, a request by the incumbent government becomes essential if the introduction of troops into the target state is to be considered legitimate.

From the perspective of the nonbifurcated actor's psycho-milieu, there-fore, both the intervention and nonintervention responses are congruent with the norms of the system identified by the actor. But in the operational milieu, there is an incongruence between the intervention response and the norms of the system. However, because the actor defines the response in terms of the dyadic interaction system, there is minimal concern with the problem of boundary definition. It is in the case of the nonintervention response that concern is displayed about the need to delineate a boundary for the system, particularly in the case of the unilateral nonintervention response where there is an inability to maintain a stable boundary.

An image is often characterized by its 'stability over time'.[96] The analysis here suggests that this characteristic needs to be qualified. Actors may form a series of divergent images when defining an ambiguous situation. The image of a situation which is brought into focus will be affected by the response which is implemented. The divergent images are stable, therefore, only in the sense that they remain available and can be brought into focus, even after the implementation of a response. This creates the possibility of establishing two different images of the same situation. This can happen in interventionary situations and the ramifications of this possibility will be examined in subsequent chapters.

CHAPTER 5

The Process of Legitimization

CLOSED systems do not exist in the 'real world'. Events in one system inevitably impinge on related systems. International actors, aware of this phenomenon, recognize that a response introduced in one dyadic inter-action system is likely to affect other dyadic interaction systems in which they participate: the effects of a response on the international system can-not be ignored. Actors acknowledge that an action designed to stabilize a system is self-defeating if a side-effect is to destabilize other systems. Unlike the chemist, working on the basis of Le Chatelier's Principle, decision-makers do not assume that the side-effects of any change intro-duced into a stable system will tend to cancel each other out; an assumption which accepts the dominance of negative feedback in a system. On occasions, feedback is positive, amplifying the side-effects and threatening general instability. This danger is particularly acute in interventionary situations. An international actor recognizes that if its definition of the situation is not accepted, whatever response is implemented may be defined as 'deviant' and the actor's adherence to the nonintervention norm will be brought into question. As a consequence, other actors in the international system may reconsider their relationship with the 'deviating' actor.

In a centralized system, when the legitimacy of an actor's behaviour is questioned, there can be recourse to the centralized authorities; if they sanction the action, then its legitimacy is confirmed. In such cases, the actor does not wish to deny the behaviour but to legitimize it. In a court of law, the objective is not always to disclaim responsibility for an action: sometimes there is an attempt to convince a jury, for example, that a defendant killed in self-defence. To do this, the defendant must get the jury to accept his definition of the situation. If the jury is convinced, then the action has been legitimized. Establishing the legitimacy of an action in the decentralized international system is not so easily achieved, but because there is a conception of a normative order, and knowing that by violating the order disfunctional systemic effects can be produced, actors do attempt to legitimize their behaviour. In this chapter, the cases demonstrate that actors are aware of the need to legitimize both the intervention and the nonintervention response; they also illustrate how the process of legitimiz-ation operates in the international system.

75

THE LEGITIMIZATION PROCESS

The extensive use of a power framework in the analysis of international relations has tended to inhibit the development of concepts related to normative behaviour, such as deviance and legitimacy. Although both concepts can be explained in power terms, 'power politics' has tended to describe and explain the anomic aspects of the international system. In the context of a power framework, order is explained by systemic acceptance of norms. Consequently, there is a realist-idealist division of opinion on the significance of the legitimization process in the international system.

Claude maintains that decision-makers do attach importance to the normative aspects of policy and so: 'In both domestic and international politics, the quest for legitimization is a persistent feature.'[1] Not all agree with this view. Easton has indicated that in the international system, unlike the domestic system, 'the impact of legitimacy is still extremely low'.[2] The disagreement between Claude and Easton cannot be explained by the relative importance which is attached to power in the international system. Claude is careful to cover himself on this issue. He argues that:

> Power and legitimacy are not antithetical but complementary. The obverse of the legitimacy of power is the power of legitimacy ... Considerations of political morality combine with more hard-headed power considerations to explain the persistence of concern about legitimacy in the political sphere.[3]

In this study it is accepted that international actors are influenced by a normative order and display a corresponding concern for the legitimization process. The ability to legitimize actions is essential in any normative order. Although a ready distinction can normally be made between legitimate and illegitimate behaviour, on the basis of established rules and a common definition of the situation, the legitimacy of an action can be contested, and whenever actors wish to ensure that their actions can be contained by the normative order, some provision must be made for the process of legitimization. Only if there is some means available whereby action can be legitimized is it possible to deal with events where there is no accepted definition of the situation; or no appropriate rules can be identified; or circumstances undermine the validity of the existing rules; or deviation needs to be condoned because of extenuating circumstances. The desire, under these circumstances, to legitimize a policy flows from the conception of the normative order.

Under conditions of uncertainty, actors prefer to have their actions legitimized because they wish to avoid the charge of deviance. Not only may such a charge hamper them from implementing the policy effectively and cause disruption in their relationships with other actors, it may also create an unfavourable image of the actor – which could persist. Irrespective of the power base of an actor, there is a common desire to project an untarnished image. For all these reasons, actors prefer to operate on the basis of legitimacy.

In the domestic system, or any system where values are authoritatively allocated, it is possible to rely on the authority to legitimize a response. The absence of an authority structure explains Easton's scepticism about the significance of legitimacy within the international system. In an attempt to apply Easton's model of a political system to the international system, it has been argued that the United Nations can be considered as an embryonic authority structure. Haas has indicated that although the Eastonian concept of legitimacy is not fulfilled in the international system, states do refer to the United Nations, which does operate, in some sense, as a source of legitimacy. Systematic attempts have been made to apply the concept of legitimization to the United Nations and other international organizations like the OAS.[4]

Although the putative ability of these institutions to establish the legitimacy of an action represents an important development, it cannot be accepted that centralized institutions are the only agents which can confer legitimacy in the international system. In fact, because of the decentralized nature of the system, the importance of a central agent which can legitimize action is diminished. In the context of the dyadic interaction system, whenever there is mutual agreement on a response, the involved actors become their own agents of legitimization. For example, if an actor accepts a request to have foreign troops on its territory, then the acceptance serves to legitimize the request. This legitimizing capacity is an essential attribute of sovereignty.

Responses cannot always be introduced on the basis of mutual accord and an alternative agent of legitimization is then sought. The hierarchical structure of the international system can play a crucial role in determining the character of the legitimizing agents in this event. Britain and France, for example, have been defined as the 'community legitimizers' in Europe during the nineteenth century.[5] British decision-makers were conscious of this role. After the Napoleonic Wars, when conservative leaders in Europe attempted to establish a consensus among the major powers in favour of eliminating the 'Jacobin challenge' which they perceived to exist in states controlled by liberal regimes, Britain denied the legitimacy of this move. After the Troppeau Protocol was issued Castlereagh wrote to the members of the Holy Alliance and indicated that Britain would endeavour to dissuade states from attempting to reduce to an abstract rule of conduct possible cases of interference in the internal affairs of independent states. The French Revolution was considered an exception because of its 'overbearing and conquering character' and Castlereagh maintained that the policy pursued in that case could not be applied to all revolutions. Britain's refusal to participate marked an absence of consensus and the autocratic states withdrew their signatures from the protocol.[6]

Although Britain can be considered as an important legitimizing agent during the nineteenth century, reflecting its assumed role as the 'balancer' in the European balance of power, British decision-makers preferred to establish a consensus among the European states rather than take an independent initiative whenever a threat to the balance of power arose. It was perceived that the Great Powers possessed a 'common responsibility' for the conduct of the smaller states which could threaten the balance, but the decision-makers felt that responsibility had to be exercised on the basis of a consensus. To this end, Britain encouraged the formation of informal machinery which could bring the Great Powers together in times of crisis. The Ambassadors' Conference held in London in 1913 at the time of the Balkan Wars was an important example of collective action.[7]

On critical issues, 'collectivity' is frequently the legitimizing agent used by states, allowing the actors to maintain that the action is being undertaken for the benefit of system stability, rather than to satisfy the interests of an individual member. Of course, it is recognized that such a policy entails costs and, when trying to foster the image of collective action, an actor will often endeavour to ensure that its action is not constrained or encumbered by additional unnecessary participants.[8] This was illustrated in 1882, when British decision-makers decided that it was necessary to send troops into Egypt. Gladstone observed that:

> We should not fully discharge our duty if we did not endeavour to convert the present interior state of Egypt from anarchy and confusion to peace and order. We shall look, during the time that remains to us, to cooperation of the Powers of civilized Europe, if it be in any case open to us. But if every chance of obtaining cooperation is exhausted the work will be undertaken by the single power of England.

However, a few days later, Granville, the Foreign Secretary, revealed that the appeal for foreign cooperation was primarily a device to legitimize the action by getting other states to identify with Britain. He stated: 'We have done the right thing, we have shown our readiness to admit others, and we have not the inconvenience of a partner.'[9]

The possibility of finding an appropriate agent which can confirm the legitimacy of an action does not always arise in the international system. In the absence of such an agent, an actor will endeavour to find some mechanism or principle to which reference can be made in an attempt to validate the definition of the situation the actor is employing and thereby identify the legitimacy of the action. In a court of law, while the jury constitutes the agent with the capacity to legitimize an action, the defendant will still have to rely on a whole series of legitimizing mechanisms to convince the judge and the jury of the validity of the actor's definition of the situation. In the international system, an actor makes use of the same procedure in the hope that other actors will accept the validity of its position.

Whether an agent of legitimization or a legitimizing mechanism is employed, it is asserted in this chapter that:

Proposition 4: When pursuing an intervention response or a nonintervention response, an actor will endeavour to gain international approval for its definition of the situation.

There are obvious advantages in ensuring that any international response is given approval by other members of the international system, but it is clearly not practical to search for approval on all occasions. Actors do not need to legitimize all their actions; most of their behaviour is routinized and can clearly be identified as legitimate. Only when the routine is broken does the need for the legitimization process become acute: the actor is then confronted by uncertainty and instability and the possibility of unintentional deviance is raised. In these circumstances, it is helpful to an actor if an agent exists which can legitimize its definition of the situation. Failing that, the actor may bring some mechanism into operation to defend its position and identify the legitimacy of its position. Neither intervention nor nonintervention falls within a routinized pattern of behaviour. These responses are implemented during times of uncertainty and instability and they raise sensitive international issues. The process of legitimization, therefore, can be considered an important element of any interventionary situation.

LEGITIMIZATION AND THE COLLECTIVE NONINTERVENTION RESPONSE

The possibility of a permanent rift between the Northern and Southern States increased the concern which British decision-makers experienced when they were confronted by the possibility of a civil war in the United States. Both sectors were important to Britain – the North for wheat and the South for cotton – and it seemed vital that both sides should accept the legitimacy of Britain's position if future relations were not to be strained. Any action short of total commitment to either side was likely to leave both parties feeling aggrieved. The British ambassador in Washington felt that the process of establishing stable relations with the bifurcated state should involve both Britain and France. He argued that the Northern Government must be made to understand that Britain had a right to communicate with the Southern Government on issues which affected British subjects and he suggested that the announcement 'should if possible be made *collectively* and in such a form as to preclude the Cabinet's pretending to find a difference between the conduct of France and Britain'.[10]

Any divergence of policy between Britain and France provided the means whereby the Northern States could reduce the legitimacy of Britain's policy. As it was, the Northern States proved to be highly successful in the way they circumscribed Britain's policy. Although the British implemented and legitimized a nonintervention system, they were unable to extend it into a mediation system. Russell could maintain that 'in Europe, Powers have often said to belligerents, make up your quarrels. We propose to give terms of pacification which we think fair and equitable. If you accept them well and good. But if your adversary accepts them and you refuse them, our mediation is at an end, and you may expect to see us your enemies.'[11] In Parliament, Palmerston insisted that mediation was out of the question 'unless a different state of things should arise, and a fair opening appear, for any step which might be likely to meet with the acquiescence of the two parties'.[12]

Although this reflected a disagreement between Russell and Palmerston, most decision-makers accepted that it was not possible to impose mediation. The British decision-makers considered that the legitimacy of granting belligerent status could be confirmed by acting in conjunction with the French, but the legitimacy of mediation depended upon the acquiescence of the two parties engaged in conflict. When the British decision-makers discussed the possibility of mediation in detail, it was also agreed that mediation was only feasible if the offer came from Britain, France and Russia.[13] Neither the British nor the French were prepared to act independently on the issue.[14]

The desire to implement policy in the international system on the basis of a systemic consensus became difficult during this period when it was perceived that the United States was an essential component of the consensus. The government in the Northern States recognized this fact and were able to bolster their own position by enacting the role of the *de jure* government. This served to reinforce the British reluctance to impose a mediation system. A need for consensus was most apparent when the civil war in Mexico was under discussion. Although the legitimacy of the Monroe Doctrine had not been accepted in Europe by 1860, there was a marked reluctance to make any major initiative in the Western hemisphere without the sanction of the United States. As the situation in Mexico deteriorated, concern among European decision-makers increased.

British decision-makers perceived a real threat that France or Spain might take independent action in Mexico. Such a move was characterized as illegitimate, so the possibility of a joint intervention was evolved for the purpose of protecting the interests of the parties concerned. When Lyons raised the issue with Seward, it was argued that the United States would provide the interest on the Mexican loan to Spain and also finance some of the claims which were being made by France and Britain. By making this offer, the Northern States were establishing their role as the *de jure* government, and also developing a policy which would undermine the legitimacy of any European action. Seward accepted that the solution was not ideal but argued that it was preferable to raising the difficult questions posed by the current situation. He preferred to postpone a more lasting solution until a 'more favourable moment'.[15]

From the British perspective, certain that Spain was about to take action, this solution was not satisfactory. Lyons argued that it would be better if the United States, France and Britain joined Spain 'in a course of action, the objects and limits of which should be strictly defined beforehand. This certainly seemed more prudent than to allow Spain to act alone now, and afterwards oppose the results of her operation if she should go too far.'[16] This argument did not carry weight with the Americans, and the formal British request for the United States to join in the intervention[17] was almost immediately turned down.[18] Lyons thought that the United States policy was 'natural under the circumstances'.[19] The British failed in their attempt to incorporate the United States within a consensus in order to legitimize a policy which was designed to operate within the American sphere of influence, and they had to resort to another agent of legitimization.[20]

When the American Supreme Court accepted that the initiation of the blockade was an unmistakable indication of war, the legitimacy of the British decision to grant belligerent status to the Southern States was unassailable. Before that point, neither the French nor the British were willing to take independent initiatives in their relations with the United States. At all points there was an attempt to coordinate policy. The importance attached to achieving a policy in Mexico which reflected a European consensus can also be partially attributed to the questionable legitimacy of any policy undertaken in the Western hemisphere while the United States was bifurcated. The ability to establish systemic legitimacy for a policy is also important when forming internal support for a policy. This will be discussed in the next chapter.

LEGITIMIZATION AND THE UNILATERAL NONINTERVENTION RESPONSE

A fear of external involvement in the Spanish Civil War preoccupied British decision-makers after the initiation of the conflict. At the end of July 1936, an official from Tangier noted: 'Italian legation are in close contact with General Franco and it has come to my knowledge from a good source that they are seeking an excuse to land forces by inciting communist elements of the local Spanish population to create an incident.' In London, it was observed as a consequence: 'It may become necessary to post an *international* armed guard on the Tangier land frontier to prevent incursions from the Spanish zone ... any suggestion of isolated action

seems out of the question.'[21] The issue soon lost its significance when
Franco firmly established himself on the Spanish mainland, but the perceived illegitimacy of independent action remained an important factor
during the conflict.

It was difficult for the British decision-makers to establish a coherent
policy towards the civil war in Spain. This was not only a product of the
desire not to alienate the parties to the conflict, but also arose from the
absence of sympathy for either side. Eden used this fact to argue that
Britain was in a 'strong position' to act as a mediator in the conflict,
'because we are known to be more neutral than any other great power
and *because a compromise is in our national interest*. The victory of either
extreme would be most unwelcome to us so that we must be up and doing
in favour of compromise whenever opportunity affords.'[22] But it was the
French who made the first initiative.

On 2 August the Foreign Office contacted the Foreign Secretary on 'a
rather urgent matter'. It was a French proposal for an agreement among
the governments concerned with the civil war in Spain to prevent any
external military assistance from reaching Spain. Mounsey commented, 'an
Anglo-Franco-Italian agreement would not be of the slightest use . . . unless
other important countries, such as Germany and also Soviet Russia, come
into line and I do not think we should *tie our hands* to any agreement which
is not practically universal'.[23] The suggestion quickly escalated. The British
expressed a preference for informal conversations, because 'summonsing
a conference on such a subject would be calculated to entail much delay,
much publicity and perhaps in the end less likelihood of quick decisions
to agree upon a reasonable amount of common identity of attitudes and
action'.[24]

The Italians, however, suggested that a commission should be established
to supervise an embargo. Germany rejected the idea, but by now the
British were moving in favour of a provision which was more elaborate
than informal conversations. They impressed upon the Germans that there
was no question of setting up 'an independent body which would have to
make decisions on whose jurisdiction might be extended in any way; it
was a question only of loosely organizing the diplomats of the interested
powers'.[25] The British persuasion was successful, and on 9 September the
first meeting of a Nonintervention Committee took place.[26] Six days
earlier, there had been a meeting of an inter-departmental committee set
up within the British Government to deal with nonintervention in Spain.[27]

Within a month, the British decision-makers moved from espousing the
virtues of informal conversation to support for an institutionalized solution,
permitting the institution to be located in London. Initially it was feared
that any kind of machinery would result in Britain giving indirect assistance to the incumbent government; in fact, the Nonintervention Committee served as an agent for legitimizing the British policy of total disen-

gagement. For the British decision-makers, the committee performed latent
and manifest functions.[28] The manifest function was to ensure that the nonintervention agreement was not being violated; the latent function was to
legitimize a policy of disengagement. It was difficult to attack or change
the policy of nonintervention because the committee demonstrated the
existence of an international consensus in favour of the policy. As the
conflict continued, it was the latent function which explains the persistence
of the committee.

At first there was an attempt to maximize support for the agreement,
because it was believed that this was a prerequisite for its success. Just
after the committee was formed there was genuine concern among the
British decision-makers about the possibility of states renouncing the agreement. Shuckburgh commented: 'The dangers of a Portuguese repudiation
of the non-intervention agreement would be so great in Europe that we
would be justified in using every possible ounce of our influence and pressure in preventing it.'[29] But even at this stage, it is possible to infer that
the Nonintervention Committee was formed as a substitute for, rather than
an instrument of, policy. A Foreign Office official noted: 'There seems
to be a great deal of apprehension as to the status and function of the
committee. This arises in part from the fact that the Governments which
have set it up have not invested it with any definite powers. This being so,
I think the position is that the committee is really a convenient way by
which the various Governments can consult together.'[30]

Within a month, there were already signs that it was more important to
maintain the committee than to perform even the limited task of consultation. When the question was raised of bringing the issue of Italian activity
on the Balearic Islands before the committee, Vansittart opposed the idea
because Britain had already taken action against Italy and had to bear the
brunt of Italian animosity. He added, 'it will only add fuel to the fire
without getting us any further.'[31] But when Eden brought up the question
of Soviet infringements before the Cabinet he argued that 'while it was
important to avoid any action calculated to jeopardize the agreement, it
seemed unavoidable to bring the evidence, where it was sufficient, to the
notice of the committee'.[32]

This in fact said as much about relations between Britain, Italy and the
Soviet Union at that time as it did about attitudes towards the Nonintervention Committee. As the months passed, it was apparent that the major
British concern was to keep the committee in operation. Shuckburgh maintained that the reason for pressing to have an impartial body on Spanish
territory

> was the necessity on political grounds of taking some steps to make the
> non-intervention agreement more effective, or at least show the world
> that the committee was itself doing something to tighten up control. To
> this extent the proposal has undoubtedly been successful in that it has

prevented the committee being broken up for a few days at least. The whole proposal in fact seems to be a very dubious one and our reason for putting it forward must be rather the need for keeping the non-intervention agreement in being than the idea that it will be of any practical effect.[33]

At the beginning of December, a new scheme for enforcing the agreement was discussed in the Foreign Office. Shuckburgh doubted the success of the scheme because he felt that Germany and Italy 'mean to make Franco win by all available means'. Despite this belief, both he and Eden supported the plan.[34] Six months later, in the Nonintervention Committee, the necessity of operating on the basis of unanimity was still supported by the British. Cranborne rejected any appeal to 'humanize' the war without Soviet approval. To do so would 'set a dangerous precedent. Non-intervention depends so very much on the existence of a united front.' Eden endorsed this view.[35] The issue was put much more bluntly in the Foreign Office by Shuckburgh, who indicated that everyone knew: 'Non-intervention having been flagrantly broken on all sides, is now little more than a *pis aller*, an expedient to avoid graver complications.'[36]

The British decision-makers experienced an apparent need to operate within a consensus at the systemic level when formulating and implementing policy during the Spanish Civil War. Britain could deflect any criticism by referring to the Nonintervention Committee. While initially it was intended to deter intervention, it was quickly employed almost exclusively as a legitimization agent. Its existence also helped Britain to dissociate from the intervention responses of Russia, Germany and Italy. Without the Nonintervention Committee, it would have been difficult for Britain to demonstrate her opposition to intervention since by this time the League of Nations could no longer effectively function as a legitimizing agent. After Abyssinia, the institution had lost much of its credibility. At the beginning of the civil war, Cecil questioned the need to bring the matter to the League of Nations. Pollock believed it would serve no purpose and would merely be 'damaging to its prestige'. Strang asserted that the Foreign Office view was that the Nonintervention Committee was 'best designed' to deal with the crisis.[37]

LEGITIMIZATION AND THE UNILATERAL INTERVENTION RESPONSE

When troops were sent to Portugal in 1826, the legitimacy of Britain's position was unquestionable, given the definition of the situation which was employed. Britain's obligation to go to Portugal's assistance when under attack had been established for centuries. Alliances are an integral component of the structure of the international system and it is assumed that their provisions will be implemented when specified conditions arise. In order to legitimize the action, therefore, it was only necessary for Canning to convince other actors in the system that the situation must be defined in terms of conflict at the systemic rather than at the subsystemic level. It was also necessary to demonstrate that the attack was not provoked.

Concern about reaction in Europe to Britain's intervention response was well founded. Despatches from Spain indicated that French officials were actively encouraging the Spanish Government to assist the Portuguese deserters, and the ambassador in Paris indicated that despite denying all knowledge of this activity, the French Government was prone to suggest that the Portuguese were antagonizing the Spaniards.[38] Earlier in the year, the Austrians had also warned Canning that 'if Spain remonstrated against the effect which the change in Portugal might produce on her internal security, the Court of Vienna could not do otherwise than support and countenance such remonstrances'.[39]

The crisis in Portugal was anticipated and Canning, appreciating that Britain might need to take direct action on some future occasion, was careful to ensure that grounds to legitimize action had been prepared. When the French sent troops into Spain in 1823, Canning extracted a pledge that there would be no attack on Portugal. It was also established that if hostilities occurred, Britain was bound to go to the assistance of the Portuguese.[40] These negotiations cannot simply be viewed in terms of legitimization. It is important to define future lines of action in negotiation[41] and this was partly an attempt to deter future French moves, but it also provided a means whereby Britain could legitimize subsequent action.

By reiterating Britain's obligation to Portugal, the legitimacy of this position was consolidated and, as the crisis approached, reference to the Anglo-Portuguese treaties increased. When Austria suggested that they would support Spanish action in a confrontation with Portugal, Canning recalled Britain's treaties 'which were known to the world'.[42] Constant references to the treaties were made in Canning's despatches to Britain's ambassadors in Europe. In his despatches to Portugal, however, while it was accepted that Britain would go to Portugal's assistance in the event of an attack, it was emphasized that the attack must be unprovoked. This factor was ignored in the other despatches because it would have reduced the efficacy of the treaties as a legitimizing mechanism.

After the precipitation of the crisis, Canning's attempts to legitimize the despatch of troops concentrated on confirming the definition of the situation at the systemic level. In his despatches, he articulated that the Portuguese deserters 'are to be considered as *foreign enemies of Portugal* – and may be acted against as such by HM Forces'.[43] Despite this assertion, Canning's reputation created a strong presumption that the intervention response was designed to assist the liberal cause in Portugal. Canning was anxious, therefore, to ensure that he alone was not identified with the instigation of the policy. Although relations between Canning and Wellington were antagonistic, the latter was asked to defend the policy in the House of Lords. Not only did Wellington have an international reputation which carried weight in Europe, he was also known to be a conservative, opposed to Canning's liberal propensities; with Wellington's support, the danger of the action being defined as internal interference was reduced. Canning wrote to Wellington:

> If you could make up your mind to say a word in the debate tomorrow in the sense of what you said at the Cabinet on Saturday (touching the evident proofs of *combination* and *design* in the simultaneous movement along the whole line of the Portuguese frontier), it would do infinite good, not in this country only, but on the continent.[44]

Two days after the intervention response was announced, the French Government formally condoned the action; in the King's Speech to the French Chamber, Spain was accused of unjustified aggression against Portugal and support was given to the counter-move made by the British.[45] Within two weeks, Metternich had also indicated his approval.[46] Since Britain's principal protagonists on this issue were France and Austria, their approval derived from an acceptance of Britain's definition of the situation rather than from the acknowledgement of the treaties. As it was, the opposition party in France denied the validity of this interpretation. Without Wellington's support, Canning's ability to legitimize the policy could have been substantially reduced. In the following chapter, there will be a discussion of the consensus formation which went on in the British political system.

LEGITIMIZATION AND THE COLLECTIVE INTERVENTION RESPONSE

The intervention response into the Russian Civil War passed through several phases, initiated by the expedition sent to Murmansk. British decision-makers did not consider that this incursion was significant and their efforts were concentrated on an inter-allied force which would operate from Vladivostok. Allied unity was a prerequisite to establish the legitimacy of this move and the absence of a consensus on the issue eliminated the possibility of any action. Difficulties arose because of the alternative definitions of the situation employed by the Allies since this affected the nature of the legitimization required. The Japanese were not prepared to take any action without approval from the United States; Britain was not in a position to act without the support of the Japanese; the United States was not prepared to participate in any action which was not sanctioned by the Bolsheviks; and the Bolsheviks were opposed to any move made by the

Japanese. The British decision-makers never fully appreciated the circuitous nature of the problem, and for several months the inability to achieve a consensus precluded the initiation of a response.

At the beginning of 1918, British decision-makers were anxious to make a move at Vladivostok when it was reported that the Soviets were plundering Irkutsk, although it transpired later that the reports were widely inaccurate. It was proposed to permit the Japanese to occupy Vladivostok.[47] Cecil feared that the Russians would perceive the move as an attempt by the Japanese to carry out the designs which were revealed during the Russo-Japanese war.[48] Some means of legitimizing the action had to be found. In a Foreign Office despatch to the United States it was argued that there was a need to land a force at Vladivostok which would be strong enough to guard the allied stores which had been left there. It was stipulated that the force would have to be primarily Japanese but that other nationalities must be included, in case the Russians should perceive the action as an invasion. It was considered essential that the United States should send a contingent.[49]

Some of the British decision-makers became extremely irritated by the need to secure American approval for any action which was taken at Vladivostok. By May it was being asked if 'we were to allow the attitude of the United States Government to paralyze us for ever in the case of Japanese intervention as it has done in the last few months?'[50] This analysis represented a considerable over-simplification. The Japanese were divided on the question of intervention and were unwilling to act in the absence of a lead from the United States. Wilson knew this but, according to Wiseman, he felt that 'it would be odious for him to use such power except the best interests of the common cause demanded it'.[51] A stalemate resulted. Foreign Office officials recognized that unless it was decided actively to support the Bolsheviks as the *de facto* government, adopting the American definition of the situation, 'there is no ground on which we can approach the United States with a view to coordination of policy'.[52]

This conclusion was based upon the American insistence that any action taken must be condoned by the Bolsheviks. Soviet participation in any consensus was essential for the legitimization of action directed towards Russia. When Lloyd George stated in the House of Commons: 'Great Britain is ready to stand by Russia, if Russia wants it', American decision-makers interpreted the statement as an acceptance of their definition of the situation and that the British now acknowledged that intervention must be preceded by an invitation. British decision-makers were irritated by that assertion and insisted that such an interpretation did not reflect the context in which the statement was made. Lloyd George argued that there was no representative government in Russia, and, therefore, no government could legitimately issue an invitation. Anxious to dispel the belief that British and American definitions of the situation now coincided, the Foreign

Office decided to have another question asked in the House of Commons which would allow a clarification of Britain's position.[53]

Without the injection of a new factor, the stalemate would have prevailed; the unresolved issue would have remained a source of irritation in Anglo-American relations until the war in Europe came to an end. The fillip was provided by the Czech divisions, caught behind the Russian border when the peace between Germany and Russia was signed. It was agreed that they should be allowed to pass through Russia to Archangel and Murmansk, where they would be transferred to France to fight on the Western front. At the beginning of June, it was reported that conflict had broken out when the Bolsheviks had attempted to disarm the Czechs.[54] Lockhart sent a note several days later in which he questioned the idea that the Czechs had been inspired by a counter-revolutionary plot. He indicated that the Bolsheviks were anxious to settle the affair amicably but felt that they must disarm the Czechs after the incident.[55] According to a report from Irkutsk, by the second week of June it was established that the conflict had been due to a misunderstanding.[56]

In spite of these reports, the situation continued to deteriorate. Lockhart wrote to the Foreign Office: 'Fate has given us in the Czechoslovakians a last chance of saving Russia and of recreating in her a new source of strength against Germany. I am alarmed at the attention which is being paid to Murmansk and Archangel when Siberian intervention will not wait, and if the Allies neglect this opportunity it will be more than deplorable.'[57] Balfour wrote to Reading in Washington: 'Lockhart's telegram causes me much anxiety. The Bolsheviks who betrayed the Roumanian army are apparently now bent on destroying the Czech army. The Czechs are our allies and we must save them if we can. The position seems to render immediate allied action on their behalf a matter of urgent necessity.'[58] The French Government agreed.[59]

The fate of the Czechs proved crucial because it radically affected the American perception of the situation. By July, Lansing wrote to Wilson and argued that the Czech involvement in Western Siberia 'materially changed the situation by introducing a sentimental element into the question of our duty'.[60] According to Kennan, an American memorandum on this subject 'reduced the Siberian situation to a simple conflict between Czechs and armed German, Austrian and Hungarian prisoners'.[61] Britain also received information which supported this position. Lockhart noted in the middle of June that the Bolsheviks were thinking of getting German help to quell the Czechs.[62] Later information indicated that there was a need for allied troops to help the Czechs in their fight against German prisoners and red guards.[63] Then on 5 July, it was decided at a meeting between Czech and allied commanders at Vladivostok to put the town under allied protection on account of the Germans and Magyars, who were inciting the population against the Czechs. The importance of sending an allied military force to support the Czechs was stressed.[64]

On 10 July, the Cabinet considered the issue. Lloyd George confronted difficulties which would arise if the United States decided not to back a British initiative. Balfour argued that the troops should be sent as soon as possible and he stipulated that the movement of allied troops to Vladivostok to protect supplies, and preserve order, could not be considered as an intervention into Russia. It was decided to send a battalion to Vladivostok immediately in an attempt to preserve order; to request action by France; to ask Tokyo to give medical assistance to the Czechs; and to inform the United States of the action and explain the reasons behind the decision.[65] A request was sent to the United States to authorize naval support for the Czechs. 'Apart from the larger question of intervention, any collapse of Czechs at Vladivostok that can be attributed to the failure of the Allies to support them there would have the most deplorable effect generally.'[66] The British were pre-empted by a unilateral American initiative to send 7000 troops to Vladivostok in conjunction with the Japanese.

Both the British and the Americans saw that the Czechs provided a mechanism which would suffice to legitimize an independent initiative of limited scope. But while the United States acted without feeling any compulsion to consult, the British did feel a need to gain retrospective approval from the Americans for the initiative. American approval was essential for the purposes of legitimization. For the French, the acquiescence of the Americans in any action taken was of even greater importance. Derby indicated that the French would do whatever the British did on the issue of sending troops. But he noted, after consulting the French foreign minister:

> At the same time he is extremely anxious that nothing should be done which would make the President of the United States think that we are forcing his hand. He pointed out to me that when the decision to send troops from Hong Kong was arrived at, the President had not so far consented to intervention and he is evidently very nervous lest the President should be irritated by the movement of troops and he begs you therefore to take every step to explain to him how the necessity for immediate action arose.[67]

The French fears were justified. When Reading saw Lansing, 'at first he was inclined to think that we had taken a first step towards intervention without consulting the United States Government.' It appears that Reading was able to convince him otherwise.[68] His argument was provided by the French, who asked the British to explain that the 'action of HMG is not dictated by any intention to start intervention, but solely with the view to ensure the safety of communication of Czech forces, order in Vladivostok and security of Allied Stores, these objects of highest importance at the moment'.[69] E. H. Carr also minuted that the French and the British were agreed that there must be no interference in Russian internal affairs and that the Czechs must give a guarantee not to support counter-revolutionary movements.[70] The Japanese also accepted that the action did not constitute intervention.[71]

The lack of consultation between the Americans and the British on this issue reflected a mutual understanding of their different definitions of the situation. The British were disturbed in case the United States would still refuse to sanction an intervention without Soviet approval. They chose not to consult in order to circumvent the refusal but initiated a response, certain that the plight of the Czechs provided a legitimizing mechanism which the Americans could not fail to accept; as a result they would at least have to condone the response. The Americans failed to consult either the British or the French, because it was feared that if they participated in the action, they would escalate the response and use the initial American action to legitimize a broader range of activity.

Once it was realized that the British and the French had taken action and could use the American initiative to legitimize a full-scale intervention, the Americans very quickly attempted to establish a boundary which would circumscribe the range of activity which they were prepared to sanction. On 10 August, a declaration delimiting the scope of American activity was issued to the Russians. The Japanese followed suit. A Foreign Office official commented: 'The two pronouncements have the appearance less of a declaration to the Russian people than of statements of policy by way of justification to the world at large.' He went on: 'This being so, it would perhaps solve the problem for us if we issued a parallel statement as to our "interventionist" policy... The publication of the occupation of Archangel would afford us an opportunity and we should thereby not give the appearance of following the American and Japanese lead.'[72]

The declaration was drafted by Cecil and it read:

> The whole Russian people can rest assured that HMG, under whose direction this action has been taken, have been activated solely by the decision to help Russia and to keep open the Northern gates of communication between her and the Allies. HMG will not retain one foot of Russian soil, at Archangel, Murmansk or anywhere else. They will leave Russia to achieve her own constitution, her own form of Government, her own settlement of internal questions. All that HMG seek to do, in concert with her Allies, is to help Russia restore herself, to secure for Russia real freedom of election for a National Assembly and thus to effect a real pronouncement of the national voice and to supply, as far as is in their power, economic relief and assistance.[73]

The declaration was clearly meant to be read by the Americans and may be regarded as a mechanism to legitimize Britain's action and help guarantee a consensus among the Allies.

INTERNAL COHESION AND POLICY FORMATION

The less certain a party is about the legitimacy of an action, the greater will be the need to seek support to legitimize the action. British decision-makers were confident that their action during the American Civil War was legitimate, and cooperation with the French sufficed to reduce any anxiety which may have been experienced. During the Russian Civil War, the British decision-makers were so lacking in confidence that they were not prepared to take action of any sort until they were certain that the United States would sanction the move. An actor will normally prefer to ensure that an action is legitimized before it is taken. Then, according to Deutsch, legitimacy acts as a 'double reinsurance, and thus a double prophecy. It promises compatibility among the various probable consequences of a value-pursuing decision and it promises the consistency of this decision and its controlling values with other values vital to the actor.'[74]

Ensuring that a response is compatible with systemic values is an important consideration for an actor and the significance of legitimization arises from this fact. But it is equally important for an actor to reconcile the response with internal values. This can be more difficult, since diametrically opposed sets of values may exist within an actor. Few responses will be able to satisfy all the values which are represented within an actor, although often the response can be reconciled with the predominant values within a political system. It is on this basis that bipartisanship can be reflected in foreign policy decisions. When an intervention stimulus occurs, however, the task is more complex, because parallels with the cleavage which exists in the target actor can often be found in the nonbifurcated actor. Consequently, there is a danger that an intervention response will alienate one extreme within the actor, while a nonintervention response will alientate two extremes. Decision-makers are aware of this difficulty, and in the next chapter there will be an examination of the way in which they endeavour to formulate policy on the basis of internal cohesion.

CHAPTER 6

The Process of Consensus Formation

CONFLICTS of opinion do not persist in the rational-choice approach to decision-making; they are resolved by calculation. The costs and benefits of various options are evaluated and, depending upon the strategy which is employed, the decision reached is designed either to maximize potential gains or to minimize losses. Rational decision-makers do not pursue a policy solely on the basis of precedent, sentiment or obligation; value considerations are only taken into account if their worth can be assessed and calculated. This amoral image of rational man is a widely-accepted description of reality. As an analytical model, many qualifications are required, but it is itself a component of reality: decision-makers are influenced by their conception of the model. While actors recognize the limitations when applied to themselves, they frequently assume that the policy of any opponent must have arisen as the result of rational calculation. International actors, for example, infer that a change in weapon deployment by an enemy must reflect an attempt to improve its strategic orientation. It is more difficult to assume that the move is simply the outcome of a struggle between different bureaucracies and may not reflect the best interests of the enemy state.

When events are analysed in this way, reification of the state takes place – rather than examining the actions of individual decision-makers, the state itself is treated as a rational actor, capable of thought and action.[1] This is a useful simplifying device for analysts and actors and it has been employed up to this point in the analysis. But in this chapter the underlying assumption is questioned and there is an examination of the level of cohesion among decision-makers when they implement a response. The cases indicate that they are sharply divided on both the regime which they favour in the bifurcated state and the nature of the response which should be implemented. Given the array of opinion, it is perhaps surprising that a decision ever gets made. It is certainly significant that the decision tends to be unanimous. The unanimity serves to reinforce the idea that international politics can best be described by the rational actor model. But this view needs to be qualified. The cases also suggest that different responses reflect different types of consensus. In this chapter there is an examination of the factors which precipitate the variations which occur when consensus is achieved among decision-makers confronted by an intervention stimulus.

THE PROCESS OF CONSENSUS FORMATION

When analysts treat the state as an autonomous entity which interacts with other similar entities in the international system, it is of course recognized that this simply represents a means of reducing a complex subject to manageable proportions. Although a simplification, it is not thought to be an unreasonable means of delimiting the area of study. It is possible to identify state behaviour and if it is assumed that decisions emerge from a process which is common to all states, then other factors become more important when explaining variations which occur in state behaviour. Attention is concentrated on the in-puts and out-puts of decision-making; these in-puts and out-puts continuously change, while the method of reaching decisions by rational calculation remains constant. A major reason why the assumptions which underlie the rational policy model do not seem unreasonable stems from the existence of the socialization process whereby individuals develop a common conception of the interests of their state and its position in the international system. There is a common ideology, and individuals who deviate from the ideology are not likely to operate in the national decision-making process. Although there are differences of opinion about the best way to deal with a situation, these differences operate within fairly narrow constraints. More apparent are the common assumptions which decision-makers share. In particular, it is accepted that the objective of decision-making is to promote the interest of the state.

The method of putting a 'black box' on the decision-making process and treating the state as a rational actor will probably always constitute an important approach in international relations. But there are alternative approaches. Perhaps the most important has been identified with the 'bureaucratic model', which stipulates that national decision-making is a complex process in the contemporary world, made up of a series of competing bureaucracies, each of which has its own set of interests; state policy is the outcome of the collective bargaining process in which these bureaucracies engage. There is, however, a substantial difference between the bureaucracies which operate in a national decision-making unit and a series of firms competing for scarce resources in a single market. In a unified state, the Cabinet constitutes a final decision-making body, and while it is true that decisions are often effectively made at the bureaucratic level, the Cabinet merely authorizing the decision, in controversial cases where there is bureaucratic conflict – and these are often the most interesting, although not necessarily the most important cases – the Cabinet must make the ultimate decision. Since most branches of government have some kind of representation in the Cabinet, the inter-bureaucratic in-fighting can extend to the Cabinet. This phenomenon explains why decisions are often not made. It is easy to see how an impasse can develop. But the fact remains that decisions very often do emerge. As Hilsman insists: 'Somehow policies do get made.'[2] Decision-making bodies have the capacity to generate consensus.

One way of circumventing an impasse is to establish a rule which implements a policy when certain conditions are fulfilled. In the United Nations General Assembly, for example, some policies can be introduced after receiving over fifty per cent of the total votes cast; other issues must receive two-thirds of the votes cast. Such a solution can lead to dissension and may fail to reveal the essence of a consensus, for it has been suggested that only unanimity constitutes consensus;[3] Quaker meetings, for example, will discuss issues until everyone agrees on a policy. But it has also been observed that there is a 'tendency of much democratic decision-making to terminate in unanimous or near-unanimous voting'.[4] This may reflect a finding of social psychologists that individuals experience a 'psychological need to perceive consensus'.[5] But because there is often unanimity in situations where 'one should expect division on substantive grounds of divided interests', Eulau has found the existence of unanimity a 'puzzling affair'.[6]

There is a great deal of debate about the way in which decision-makers move from the point where there are basic disagreements about policy to where a decision is unanimously agreed upon. Buchanan and Tullock suggest that 'if costs of decision-making could be reduced to negligible proportions, the rational individual should always support the requirements of unanimous consent before political decisions are finally made'.[7] This assumption is 'untenable', according to Eulau, because it contains the presumption that 'human beings are invariably rationally calculating, in the sense that they seek to maximize personal benefits by some hedonistic calculus and make choices, including the decision about how to make decisions, in terms of least cost'.[8]

Eulau suggests, in preference, that a typology is necessary to locate empirical situations where unanimous decision-making occurs.[9] Along one dimension he distinguishes the way in which decisions are handled. He separates *formal patterns* of decision-making, where the process is 'routinized and bureaucratized', from *informal patterns*, where decisions are made by 'traditional interpersonal arrangements'. Located between the two and possessing both formal and informal characteristics, there is the *political* way of making decisions, which takes account of 'bargaining and trades'.

On the second dimension, he examines the way in which individual and group interests are articulated. By *interest articulation*, he means 'the ways in which individual or group interests are structured in the perceptions and verbalizations of the decision-makers'. He differentiates between *interest diffuseness*, which arises when demands do not constitute a hierarchy of preferences which would give priority to one demand over another; and *interest specificity*, which occurs when demands can be located within some hierarchy of preferences.

Using these two dimensions, four major types of consensus formation can be elaborated (eliminating the formal patterns of decision-making, where the need to formulate a consensus is not necessary). The first type of consensus reflects an informal type of decision-making where there is no conflict between group and individual interests. There are specific group interests which the individual accepts. Individual interests, therefore, do not affect the group decision-making process and there is no cause for division. This is defined as an *ancestral* consensus and it is argued that even in complex modern political systems there are many areas where consensus rather than conflict dominates the situation. Unanimous decision-making, however, normally operates in an environment which reflects the existence of conflict. A *false* consensus can emerge in a situation of informal decision-making where individuals do have specific interests and there is no hierarchy of group interests which can be used to resolve individual conflict. In this situation, when a consensus does emerge it is based on 'the habit of handling decisions consensually and the need to maintain group solidarity'; the consequence is that individual interests, though specific, 'are suppressed or concealed in the name of the group'. The third form of consensus operates in a political environment where there are specific interests for the group, but not for the individuals. Here, 'unanimity, if it occurs, probably stems from successful trading and bargaining among individual members'. This constitutes a *bargained* consensus. Finally, Eulau postulates decision-making in a political environment where group interests are diffuse while individual interests are specific. He suggests that unanimity in this context is difficult to explain because in the absence of any articulated group interests, the decision situation will appear ambiguous to the decision-makers and consequently a *projected* consensus is formed.

> The individual decision-maker will tend to project his own preferred interests on the group as a whole. Not knowing where others stand, such projection provides the individual with a perceptual anchorage point. He expects others to decide in the way in which he himself decides. This psychological ordering of the ambiguous situation involves a great deal of perceptual distortion. But it may have the effect of creating a cognitive environment in which psychological pressures towards a unanimous decision become very great. If it is believed that everybody agrees with everybody else, the image of unanimity can serve as a kind of projective screen from responsibility for failure to resolve an issue in those terms

in which it was originally defined by the individual with specific interests himself. Unanimity may be said to be projected.[10]

So, a place also has to be made for a projected consensus. When the cases are examined, it will be seen that aspects of these different types of consensus can be seen in situations where decision-makers have to respond to an intervention stimulus. But before examining the cases, it is necessary to examine the different cleavages which can occur among decision-makers under these circumstances.

THE INTERVENTION STIMULUS AND CONSENSUS FORMATION

When Castlereagh elaborated his opposition to an 'abstract principle' which gave Great Powers the right to interfere in the domestic affairs of other states, one of his objections was that it had the

> air of dictation or menace, and the possibility of its being intended to be pushed to a forcible intervention is always assumed or imputed by an adverse party. The grounds for intervention thus become unpopular, the intention of the parties is misunderstood, the public mind is agitated and perverted, and the general political situation of the government is thereby essentially embarrassed.[11]

The White Paper in which this statement is contained provided the basis for a norm of nonintervention which has persisted through time, and Castlereagh's belief that intervention will occasion political instability continues to reinforce the norm.

The intervention stimulus itself, however, is sufficient to engender political conflict, dividing individuals in the political system. Two relevant lines of cleavage can arise. One divides the supporters of the incumbent government from those of the insurgent government and can be termed the *regime cleavage*; the second separates those who favour intervention from those who favour nonintervention, and can be called the *policy cleavage*. These cleavages are not restricted to divisions between groups with different value systems. Often, within the policy-making structure, real differences occur about the nature and direction of a response to an intervention stimulus.

Rae and Taylor isolate three properties of cleavage which will affect the level of stability within a community when cleavages form. *Crystallization* is the proportion of a community which finds itself 'committed to any recognizable position on any given cleavage'. *Fragmentation* is the degree to which the cleavage will 'set members of the community against each other'. And *intensity* is the level of commitment with which a group adheres to an issue. It is the last property which can be most significant, because as the intensity rises, cross-cutting cleavages, which diffuse the effect of crystallization and fragmentation, can break down, and polarization can occur. Rae and Taylor consider intensity a central issue in political analysis and one which raises many methodological difficulties.[12]

Identifying the intensity of feeling which an individual experiences when confronted by an intervention stimulus is not easy. Some light can be shed on the problem by reference to a 'new and still evolving framework for distinguishing different patterns of personal involvement with the national system'.[13] Rather than identifying intensity in the first instance, Kelman has established a typology of the ways in which an individual can form an attachment to a political system; then he makes certain inferences about the levels of intensity within the typology. A distinction is made on one dimension between sentimental and instrumental attachments. The sentimental attachment indicates an ego-involvement with the state and consequently the individual feels the system is 'a reflection and extension of himself'. The instrumental attachment arises when the individual perceives the system as 'an effective vehicle for achieving his own ends'.[14] Such attachments extend beyond the political system in which an individual is located. Many Arabs, for example, formed a sentimental attachment to Nasser and expressed personal grief when he died. But often, such an attachment takes a purely instrumental form. Businessmen in Europe, for example, may have felt an attachment for King Faisal in Saudi Arabia, not because of any personal regard, but simply because of his ability to guarantee stability in the area. If he had lost this ability, their attachment would have been transferred.

Kelman has evolved a number of hypotheses which relate this framework to the question of intensity. In particular, he suggests that 'sentimentally attached individuals are more likely to conceive an intergroup conflict in competitive zero-sum terms, while instrumentally attached individuals are more likely to see the possibility for cooperation and a non-zero-sum orientation'.[15] If this hypothesis is correct, then the type of consensus which emerges when decision-makers establish a response to an intervention stimulus will depend partially upon the ways in which the decision-makers identify with the bifurcated actor.

The nature of the consensus will also be affected by the way in which the decision-makers are divided by regime and policy cleavages. The cases show that in practice it is possible for decision-makers to be divided by both cleavages and in terms of a sentimental or instrumental attachment for the regimes in the bifurcated actor. The composition of any consensus which forms, therefore, can be very complex. However, there is clear bias in favour of a consensus forming around nonintervention. For example, the regime cleavage may divide supporters of the insurgent and incumbent governments, but if both fall on the same side of the policy cleavage, and favour nonintervention, a unanimous policy will quickly form. The consensus will contain diametrically opposed viewpoints.

Unanimity is less likely to emerge when all decision-makers can be found on the other side of the policy cleavage, and favour intervention; but normally, when there are two interrelated lines of cleavage, it is likely that there will be a degree of 'overlap': the concept is a product of *cross-cutting cleavages*, which occur whenever 'two cleavages divide a community along different axes'.[16] The degree of 'overlap' is defined as the extent to which 'the crystallized portion of the community on one cleavage is the same as the crystallized portion on another'.[17] So, while nonintervention provides common ground for supporters of the insurgents and the incumbents, the policy of intervention creates a division. To be successful in terms of voting strength, decision-makers favouring an intervention response must outnumber the group which supports intervention in favour of the opposite party and the two groups which favour nonintervention. Given this bias in favour of nonintervention, it is not surprising to find that the unanimity for intervention or nonintervention reflects different types of consensus. In particular it is stipulated that:

> *Proposition 5: An intervention response reflects a false or projected consensus; a nonintervention response reflects an ancestral or bargained consensus.*

The position clearly indicates that a consensus formed in favour of a nonintervention response reflects a much higher level of basic agreement than the response which forms in favour of an intervention response. In the case of an intervention response, the agreement is purely superficial: the decision-makers either deliberately suppress their own preference, or else the implications which underlie the consensus are distorted in such a way that there is likely to be a high level of misunderstanding between the decision-makers. Whether the consensus reflects a false or a projected consensus, it is likely to have serious ramifications for subsequent developments in the situation.

CONSENSUS ON THE UNILATERAL INTERVENTION RESPONSE

There was near-unanimity at the Cabinet meeting which decided to send troops to Portugal. 'Lord Westmorland was the only one in the Cabinet who made any objection to the troops going, and it was very foolish of him for there can be no doubt that this hostile invasion has been effected with the knowledge, if not with the active assistance of the Spanish Government.'[18] Despite this common definition of the situation, policy and regime cleavages existed within the Cabinet and this consensus, which was so easily formed, masked fundamental differences between the members of the Cabinet.

Division within the Cabinet was apparent during the initial stages of the crisis. As early as August, Wellington indicated to his friends that if the Cabinet pursued measures which he thought likely to bring about war, 'he would quit the government, for he would not be implicated in counsels he thought so disastrous to the country'.[19] At the beginning of September, Liverpool, the Prime Minister, was warned by a friend that 'if efforts are not made to prevent collision between Spain and Portugal and if that collision should take place, he [Wellington] will, I am certain write to you that he must withdraw from the Cabinet'.[20] Within a week, it was remarked: 'However grand Lord Liverpool may write, you may depend upon it that he is sufficiently alarmed. If you had heard him on the Portuguese question in the Cabinet last Saturday, you would have seen how unwilling he is not to attend to the Duke's wishes.'[21]

Wellington was certainly not in a mood to compromise in order to minimize conflict and maintain cohesion within the Cabinet. He felt: 'The state of the Cabinet and of the whole party, the sort of fusion Mr. Canning has effected with the Opposition, and the ill-humour and almost open hostility of old supporters of the Tory Party make the whole concern so very disagreeable that I would do anything to be out of it and see the Government broke up. I hope and believe it will happen soon.'[22] Support from Wellington was important to the Government and Canning and Liverpool altered their policy on several issues to accommodate Wellington.[23] But on occasions it was not possible to placate Wellington because of the possible reaction of other members of the party. Liverpool, for example, refused to allow Wellington's brother to become a bishop, and the Duke was 'excessively angry, and I am certain will not forgive it and, though he will not quarrel upon this subject, it will make him disposed to quarrel the first opportunity'.[24] At the same time, opponents of the Duke argued: 'The catalogue of favours bestowed upon the Duke's family is in very bad taste.'[25]

Despite this evidence of conflict, Wellington participated in a very active way in the consensus which initiated the intervention response. But he did not do so with a sense of conviction. Canning believed that he had out-manoeuvered Wellington and he wrote to a friend that he had sent a message to Wellington concerning the arrival of the British troops in Portugal 'partly for his information, but in great part also to plague his heart, as you will perceive'.[26] It was observed in a letter to Bathurst that Wellington 'betrayed bitter feelings' about the Portuguese intervention.[27] Wellington's cooperation can be explained in the same terms that Whig and Tory leaders used to justify their cooperation in a coalition government. Ellenborough, a Tory, wrote: 'I thought there had seldom been circumstances under which there was less of personal pleasure in belonging to a Government; but there had seldom been circumstances under which to abandon the administration on trifling grounds would have been more criminal. The corn question, the Russian question and that of Portugal would all have been decided differently had there been a Whig Government.'[28] And Palmerston, a Whig, argued in the same vein that 'if we all went out there would be formed a purely Tory Government, that would speedily throw over all those measures on which Canning had founded his fame. We should immediately break with Russia, probably also with France, back out of the Greek treaty, and unite ourselves with Metternich, and adopt the apostolical party in Spain and Portugal.'[29]

Although Westmorland was the only Tory who actively opposed the decision to send troops to Portugal, there is evidence that others were hostile. Canning expressed gratitude to Peel who had 'both on the South American question and the recent demonstrations in Portugal concurred in supporting him against his other colleagues'.[30] The level of hostility can be observed when Canning came to form his own government in February 1827. Abercromby noted: 'Considering the state of Europe, the ground he had taken with respect to Portugal and the condition of Ireland, it will be beyond even his skill to defend the honesty of the principle on which his government will be founded. It is in fact founded on a systematic exclusion of all honest principle.'[31]

Given this sharp policy cleavage which can be seen to exist retrospectively, the consensus which existed when the move was initiated must have reflected more than a common definition of the situation. Both Canning and Wellington came to the situation with certain predispositions which had developed during the previous three years. It was the convergence of these predispositions which permitted the consensus to occur. In both Spain and Portugal, the Absolutists lost control at the end of the Napoleonic wars and were replaced by Liberal governments, but in Portugal, unlike Spain, they regained control without external assistance, though in conditions of rebellion and division.

In July 1823, the Portuguese Government requested the British to send a fleet and 6000 men; Canning agreed to send the ships, but not the troops. Arbuthnot observed: 'The Duke is greatly annoyed at this, for Palmella [Foreign Minister] at the end of his letter, says that he applies to England *first* and hints that, if she refuses, he will then go to France.' Wellington wrote to Canning and urged that he should send troops because by sending the ships he had yielded the principle. He suggested that public agitation against the policy could be eliminated if it was explained that the troops were being sent at the request of the Portuguese Government and that the troops would only be used against forces which were 'in arms' against the government. While Wellington supported the government and was willing to lend them support, Canning favoured the rebels but was certainly not prepared to offer any formal assistance.

Wellington perceived the situation in these terms:

The Duke said he did not believe Mr. Canning would send troops, and explained with the utmost bitterness that every day showed more and more the irreparable loss we had sustained in Lord Londonderry and what a misfortune it was to have Mr. Canning, who was for yielding every point to the Revolutionists and who, every day, sunk us lower and lower in the political scale. He ended his letter by saying he hoped Mr. Canning had made up his mind to Portugal being occupied by French troops and entered in the interests of France.[32]

At this point, there was little support for a policy of intervention; although a regime cleavage did exist, this did not fragment the consensus which favoured nonintervention. Canning and Liverpool apparently felt it necessary to demonstrate the crystallization which existed on this cleavage. Wellington was asked to meet Canning and Liverpool to discuss the matter. No discussion took place, and at the Cabinet meeting which followed the proposed meeting, the decision concerning Portugal was taken. In the Cabinet, Liverpool asserted that it would be necessary to call Parliament in order to sanction troops being sent to Portugal.

The Duke begged to know why this was necessary, and Lord Melville proved in '86 Mr. Pitt had sent troops to Holland without consulting Parliament, and the Duke maintained it was the King's Prerogative, if money was not sent, to act in such a case without Parliament. He said if it was necessary to call Parliament that ended the matter at once, for that such a discussion must do mischief and at once do away with the *secrecy* upon which Palmella had insisted. The Duke, however, clearly saw that the whole thing was settled, and that he was only had up to town to let him see that the Cabinet thought differently from him. He is very angry.[33]

Rebellion continued in Portugal the following year. By May, the fragmentation within the Cabinet had increased along the policy cleavage. Nonintervention was still favoured. But some, particularly Wellington, felt that :

Portugal is our old and most faithful ally; our honour is concerned in her independence and, if foreign powers, France for instance, say 'We will not allow this anarchy to continue', what are we to do? We cannot refuse aid ourselves and yet forbid others giving it. There could be no answer to this, and it was agreed to leave the question open. Indeed, until a request was made by Portugal for troops we could not send them.[34]

A request soon followed, after a rebellion by Dom Miguel. Canning was anxious not to send British troops, fearing that this could legitimize the position of the French troops in Spain, but it was difficult for him to answer Wellington's charge in the Cabinet that the French could use the disturbance to send troops into Portugal. He agreed tentatively to send Hanoverian troops. When this became known, the French quickly reacted, giving an assurance that France had no designs on Portugal. Satisfied, Canning cancelled the order to send the Hanoverian troops. Wellington was furious. As he saw it 'Polignac went and protested. In short, France has bullied us out of it.'[35] He also attributed the policy reversal to the protests against the move in the Whig newspapers, believing Canning had 'taken fright and is making all sorts of difficulties'.[36]

By 1826, there was substantial fragmentation within the Cabinet, and crystallization occurred along both the regime and policy cleavages. The implementation of Pedro's liberal charter substantially altered the situation. Although Canning was concerned in case the charter should precipitate revolution, its adoption created a sentimental tie with the incumbent government. The sentimental attachment which Wellingon had experienced for the incumbent government correspondingly declined. It was now he who favoured the insurgents. But the position which he had consistently maintained since 1823 made it difficult for him to oppose Canning's decision to send troops to Portugal when the incursion across the Spanish frontier was presented as a *casus foederis*. Moreover, it was impossible for Wellington to impose a nonintervention system, given the importance which he had already attached to a threat of an invasion by the French troops.

There were both false and projected elements to the consensus which formed around the decision to send troops to Portugal. Both Canning and Wellington were well aware that their positions were substantially different on this issue and that it was necessary for Wellington to submerge his specific interest in the situation. This element of falsity in the consensus is apparent when the attitude of the two decision-makers is compared on related issues. When Wellington justified the position adopted by Britain, he also maintained that 'the perfidious acts of aggression in Portugal ought to be attributed to the servants of the Spanish Government than that Government itself. They ought to be looked upon as the acts of the captaincy-general of the provinces, and even the ministers of the King of Spain, than ordered or advised by His Catholic Majesty.'[37] The tone which Canning adopted was very different. While he was careful to argue that the British response was legitimate even if the act of aggression did not have 'the authority or the suggestion of the Government', he asked 'if all that has occurred on the frontiers has occurred only because the vigilance of the Spanish Government has been surprised, its confidence betrayed and its orders neglected ... let us see some symptoms of disapprobation, some signs of repentance, some measures indicative of sorrow for the past and sincerity for the future'.[38]

Canning went much further than this in the process of defending the policy which he favoured. As he explained to Granville:

If I know anything of the House of Commons from 33 years of experience, or if I may trust to what reaches me in reports of feelings out of doors, the declaration of the obvious but unsuspected truth, that 'I called the New World into existence to redress the balance of the Old', has been more grateful to English ears and to English feelings, ten

thousand times, than would have been the most satisfactory announcement of the intention of the French Government to withdraw its army
from Spain.[39]

It was observed at the time that the opposition were more affected by
Canning's speech than were the government's followers. The reason for
the cool reaction was explained by Wellington, who believed 'we pass in
Europe for a Jacobin Club. However, as yet, we have only boasted we are
such a body. Our acts do not yet prove it.' He added as a post-script: 'I
see in the despatches to Vienna and Paris that we are now explaining away
the meaning of our speeches.'[40]

Although Canning was conscious to some degree that his position
diverged from Wellington's there were occasions when he did seem to
'project his own preferred interests on the group as a whole'. For Canning,
the principal reason for sending troops to Portugal related to the systemic
problems created by the presence of the French troops in Spain. From the
beginning of 1826, he had been preoccupied with the problem.

> For the early part of the session we shall have our hands full of our
> internal difficulties: but these very difficulties, though not in any degree
> attributable to the Government, and though particularly alien to my
> department, will yet certainly produce a general temper of disquietude
> and dissatisfaction therefore and may perhaps so far extend the influence
> of those sentiments to me, as to render my assurances (in the face especi-
> ally of what appears more or less visible to the uninstructed eye) of the
> necessary and innocent continuance of a French force in Spain much
> less satisfactory than they have been admitted to be in former sessions.[41]

The French assurances were also much less satisfactory to Canning.
Writing on the need to remove the French from Spain, Canning noted to
Granville:

> A good opportunity will arise when, after the settlement of the dispute
> between Spain and Portugal, we withdraw our troops from Lisbon. But
> once there, he must not expect that we will under any circumstances
> withdraw them leaving the French army in Spain. *This,* however, you
> need not say to Villele: rather present the matter to him in a contrary
> sense, as intended to afford him the means of getting out of his difficulty
> with honour.[42]

It was Wellington who prevented Canning from projecting his own interests
in the situation on to other decision-makers. He insisted that:

> Whatever may be your ultimate determination respecting the French
> troops in Spain and His Majesty's troops in Portugal, it is obvious that
> you do not send the latter because the French troops are in Spain; and
> it is as well not to give any person even a pretext for saying that we
> had been seeking for an opportunity of adopting this measure with a
> view to get the French out of Spain.[43]

Wellington and Canning were projecting different specific interests onto the
same situation. The level of perceptual distortion is even more apparent

when Canning had to deal with other actors in the international system. He was unable to appreciate that they might also be working on the basis of a false consensus.

When the British announced their decision to send troops to Portugal, the French Government came under severe attack. The ultra-royalists dismissed all the reasons which the British gave in support of their actions. It was argued: 'The question for England is not whether she wants to reign in a particular part of the Peninsula; she aspires to domineer over the whole of it.'[44] They believed that the French Government should have given assistance to Ferdinand to crush the constitutionalists in Portugal. The more moderate royalists were also furious with the speech made by Canning and they resented, in particular, 'the galling assumption of superiority in political management'. The French Government also came under attack from the liberals, who argued that the situation had arisen because of the support which France had been giving to Ferdinand.[45]

Public support for Britain's position was given by the French Government, in spite of this criticism. At the same time, in private, Damas informed Granville that while they did not deny that the *casus foederis* had occurred, they regretted the British action because it meant that the decision to withdraw from Spain would have to be suspended.[46] When Polignac, the French ambassador in London, met Canning he spelled out the situation even more clearly and indicated that while they had made the 'expression of their sentiments as inoffensive as possible', the French Government was concerned because of the likelihood that the conflict would be ended quickly and the British presence might well be looked upon as an 'occupation'. Canning was disturbed by the discrepancy in the French position as described by Granville and Polignac.[47]

Granville went to see Damas again, who indicated that the French did accept that the *casus foederis* had occurred and Granville felt that the public declaration admitting the *casus foederis* was 'so satisfactory I did not think it necessary to push to an extremity unpleasant to the Baron de Damas an explanation of the discrepancies which you wish to have cleared up'.[48] Canning replied that if the French Government did not have complete confidence in Polignac 'it may not be improper to suggest in a friendly manner that ... it might be advisable to abstain as much as possible from employing him'.[49] The inability to distinguish between public and private statements suggests that the projected element of the consensus was very high. The difference between the public and private statements made by the French decision-makers was certainly no greater than the discrepancy between Britain's position as expressed by Granville and the position expressed by Canning in public, where he maintained:

> The French army in Spain is now a protection to that very party which it was originally called to put down. Were the French army suddenly removed at this precise moment, I verily believe that the immediate

effect would be to give full scope to the unbridled rage of a fanatical faction, before which, in the whirlwind of intestine strife, the party least in numbers would be swept away.[50]

Canning was unable to draw the comparison and this suggests that once the decision had been made to send troops to Portugal, there was a need to preserve an 'image of unanimity' and this extended to the decision-makers in other actors. The nature of the cognitive distortion which this involved will be examined in the following chapter.

Consensus on the collective intervention response

The emergence of the Bolshevik Government was the source of substantial cleavages within the British political system. Mayer observes that 'until 1917, the political truce was respected almost unanimously by Conservative, Liberal and Labour Parties .... However, after 1917, war weariness and the Russian Revolution combined to undermine Britain's political truce.'[51] The cleavages widened with time. By the end of 1919, Hoare noted the 'unfortunate fact' that attitudes towards Russia were divided along party lines.

> The principle of continuity in foreign policy is in danger of being abandoned. The chances of a general election within the next year must be reckoned with and also the possibility that it may result in the establishment of a government largely dependent on labour support. Should that be the case and should no definite Russian policy have been adopted it will become one of the main subjects of discussion and agitation. Such a result would be deplorable both because it would adversely affect the general situation in England and also because it would render it more difficult for the Government of the day to induce the French and other allied Governments to accept their Russian policy.[52]

This view is over-simplified. All parties were divided by regime and policy cleavages. Wide cleavages existed within the Cabinet, as a conversation recorded by Jones shows.

> Balfour stated that 'the atmosphere at Petrograd makes Lockhart regard Bolsheviks as agents of light'. Lloyd George replied that this 'Rather proves they are. The criticism of the Bolsheviks always comes from those 3,000 miles away from them.' Balfour went on 'I make a modest suggestion that the Bolsheviks are not angels of light.' After the meeting, Lloyd George remarked to Jones, 'You see, the moment we get to fundamentals we are "Poles apart".'[53]

From the beginning, Lloyd George demonstrated a sentimental attachment for the Bolsheviks. He remarked to a friend, shortly after they took control: 'The Russians are engaged in an interesting experiment: they are beginning with a clean sheet. What they do with it remains to be seen.'[54]

Two years later, he remained sympathetic, maintaining that Lenin was 'the biggest man in Politics. He had conceived and carried out a great economic experiment. It looked as if it were a failure. If so, Lenin was a big enough man to confess the truth and face it.'[55]

On the other side of the regime cleavage lay Churchill. Riddell reported that Churchill was extremely bitter about the Bolsheviks.[56] He 'dilated at length on the Bolshevik danger to civilization' and gave concrete reasons for his prejudice.

> The Bolsheviks are fanatics. Nothing will turn a fanatic from his purpose. Lloyd George thinks he can talk them over and that they will see the errors of their ways and the impracticability of their schemes. Nothing of the sort! Their view is that their system has not been successful because it has not been tried on a large enough scale and that in order to secure success they must make it world-wide.[57]

Churchill possessed a sentimental attachment for the anti-Bolsheviks and his beliefs were later crystallized in *The World Crisis* where, according to James, he draws 'a warmly over-sympathetic portrait of Nicholas II, and portrayed Russia at the beginning of 1917 as being on the verge of victory when "Despair and Treachery usurped command at the very moment when the task was done ... with victory in her grasp she fell upon the earth, devoured alive, like Herod of old, by worms".'[58]

The regime cleavage gave rise to a policy cleavage. In April 1918, Lloyd George feared that the British were treating the Bolshevik Government 'as if it were no government. Under the old regime you would not have gone to Murmansk and Vladivostok without the Tsar's permission.'[59] He insisted that he 'had no fear that Bolshevism was a formidable menace to the internal peace of this country'.[60] Lloyd George believed that it was necessary to come to terms with the Bolsheviks, while Churchill was anxious to send an allied force into Russia to crush the Bolsheviks. The two cleavages, however, proved to be cross-cutting, and there was considerable fragmentation among the decision-makers. Hardinge, for example, agreed that Britain must come to terms with the Bolsheviks; but he was careful to distinguish his views from those of Lloyd George whose 'motive was in reality a certain amount of sympathy with the Bolsheviks whom [he] regarded as having overthrown an autocratic government under the influence of a policy of self-determination'.[61]

There was unanimous support to send troops to Murmansk and later to Vladivostok; in view of the sharp cleavages which existed within the Cabinet, such a consensus could only occur because the specific interests possessed by both extremes were suppressed, reflecting false and projected elements of consensus. The extent to which Lloyd George had to suppress his specific interests has been described by Nicolson, who believed that Lloyd George's views were 'anathema to the French and to his own Tory supporters in the coalition Cabinet. He refrained, therefore, from openly admitting these objectives, and at times he would openly deny them. But they persisted. He would return to them again and again.'[62] Lloyd George constantly had to modify his own views in order to operate within a consensus, and the following year, when 'Tory members of his own Cabinet, representing conservative opinion in England, strongly protested his "soft" line on Bolshevism, Lloyd George came out in favour of continued intervention and further aid to the anti-Bolsheviks'.[63]

Consensus was achieved by a process of interest aggregation. A cluster of issues was related to the intervention response and decision-makers identified with different combinations. The specific combinations of interests were not always exposed. While Lloyd George had to suppress his interest in coming to terms with the Bolsheviks because it was not compatible with the policy which was being pursued, Churchill had to disguise his interest in the suppression of Bolshevism because it was decided to exclude this from the list of stateable interests. Lockhart did not appreciate this modification had taken place, and he remarked later: 'One lesson that period should have taught me is that the man in London has a thousand advantages over the man on the spot. Then I was too young to profit by it. During the next year I was to acquire it by the bitter experience of being the man on the spot.'[64] He was specifically informed by Balfour that 'suppression of Bolshevism' was not a British interest.

The extent to which the consensus was false was even more apparent at the inter-departmental level. By the end of the war, relations between the War Office and the Foreign Office were so strained that it was necessary to establish a Russian Committee to try to unify action between the two departments. Disagreements about which parties in Russia should receive aid became so acute that the War Office refused to supply the Foreign Office with the relevant information.[65] Even within the Foreign Office there was sharp disagreement. Carr maintained: 'It may be said that the Bolsheviks would not keep the terms of any understanding which may be arrived at. This is possible. In this case no harm will have been done by an attempt to arrive at an understanding and we could have a much clearer case to present to public opinion in this country.' Cecil disagreed and 'strongly deprecated the idea of ever coming to any sort of political understanding with the Bolshevik Government'.[66]

The British decision-makers were extremely sensitive about the cleavages which existed between them, and the need to preserve a superficial consensus. During the Paris Peace Conference, Clemenceau attempted to exploit the differences which existed between Balfour and Lloyd George by consulting Balfour on certain sensitive issues. Lloyd George became extremely angry and threatened that 'if Clemenceau persisted in this tactic he would return to England and leave Balfour without any authority to make a final decision'.[67]

However, specific interests submerged in order to achieve consensus were given some exposure at the national decision-making level. This was less true at the systemic level. The intervention response was only possible with the cooperation of other states. There was a conscious effort to retain this consensus, creating an element of falsity. For example, when the Chinese heard that the Allies were sending troops to Vladivostok, they asked for Britain's opinion. A Foreign Office official noted: 'As usual we shall no doubt have to conform our views to the Japanese on this matter; and we had better give no answer until we know what their answer is going to be.'[68]

Policy also had to be modified in order to maintain inter-allied consensus. Britain attempted to pre-empt allied policy on one occasion by deciding to give the anti-Bolshevik Omsk Government *de facto* recognition. It was then discovered that the French were not prepared to follow such a step, because the Americans were 'not prepared to do so'. They argued that, like the Americans, they could not give a government formal recognition 'until quite satisfied that it is likely to be on a permanent basis'. A Foreign Office official commented, 'if we wait till "quite satisfied" anything in Russia is on a "permanent basis" we shall wait till Doomsday'.[69] Nevertheless, it was decided not to take an initiative.

Information flows were affected by the awareness of the false consensus which operated at the inter-allied level. At the beginning of July 1918, just before the United States decided to go to the assistance of the Czechs, the British learned that the Germans intended to turn East again and break the Treaty of Brest Litovsk. If this were true, then it tended to undermine the argument that intervention was necessary in order to draw the Germans back to Eastern front. Cecil decided that this information should be passed on to Paris but not to Washington, where extreme reluctance about intervention had already been expressed.[70]

Sensitivity to the nature of the consensus was not always present and a projected element to the consensus existed. The British were very slow to realize that the desirability of intervention was disputed in Japan[71] and they seemed incapable of accepting that the Japanese had no intention of moving West of the Urals – an important aspect of Britain's policy.[72] But it was relations with the United States which became particularly strained because of the inability of the British decision-makers to appreciate that there was a divergence between British and American interests.

A memorandum was sent to Wilson in June 1918 in which it was argued that even if Germany could be defeated on the Western front, the outcome could not be decisive because of Germany's control of the Eastern front.

> Unless, therefore, Russia can reconstitute herself as a military power in the East against the time when the Allied Armies are withdrawn, nothing can prevent the complete absorption of her resources by the Central Powers, which would imply world domination, and the only way by which the resurrection of Russia can be brought about is by immediate Allied military intervention in to that theatre.[73]

Arguments of this sort failed to impress the Americans[74] but they continued to be made. There were some arguments which were employed which were not only dismissed, but caused active resentment in Washington. According to Fowler:

London was slow in realizing that the consideration of keeping the 'road to India' safe was an argument which aroused resentment rather than sympathy in the United States. Indeed reference to the security of India was such a ritual for some British officials that they introduced it into papers on almost any subject. Reading on March 10 cautioned against the mention of India in messages directed towards the Americans, yet the practice continued well into April. It finally ceased when Wiseman, in London, pointed out the danger of leading Americans to assume that 'Japanese intervention is intended to secure the British position in India rather than as an effective factor in the present fighting in Europe'.[75]

When the Americans, Japanese, French and British did eventually introduce the intervention response, the consensus did not emerge from a coordinated policy, but because of the common perception of the position of the Czech troops. Some British decision-makers, however, had great difficulty coming to terms with the fact that the 'consensus' did not reflect a set of common interests. They insisted on projecting their own interests onto the situation. When the Americans categorically refused to expand the initial action into a fully-fledged intervention, Cecil was particularly irritated. 'The Americans are maddening. Ask all our American experts if they can suggest any way out of this impasse – I can think of none.' One of the Foreign Office officials, however, understood the significance of operating in the context of a projected consensus. He commented on Cecil's inquiry: 'I think that we must remember that at Washington we are regarded as being liable to panic – and in this instance, as Mazaryk himself seems quite cheerful, I fear we may be exposed to the suspicion not only of panicking but also of being too ready to snatch at the first chance of committing the United States more deeply than the latter are willing to do.' He went on to say that Americans always argued that they were too deeply committed in other areas to expand their operations in Russia. The official indicated that the British never discussed this issue. 'The Americans are maddening partly because we never argue with them on their own ground.'[76]

Although this element of projection existed at the inter-allied level, the level of projection was much higher among the British decision-makers themselves. The interests expressed by the two extremes were mutually incompatible. Mayer has argued that 'in order not to endanger Allied unity, the British and French Cabinets had an indefinite postponement of a full-blown inter-Allied war-aims debate which was likely to give rise to serious policy divergences'.[77] And in the House of Commons, when members made repeated requests for a statement of British aims in Russia, they were informed that it was 'not in the national interest that any such information should be given'.[78] But it would seem that discussion was as much a threat to intra-allied as inter-allied unity and it was for this reason that it was postponed. In the next chapter, there will be a discussion of the way in which decision-makers reconciled themselves to the divergent positions in the consensus.

CONSENSUS ON THE COLLECTIVE NONINTERVENTION RESPONSE

One historian who has examined the reaction of Britain to the American Civil War has observed that as his investigations proceeded, 'it became progressively more clear that the great crisis in America was almost equally a crisis in the domestic history of Great Britain herself'.[79] The crisis did not arise simply from the interruption in trade between the two countries; the Southern States over-estimated the importance of this factor. As Russell, the Foreign Secretary, indicated at the time, the South failed to remember 'the lesson so often taught by experience, that stopping the supply results in stimulating it elsewhere . . . in answer to all the arguments they are apt to repeat their senseless cry that "cotton is king".'[80] In retrospect, it can be seen that the shortage of cotton served to raise prices and reduce the industry to a more efficient size.[81] Moreover, this instrumental attachment to the South was matched by an equally important tie to the North in the form of wheat, necessary to feed the British industrial workers.[82]

The crisis reflected the conflict in political principles which were raised during the civil war. Many British conservatives had a strong sentimental attachment to the Southern States,[83] which was shared by Palmerston, who had great sympathy for the Southern cause. After the severe defeat sustained by the North at Bull Run, he noted that putting a uniform on men did not create an army and that while the South were fighting for what they believed to be their vital interests, the North were fighting for an idea entertained by professional politicians.[84] His attitude towards the Northern States was affected by his general opinion of democracy. 'The history of the world in all times and countries shows that Power in the hands of the masses throws the scum of the community to the surface and that truth and justice are soon banished from the land – we should all fare in the same way under the sway of Bright and his associates.'[85] Even Gladstone, a liberal, favoured the Southern cause because of his belief in the right of self-determination.[86]

Only the radicals possessed a sentimental attachment for the Northern States. They were deeply affected by the outbreak of the war. Cobden was 'broken down in heart and feeling' by the outbreak of the war, according to Bright.[87] For them, the issue was very stark: 'it was obvious from the first that a Southern victory would mean, in fact, a victory for slavery'.[88]

It was this factor which complicated the issue. Palmerston could contemplate bifurcation with equanimity and before the outbreak of the civil war he forecast to Queen Victoria 'the approaching and virtually accomplished Dissolution in America of the great Northern Confederation'.[89] But he was also strongly opposed to slavery,[90] and Russell insisted in Parliament: 'It is our earnest wish that the sin and stain of slavery must cease.'[91] Only a victory by the North could bring about this end.

There was, therefore, no clear regime cleavage. The South was favoured in terms of the abstract right of self-determination, but the North had a claim to support on the grounds of the abolition of slavery. A policy cleavage never emerged. The radicals were uncertain about the position which they should adopt. Cobden noted at the beginning of 1862 that he could not see his way through the 'American business. I don't believe the North and the South can ever lie in the same bed again.'[92] There was no pressure applied to intervene on the side of the North. According to Jones, most conservatives failed to take any great interest in the war and adopted a policy of neutrality, eliminating pressure to intervene in favour of the Southern States.[93]

The consensus within the Cabinet favouring nonintervention cannot be attributed to homogeneity within the group; it was formed in 1859, and, according to Southgate, marked 'the deliberate recreation of the two-party system which had broken down in 1846'.[94] This was achieved by uniting the Whigs, the Peelites and the Manchester School, led by Cobden. Palmerston's restraint during the civil war has been attributed to his desire 'to preserve his coalition government by avoiding discord',[95] and it has also been suggested: 'The Palmerston-Russell ministry held office by a somewhat uncertain tenure through the silent acquiescence of a large element in the ranks of the conservatives, who recognized in the Prime Minister one of themselves.'[96] Palmerston himself seems to have been aware of the problems of consensus formation. He wrote to Russell: 'As to Cabinets, if we had colleagues like those who sat in Pitt's Cabinet, or such men as those who sat with Peel, you and I might have had our way on most things, but when as is now the case, able men fill every department, such men will have opinions and hold to them.'[97]

During the formation of policy for the civil war in America, however, it would seem that individual interests were not sufficiently crystallized to give rise to conflict when the decision was made. The ancestral element extended beyond the Cabinet. Disraeli, the leader of the opposition, indicated that he had 'exerted whatever influence he might possess in endeavouring to dissuade his friends from embarrassing Her Majesty's Government in their position of "politic and dignified reserve"'.[98] And when a Member of Parliament wished to table a motion concerning the recognition of the Southern States, Russell said that he could not, of course, prevent him from doing so, 'but looking to the interests of the public service, I cannot say that I think it desirable that it should come on'.[99] The motion was voluntarily postponed *sine die.*

CONSENSUS ON THE UNILATERAL NONINTERVENTION RESPONSE

When conflict was initiated in Spain, the divisions which were exposed in the political system found their counterpart in other European countries. Mowat notes that the war affected the British political scene; it 'widened existing divisions between right and left (terms hardly used in the political scene before this); it brought bitterness and class-consciousness into foreign policy, and so into domestic politics to an extent unknown before.'[100] A regime cleavage quickly established itself. At the onset of the war, Churchill made an assessment of the predispositions of the British decision-makers in a letter to Corbin, the French ambassador in London. He felt that 'if France sent airplanes, etc., to the present Madrid Government and the Germans pushed in from the other angle, the dominant forces here would be pleased with Germany and Italy and estranged from France'.[101] Corbin reported back to France that there was a strong pro-rebel feeling in the British Cabinet.[102]

Sentimental attachments developed for both the incumbent and insurgent governments and these gave rise to strongly worded minutes when it appeared that policy was moving in favour of one side or the other. When Eden discussed breaches of the nonintervention agreement in the House of Commons and indicated that 'there are other Governments more to blame than those of Germany and Italy', Collier, a Foreign Office official, expressed surprise and went on:

> There was some evidence that the Spanish revolt had originally been prepared with the connivance if not the instigation of the Italian Government, and that the Soviet Union, for their part, only began to supply arms to the Spanish Government when it was apparent that the Italians and Germans didn't intend to observe the nonintervention agreement. What really disturbs me is therefore the growth of a belief in Liberal and Labour circles (and not in those circles only) that the Government has been induced by people whom I have heard described as 'Conservatives first and Englishmen afterwards', to adopt a policy of conniving at Signor Mussolini's now avowed policy of spreading Fascism throughout the world as an antidote to Communism and of seeking to come to an understanding with him that would leave him free to pursue this policy without fear of British opposition.

Collier went on to say that he had always assumed these fears were groundless, but in view of the 'talk of an agreement with Mussolini without any mention of a settlement in Spain I must confess doubts'.[103]

For some decision-makers there was an important instrumental attachment to the Fascists which over-rode any potential sentimental attachments for the Republicans. Vansittart stated 'we simply have not the wherewithal to face trouble on three fronts' and as a consequence it was necessary to come to terms with Italy.[104] The perception of developments in the international system also strengthened the instrumental attachment to the insurgent government in Spain. Mounsey, Cadogan and Eden all felt that if the insurgents were defeated, a communist regime would take over; it was felt that this eventuality must be prevented.[105] Within the Cabinet there was a strong desire to foster good relations with Franco. The First Lord of the Admiralty indicated that he 'did not wish to appear as a protagonist against General Franco, if only for the reason that the insurgents held the part of Spain in which this country was most interested'.[106]

The crystallization which occurred in favour of Franco was matched by the crystallization which occurred on the other side of the cleavage in favour of the Republicans. Within the Labour Party and the TUC there was a strong sentimental attachment for the incumbent government and the political left would have been outraged by any attempt to assist Franco.[107] A consensus within the political system could only be achieved by submerging the specific interests on either side of the cleavage which favoured support to either the insurgents or the incumbents. A policy of nonintervention permitted these specific interests to remain submerged. Both sides had to compromise and the consensus reflected a political bargain.

The adopted policy was dictated by the knowledge that if any other were formulated, it would 'give the opposition an opportunity for attacking the Government for failing to support democratic principles'.[108] It was appreciated that any move in favour of Franco would create intense hostility in Britain and would be very difficult to defend in Parliament. When Chamberlain was Prime Minister, he maintained: 'If HMG were to grant belligerent rights at this juncture, however, it would be said by their opponents that this revealed the Government's policy in its true light, which they had always claimed was support for Franco.'[109] It has been suggested that the British Government persuaded the French Government to put forward the nonintervention scheme in order to silence the British left;[110] although this was not the case, it was admitted later by Attlee that the attitude of the French Government 'hampered us in bringing pressure on our own Government'.[111]

The nonintervention policy represented an acceptable compromise; this bargained consensus represented the lowest common denominator which was acceptable to all groups. The policy reflected group specificity, but individual specificity of interests did exist and they were suppressed in order to permit the consensus to emerge.[112] Even the Labour Party and the TUC gave their support to the policy.[113] This made it a difficult policy for the government to sustain because of the danger that individual specific interests would emerge. The refusal to accept Franco's agents in Britain reflected pressure from the left,[114] but there was corresponding pressure from the right. As Mounsey observed:

> The fact that we are producing proposals of our own to the Nonintervention Committee without prior agreement with France should do something to remove the suspicion that we are bound through France to Valencia . . . it is by our acts that we should be judged, not by our words; and if some of our humanitarian work could benefit Franco rather than Valencia that would be our best reply on the point of partiality.[115]

In the next chapter there will be a discussion of the perceptual distortion which was necessary in order to allow individual specificity of interests to be submerged beneath the group specificity which prevailed.

DECISION-MAKING AND CONSENSUS FORMATION

Holsti has maintained: 'The range of variation among foreign policy leaders on *politically relevant attributes* is quite restricted. Without necessarily falling prey to the overly-simple conceptualization of politics, the premise that the range of individual variations among foreign policy elites is smaller than that of the general public is eminently reasonable.'[116] It has also been suggested that as the stress within a situation increases, group pressures will build up to enforce conformity within the group.[117] The analysis here indicates that these conclusions must be modified. Substantial cleavages can exist among decision-makers and yet consensus can be achieved while individual specificity of interest is maintained.

Such a situation can partially be explained by the process of interest aggregation,[118] where a single policy promises to satisfy a series of divergent interests. The process has been described by de Rivera, who suggests that 'when a person attempts to convince others of a point he builds an argument which is directed to their concerns and is a selection of a portion of the truth'.[119] The situation can also be explained in terms of perceptual distortion. Some distortion is bound to occur when interests are aggregated, since the individual will be aware that there are members of the consensus who are operating on the basis of mutually incompatible interests. The process which permits decision-makers to pursue a policy under such conditions will now be examined.

CHAPTER 7

Consistency and Dissonance

RATIONAL man, working with perfect information, can always formulate a policy which will optimize his position. Under real conditions the nature of decision-making is very different. Before decisions are made, the decision-maker experiences pre-decision conflict while the relative costs and benefits of various options are considered. These rarely point unambiguously in one direction, but because decision-makers desire to be rational, Simon has argued that they implement 'bounded rationality'; a simplified model of the real situation is constructed and the decision-maker behaves rationally with respect to this model.[1] He uses the model to choose between the options and once the decision is made, conflict is resolved. However, some social psychologists have suggested that the conflict is replaced by post-decision dissonance, which occurs because 'the decision in favour of the chosen alternative is counter to the beliefs that favour the unchosen alternative';[2] the level of the dissonance will therefore increase with the importance of the decision taken, the attractiveness of the unchosen alternative, and the amount of cognitive overlap.[3]

It might be thought that the level of dissonance experienced by an individual will reduce when a decision reflects a consensus within a group, but as was shown in the previous chapter, the emergence of a consensus does not necessarily imply agreement among decision-makers; considerable divergence of opinion and basic conflict can be contained by a consensus, either by the suppression of individual interests, some kind of bargaining process, or by means of projecting different individual specific interests onto the decision which is arrived at collectively. The consensus, therefore, may mask a set of cleavages which divide the group. In this chapter, there is an examination of the way individuals operate within a consensus which initiates a policy inconsistent with their accepted beliefs. It is suggested that, consciously or unconsciously, a series of techniques is employed, designed to reduce any inconsistency between the decision implemented and related beliefs which are held by the decision-maker.

115

DISSONANCE AND DECISION-MAKING

The sharp distinction which is made between pre-decision and post-decision processes distinguishes the cognitive dissonance theory from other cognitive consistency models[4] and it is particularly relevant in this context because it has been so closely related to the process of decision-making.[5] When the theory was first formulated it was argued not only that dissonance would occur after any decision, but also that the individual would always attempt to reduce the dissonance. It followed from this assumption that before a decision is taken, alternatives will be viewed in a more 'impartial' and 'objective' light[6] than after the decision is taken, when the individual will be looking for information which supports the decision and avoid information which invalidates it.[7] Information, in other words, will be selected to substantiate the model of reality which has been accepted.

Extensive criticism has been levelled against the theory of cognitive dissonance; as a result it has been substantially revised. A major objection relates to the implication contained in the theory that, in post-decision situations, the individual

> ... in order to stabilize his decisions, must, to some extent, maladapt himself to his environment. Thus presumably the more evidence a person gets that his decision was wrong, the more ardently will he support his original decision (until he belatedly revokes his decision). Maladaptive behaviour obviously occurs but its occurrence is not proof that it must occur as a result of such a basic psychological function as decision-making.[8]

Festinger has now accepted that 'simply making a decision does not guarantee the onset of dissonance-reduction processes',[9] and argues that 'commitment' to a decision is necessary to initiate the process.[10] An alternative formulation, which is preferred, has emerged from the result of an experiment by Deutsch, Krauss and Rosenau, which indicates that:

> When a person experiences dissonance after making a choice, he is attempting to defend himself against a perceived implication of his choice which is contrary to his self-conception. It is the inconsistency between the cognition of self and choice, rather than the inconsistency in the selection of one alternative rather than another, that is critical to the occurrence of post-decisional dissonance.[11]

The authors argue that this hypothesis is a specific formulation of the general proposition derived from Heider's theory of cognitive consistency 'that any event (x) which is conceived to be a function of the characteristics of a person (p) and of his environment (e) will tend to be perceived in such a way that the perception of p, e, x, and their interrelationships are not inconsistent with one another'.[12] When a triadic relationship is established which links the individual with two related points of cognition, four possible triads can be formed, if the relationships are defined in terms of association and dissociation. Two of the triads are balanced; two are unbalanced.[13]

Defining the points of cognition as either nonintervention and stability, or intervention and instability, the triads demonstrate the consistency which underpins the norm of nonintervention. In the first triad, the decision-maker (P) favours a stable environment (E) and the policy of nonintervention (x) which he believes will foster a stable environment. The associative relationship between the three points of cognition establishes cognitive consistency. If the decision-maker comes to believe that there is a dissociative relationship between nonintervention and a stable environment, as in the second triad, the model reflects inconsistency. Balance is restored in the third triad where the decision-maker (P) wishes to eschew a policy of intervention (x) which is not compatible with a stable environment (E). Finally, imbalance returns when the decision-maker (P) wishes to avoid an unstable environment (E) and the policy of intervention (x) while at the same time believing that intervention is a policy which will maintain stability.

An intervention response will give rise to a high level of dissonance, partly because the divergence which occurs between the operational and psycho-milieus will give rise to a large volume of information discrepant with the model of the situation which has been established, but also because of the need to suppress individual interest specificity for the purpose of establishing a consensus. False and projected consensuses are likely to cause dissonance for the component members.

The theory of cognitive dissonance has been attacked because it 'can predict almost *any* result which an experiment may find ... Such a situation means that we are never sure *before* any experiment is conducted which of the many possible results may occur.'[14] While this may be true, the fact remains that the theory has 'pointed to some very interesting questions about post-decisional processes'.[15] The model of reality established will not only indicate which alternative to choose, but also structure the environment in such a way that the information received is rendered consistent with the policy adopted. Dissonance does not simply give rise to an avoidance of discrepant information; active steps are taken to cope with inconsistent information. The process has been described in terms of self-justification or rationalization.

DECISION CONFLICT AND DISSONANCE REDUCTION

The importance of dissonance reduction relates to the level of conflict which precedes the decision. If there is very severe decision conflict, then an elaborate process of dissonance reduction will have to be implemented. Abelson has suggested that there are four distinct cognitive mechanisms which can be employed in the process of dissonance reduction.[16] The first is *denial*, the mechanism most frequently employed. In this instance, the validity of information which creates dissonance is denied. It amounts to a simple refusal to accept information which will create dissonance. Arguments tend to be dismissed rather than refuted and the utility of the tactic is enormous because of the ease with which it can be operated. Although it may appear a very crude method of coping with disagreeable information, the ubiquity with which it is employed tends to substantiate Abelson's contention that it will be the first move made when information received is likely to increase the level of dissonance. It can be manifested in a variety of forms: a teacher may 'ignore' the bad behaviour of a child whom he believes cannot be disciplined; or some information may be specifically 'excluded'. Janis suggests that Wilson employed both these tactics during the First World War, when he wished to keep the United States out of the war. He 'ignored' information which would have indicated that the Germans were implacably hostile and he refused to meet the German ambassador because this might have presented him with information which was dissonant with his definition of the situation.[17]

Denial will not always serve to reduce dissonance and in some cases inconsistency cannot be denied, in which case dissonance can be reduced by implementing a process of *bolstering*. Here, the decision is reinforced by a series of arguments designed either to increase the attractiveness of the decision or to decrease the significance of the inconsistent cognition. To use a familiar example, if an individual finds that he can no longer deny an associative relationship between smoking and cancer and he is frightened of cancer, then he will experience dissonance each time he smokes a cigarette. He can bolster the decision to smoke by deciding that smoking is good for his nerves and that if he gives it up, he will make life intolerable for his family. He may hear from a friend that if he gives up smoking he will put on weight, something he wishes to avoid. In addition, he believes that heavier people have a greater chance of dying from heart failure. At the same time, he can diminish the significance of cancer by pointing to information which indicates that a cure for cancer will soon be achieved, and also the statistic which indicates that the risk of being killed in a car is much greater than the chance of dying from lung cancer.

The process of bolstering assumes that the actor favours one cognition which allows the significance of the second to be diminished. A move of this kind is not always possible, for the actor may feel strongly about two inconsistent cognitions. One way of circumventing the inconsistency between the two cognitions is by a process of *differentiation*. This involves creating a series of arguments which invert the apparent associative or dissociative relationship between the two inconsistent cognitions, thereby creating a balanced triad. Galtung has suggested that this tactic was employed by the White Rhodesians when Britain imposed sanctions after the unilateral declaration of independence.[18] The strong distaste the Rhodesians felt for the sanctions created an unbalanced triad in view of the associative relationships which existed between Britain and the Rhodesians, and Britain and the sanctions. Since the Rhodesians were not willing to alter their attitude towards either Britain or the sanctions, the only way a balance could be restored was by establishing a dissociative relationship between Britain and the sanctions.

This was done by differentiating between Britain and the Labour Government. The Rhodesians used the Queen as the symbolic head of Britain and established a dissociative relationship between the Queen and sanctions and also between the Queen and the Labour Government. The differentiation was furthered by establishing an associative relationship between the Labour Party and the Communists. In this way, it was possible to invert the relationship which had existed between Britain and sanctions; it was perceived that Britain also disliked the sanctions, balancing the original triad. This is an important device frequently employed by decision-makers. For example, the Americans differentiated between communism in the Soviet Union and the communism practised by Tito after Yugoslavia broke away from the Soviet bloc; the one was associated with totalitarianism and the other with national independence.

If it is not desirable to invert the relationship between two inconsistent cognitions, there is a fourth way by which dissonance can be reduced and which can accommodate this requirement; it involves the process of *transcendence*. The process is not frequently employed because of the cognitive complexity required to implement it. To establish a cognitive balance while at the same time sustaining the inconsistent relationship, it is necessary to formulate a new idea which demonstrates the compatibility of the inconsistent cognitions when viewed from a transcendent level. For example, it was difficult for some religious sects to accept Darwin's theory of evolution because it contradicted the Bible; others reconciled the difference by distinguishing between literal and figurative truth; this provided the transcendent idea which reconciled the inconsistency. In a political context, de Gaulle was able to rationalize his participation in the European community with his belief in the destiny of France, by the notion of *Europe des Patries*. His conception of Europe as a 'third force' managed to capture national and supranational overtones.

The process of rationalization is normally related to intra-personal conflict and it is implied that the process is largely unconscious. But it is possible to observe the process in operation at the inter-personal level. Individuals are conscious of the need to rationalize and will often assist others in the process. If a girl is jilted, friends may pass on information of a derogatory nature about the boy which they previously concealed, in an effort to placate the girl. The process can become institutionalized and this has aroused the interest of sociologists. Goffman examines the process in terms of 'cooling-off the mark'.[19] The mark is the victim of a con-man's trick. Since the trick will be repeated many times, it is important that the mark should not disclose the nature of the trick. After it has been performed, therefore, one of the con-men will remain with the mark in order to pacify him and ensure that he does not inform the authorities. The con-man is only required to reinforce the natural inclination of the mark, who will not be anxious to publicize his gullibility.

Whenever decision-makers endeavour to establish a consensus and it is appreciated that individual interest specificities are being violated, there will often be a conscious attempt to implement a mechanism to reduce the resultant dissonance. For example, in February 1972, when the Labour Party in Britain voted almost unanimously against the government on the terms of entry into the Common Market, the Chief Whip stressed that the consensus represented a vote of no-confidence in the government. In this way, he helped to reduce the dissonance experienced by those members of the Labour Party who had voted in favour of Common Market legislation the previous November.

An intervention stimulus always provides a source of potential conflict for the decision-makers of an external actor. A regime cleavage will frequently occur and this can precipitate a policy cleavage, although this cleavage can also occur independently. Provided that the interests of the individual decision-makers remain diffuse, the level of conflict will be minimal; conflict will only develop when individual interest specificity occurs. A consensus may not reflect the interest specificities of all the constituent members; this will affect the level of post-decision dissonance experienced after the response is initiated. If the response does not reflect the preferred option of an actor, he will feel much less pressure to defend the option in the face of dissonant information subsequently received. On the basis of this assumption, it is stipulated that:

Proposition 6: In an interventionary situation, decision-makers will experience dissonance when there is either a false or projected consensus which reflects their interest specificity, or a bargained consensus which fails to reflect their interest specificity.

Abelson has asserted that when an actor experiences dissonance, there is a 'hierarchy of resolution attempts based upon the relative ease of achieving success with each of the methods'.[20] While this may apply at the level of intra-personal conflict, it is contended that at the inter-personal level there will normally be a variety of mechanisms for reducing dissonance employed simultaneously. Sometimes the mechanisms will be employed unconsciously; on other occasions they will be introduced consciously in order to reduce dissonance among some members of the group. No attempt is made, however, to distinguish between the conscious and unconscious attempts at dissonance reduction in the analysis of the cases which follow.

DISSONANCE REDUCTION DURING THE UNILATERAL INTERVENTION RESPONSE

Conflict, reflecting a policy cleavage which separated Wellington and Canning, existed within the Cabinet for several years before the stimulus which precipitated an intervention response occurred. Canning had always refused to take action in Portugal on the grounds of nonintervention. On occasions, Wellington dissented from this position, although he accepted the importance of the nonintervention norm. When his consistency on this point was challenged, he argued that on previous occasions 'troops were to be granted for a *specific purpose* (to quell a mutiny of troops) which he had no objection to, but what is now wanted is a guarantee of the form of government that may be established generally, which would cause our Parliament to interfere in every act of the Portuguese Government and is a thing he could not sanction'.[21]

When the crisis developed, ambiguity within the situation allowed the emergence of several divergent images, serving to increase the level of conflict between decision-makers. The existence of conflict was demonstrated by Wellington's threats to resign. But Canning also experienced predecision conflict and this is reflected in the stern warnings which were sent to A Court in Lisbon, who was informed that 'While HMG have been straining every ounce of influence and authority in Europe, and with entire success, to avert foreign aggression from that Kingdom, the Rulers of it have succeeded, on the other hand, in wantonly and provokingly furnishing materials for a civil war.' He added, 'Here fortunately we have no treaties to compel our interference or to fetter our direction.'[22]

These positions were reversed when the intervention response was formulated. Far from resigning, Wellington supported the despatch of the troops, while Canning praised the forbearance of the Portuguese Government. Both were aware, however, that they were participating in a false consensus. The resultant dissonance was reduced by the mechanism of differentiation.

A close friend provides a very clear indication of Wellington's profile of the situation, indicating that 'it is curious to remark upon Mr. Canning's eagerness to send out troops now, and his positive objection three years ago, when this very means was urged upon him by the Duke. The object then, however, was to uphold an established Government and *to keep the peace*; now I am certain Mr. Canning hopes that it will blow up a war.'[23] Canning was equally sure that Wellington did not welcome the response but after being outwitted by Canning, he had to accept the move. For this reason, he was sure that the news of the troops' arrival in Lisbon would 'plague his heart'.[24] Wellington was under no illusions about Canning's attitude.

When Canning 'received despatches from Sir Wm. A Court stating the entry into Portugal of the Portuguese deserters, with *arms* furnished by Spain and a promise of artillery from Badajos' he sent them to Wellington, 'somewhat triumphantly observing that *now* there could be no doubt what our duty to Portugal was'.[25]

Although Wellington and Canning experienced a need to differentiate their positions, there was a common area of dissonance which the response created. Both decision-makers were firmly committed to the nonintervention norm and both, on occasions, had defined the despatch of troops to Portugal in terms of intervention, thereby establishing a dissociative relationship between the despatch of troops and the nonintervention norm. The alternative images which had developed during the crisis permitted an associative relationship to be established between these two points of cognition by differentiating between the definitions of the situation as a civil war and an invasion. Once the differentiation could be established, the dissociative relationship could be inverted, creating cognitive consistency. By sending troops, it would be possible for the Portuguese to resolve their internal differences without a threat of external interference. The despatch of troops, therefore, reinforced the nonintervention norm.

Once the response was formulated, information which substantiated this image of the situation was used to bolster the definition; dissonant information was denied. Although Canning had been sent information which demonstrated that the Portuguese had engaged in provocative activity,[26] he accepted the reports which indicated that the Spanish authorities were informed six weeks before the invasion that such a move was planned, invalidating the argument that they had been taken by surprise[27] and undermining the credibility of the promise to disarm the Portuguese deserters and place them in the interior of Spain.[28] When the intervention response was formulated, however, he felt that he must 'in justice add that it is not the fault of the Portuguese. The forbearance of the Government has been superhuman.'[29]

The model of reality based on these cognitions excluded the possibility of the British reversing their decision. While Canning could assert that 'it must never be forgotten that the means of effectively removing it [the British expedition] can only be found at Madrid and not at Lisbon',[30] he also insisted, in a despatch to Granville, that the French could see

> ... how tenderly Spain is even now treated in His Majesty's message, and how carefully an opening is left for explanation, disavowal, or redress. But you will not hold out an expectation that anything can now prevent the departure of the troops for Lisbon. Whether from want of sincerity on the part of the Spanish Government in making its agreements, or from want of power to execute them, is practically unimport-ant – but from one cause or another ... no reliance could be placed on any engagement which His Catholic Majesty might contract so long as Portugal is unprovided with effectual means of defence.[31]

Once this model was established, Canning denied the possibility of alternative settlements. For months, Lamb, in Madrid, had insisted that one reason for Spanish intransigence was the presence of the French ambassador, De Moustier, who encouraged subversive activity against the Portuguese. Canning accepted that his recall in October 'would probably have prevented the mischief it is now intended to remedy',[32] but denied in December that de Moustier was of significance and described the move as 'moonshine'.[33] It did not precipitate any modification of the model of reality which he was employing.

Even when the intervention response was being implemented, Wellington was less prone to establish a rigid model of reality. His image was more flexible and capable of absorbing alternative images. After receiving despatches from Beresford, defining the intervention stimulus in terms of a civil war, Wellington wrote to Canning, 'It appears to me that he has mistaken the case. At all events he has taken a view of it different from the one on which we are about to act, and it is very desirable that he should be set straight.'[34] It is possible that the decision created much less dissonance for Wellington; it reflected a policy which he had previously advocated and he perceived the situation in terms of very limited objectives. He wrote to Bathurst, Secretary for War: 'I am delighted to find that the troops are off . . . . They will probably move across the Douro, in cooperation with some Portuguese troops. But if this is done *in style* there will be an end to the insurrection, and there will be no war. By the time Parliament will meet again this matter will probably be cleared up.'[35]

For Canning, it was a response which he had strenuously avoided in the past, and he was determined that the troops would not be removed until after the French had left Spain. Wellington undoubtedly heightened Canning's dissonance by insisting that this was not the reason why the troops were being sent. This helps to explain Canning's strong desire to differentiate the positions of Wellington and himself. He was very sensitive to any criticism of his position. When Beresford, who had helped to organize the Portuguese Military, returned from Portugal, he commented on the incumbent regime in Portugal as a 'wretched party our policy has been supporting in Portugal, and the truth was that Mr. Canning was afraid to hear the truth on this subject; and he being aware of my opinion, never saw me after my return from Portugal.'[36]

Canning insisted upon defining the situation in terms of foreign aggression; in order to maintain the consistency of the model, therefore, the Portuguese had to be completely innocent and the Spanish authorities totally responsible. There was no possibility of the nonintervention norm being violated. Wellington accepted that the situation was more ambiguous.

It may be the case that these hostile bodies have joined themselves, or have been joined by insurgents in the country, or other troops who may have passed over. So much the worse for those who have joined them.

There can be no choice on a battle field, and no matter how strongly we may desire and sincerely intend not to interfere in the internal concerns of Portugal, we cannot allow a hostile corps sent in from Spain to exist in Portugal if we have the means of destroying it or driving it out.[37]

It can be inferred from the theory of cognitive dissonance that Canning must have experienced greater pre-decision conflict and, therefore, a higher level of post-decision dissonance than Wellington. A higher level of rationalization was employed by Canning when the decision was being implemented. The consequence of this divergence will be examined in the next chapter.

DISSONANCE REDUCTION DURING THE COLLECTIVE NONINTERVENTION RESPONSE

The nonintervention response to the stimulus created by the American Civil War was formulated and implemented in the absence of individual interest specificity. Since individual interests were diffused, group specificity dictated the nature of the response. Individuals, therefore, did not have to distort their perception of the situation in order to participate in the consensus which favoured a nonintervention response. As a result there was very little pre-decision conflict and the implementation of the response gave rise to virtually no dissonance.

The close correspondence between the operational and psycho-milieus meant that information which was received about the situation was easily accommodated by the model which had been formed. New information was not a source of dissonance and so the techniques of rationalization were not employed. There was, however, great concern about the accuracy of the model which had been employed to define the situation. A year after the war started, Russell insisted: 'Events have confirmed our judgement. A revolt which 400,000 men and twelve months of regular war had failed to subdue could not be treated as a local riot'. The word 'riot' was then crossed out and replaced by 'insurrection'. Russell went on: 'It was idle to say that foreign support had given its strength and its vitality to this insurrection. Its extent and its duration had much deeper causes.'[38] The second 'insurrection' was then replaced by 'movement'. It is apparent that Russell found it difficult to characterize correctly the secessionist states. The initial words did not correspond to the model which depicted a bifurcated state. It was important to the British decision-makers that the correct image of this model was projected.

DISSONANCE REDUCTION DURING THE COLLECTIVE INTERVENTION RESPONSE

The individual interest specificities of British decision-makers diverged widely during the period when the response to the Russian Civil War was formulated. At one extreme, Churchill wished to eliminate the Bolsheviks, while at the other, Lloyd George wished to bring about some kind of reconciliation. Both of these interests had to be suppressed when a consensus on the intervention response was formed. Because of the divergence of interests, there was a high level of pre-decision conflict. The existence of the conflict was reflected by the inability to establish a set of consistent cognitions with which to formulate a model of reality. This is illustrated in two despatches sent out simultaneously by Balfour. In the first, he strenuously denied that it was Britain's intention to suppress the Bolsheviks;[39] in the second, he observed to the Americans, 'Our intervention would, I think, cause the downfall of the Bolsheviks but if it is to retain its element of surprise . . . we cannot afford to waste time.'[40]

Establishing a consistent model was also complicated by the constant stream of reports from Lockhart which indicated that the Russians were strongly opposed to an inter-allied contingent operating in Russia when the majority of the troops would be Japanese. A dissociative relationship existed between the cognition of the Russians and the cognition which favoured the policy of sending troops to Russia. An inversion of this dissociative relationship became possible by the mechanism of differentiation. Once this was achieved, a consistent model of reality could be established.

A differentiation was developed between the Russians and the Bolsheviks. Such a distinction had already been made before the revolution. Carr observed in October 1918: 'It is interesting to note that the Russians are more afraid of the Bolsheviks than the Germans' to which Cecil added, 'They have good reason to be.'[41] In the Foreign Office it was argued that the Bolsheviks were either Jews or Letts. This belief was so firmly entrenched that it was necessary to form elaborate hypotheses to explain evidence which contradicted it. Before the revolution, when the Russian Government captured a Bolshevik stronghold, 'A quantity of anti-semitic literature was found, including coloured post-cards illustrating ritual murders. This find is sufficiently strange in view of the fact that many Bolsheviks are of Jewish origin; it can best be explained on the supposition that the whole plot was the work of the Germans who thought that a massacre of the Jews, never a very difficult thing to arrange in Russia, would lead to general butchery and disorganization.'[42]

The distinction between the Russians and the Bolsheviks was further accentuated by another belief propagated before the revolution, particularly by Buchanan, Britain's principal representative in Russia, which was that the Bolsheviks were in German pay. When the Bolsheviks were established as a government, the significance of the relationship between the Russians and the Germans increased. In a memorandum to the Cabinet, Cecil observed: 'On the whole, since the outbreak of the Bolshevik revolution almost every step taken by the Bolshevik Government has been precisely that which would have been most desired by the [German] General Staff.' When he questioned the function of the volunteer force which was being established by the Bolsheviks, Cecil argued 'it might be useful to apply to the future the rule that seems to have governed the past and enquire what would the German General Staff be likely to wish at the moment'. He suggested that the volunteer force was going to be used to supply the Germans with supplies and labour. 'For this no doubt Trotsky's volunteer army controlled in German interests would be sufficient and with a little dexterity it would be possible to conceal at any rate for some time that it was being used in favour of Germany.'[43]

Balfour also doubted the independence of the Bolshevik Government. While he was prepared to accept the view of those who knew Lenin and Trotsky, he went on: 'If they should say that Lenin and Trotsky are fanatics but not traitors, I accept the statement without reserve. I should, however, have expected that in that case a diligent search would have detected some aspect of Russian policy which was favourable to the Allies and unfavourable to Germany. I cannot find it.'[44] On another occasion, Balfour remarked: 'The Bolsheviks have striven by words and deeds to destroy the fighting spirit of the country: they have reason to be proud of their success.'[45]

This predisposition to view the Bolsheviks as German agents was bolstered by the nature of information which was absorbed and accepted. The Foreign Office wrote to Lockhart: 'We receive reports of the arming of enemy prisoners in Siberia and it is being stated that this is being done under Bolshevik instruction. Such proceedings seem hardly reconcilable with the anti-German protestations of Trotsky.'[46] Ullman has dismissed the idea that this constituted a serious threat to the Allies, or that the Bolsheviks did seriously carry out such a policy. He goes on: 'Even more improbable was the fear, first expressed early in January and reiterated again and again in succeeding months, that the Germans would dismantle submarines in the Baltic, ship the parts all the way across Russia and Siberia by railroad, and then assemble them again in Vladivostok to menace shipping in the sea of Japan.'[47]

Constant efforts were made by Lockhart to counteract the image which had been formed of the Bolsheviks. He denied that Trotsky could be considered a German agent[48] and insisted that the 'most fundamental mistake in our policy' related to this idea. 'Whatever the Bolsheviks may be, they are not working for the German Government.'[49] Decision-makers in London coped with this dissonant information in a number of ways. Apart from denying that they had any intention of suppressing the Bolsheviks, they also insisted: 'We shall be glad to do all we can to help the Bolsheviks to resist the Germans.'[50] Lockhart's views were further deflected by the complaint that the Bolsheviks 'did nothing to help themselves and that their major attack was against Rumania which could, in fact, form the major bulwark against Germany.'[51]

Attacks were also made on Lockhart's judgement.

Where Mr. Lockhart seems to be hopelessly at fault is in talking of 'Russia' and the half-crazy international anarchists who are now in control of most of the country, as if they were one. We see the Russians of the Ukraine welcoming the Germans as saviours from the Bolsheviks and know that this feeling is shared by all respectable classes in Russia. Although general nausea has no doubt been caused by the German peace terms, it is not under the Bolsheviks that any effective resistance to Germany will be made. We must use and are using the Bolsheviks for all they are worth, but any undue encouragement of them will neither raise effective Russian support at present nor Russian gratitude in the future.[52]

Lockhart persisted in questioning the intentions of the Foreign Office:

In spite of our good intentions there has been a consistent if unconscious support of counter-revolutionary movements at a moment when counter-revolution can only be favourable to the Germans. Money has been given, with or without your support, for most suspicious purposes. With very few exceptions your agents have had only one policy, viz. to prove that Bolsheviks are pro-German and our secret service has naturally had no difficulty buying a wonderful collection of documents. Some of these documents have been published in Pravda as an hilarious illustration of what England and France believe.

He went on:

Further, all our information is received through bourgeois circles. These are naturally prejudiced and are only too ready to believe any story however incredible against the Bolsheviks. I do not complain, I simply point out the gulf which exists between the totally different points of view. You say that if I can make the Bolsheviks realize facts as they are I shall render a great service. In short you ask me to persuade the Bolsheviks to adopt the English point of view. It is impossible.[53]

Warnings were sent to Lockhart by his wife and friends that his reports were making him unpopular in official circles.[54] Much of the time his reports were not taken seriously by Foreign Office officials; although they did irritate some officials. General Knox observed: 'Practically the only official telegrams we receive from Russia are those sent by Mr. Lockhart and Mr. Lockhart apparently sees no-one except Bolsheviks. His messages reflect only Bolshevik views.' Knox was concerned that Lockhart's advice was 'in a political sense unsound and in a military sense criminally misleading. Why is he retained in Russia?' A Foreign Office official commented that Lockhart must either be told not to give military advice or be recalled. Cecil added that Lockhart should be informed of British policy and told 'that it was his job to support it'.[55]

News of this displeasure about officials who did not send information which conformed with the established image of reality was not slow to reach Russia. In June, Lockhart, after meeting an official who had just arrived from London, felt impelled to send a despatch in which he said he had been informed that Balfour was 'displeased by some of my despatches and fears that I have become a convert to Bolshevism'. Balfour denied the suggestion,[56] although there is one report from Lockhart on which Foreign Office comments indicate quite clearly that they considered him to be a tool of the Bolsheviks.[57]

But Lockhart was not the only official to have his advice ignored. Hicks, an official in Russia, went to investigate the report that the Bolsheviks were arming prisoners in Siberia. He indicated that there was no appreciable danger to the Allies. Ullman states that his report was dismissed out of hand and that the War Office went so far as to demand his immediate recall after they received his report.[58] Journalists were also classified as Bolshevik supporters if their views got out of line with official policy, and the censor ensured that dissonant information was eliminated. It reflected what Price called a 'conspiracy of silence'; he believed that only reports favourable to the intervention were allowed to pass. Scott, the editor of the *Manchester Guardian*, was forced to suppress information Price was sending, which indicated that the Bolsheviks were willing to compromise with the Allies.[59] The Foreign Office felt: 'It will do no great harm to keep the Bolsheviks waiting a little, while public opinion in this country is being enlightened as to what Bolshevik rule really means.'[60] Balfour was anxious to give maximum publicity to stories of Bolshevik atrocities, although he did feel that it was necessary to wait for confirmation before releasing them.[61]

Decision-makers in London, therefore, maintained cognitive consistency by establishing an associative relationship between the Bolsheviks and those officials who sent dissonant information. Parallels were never drawn with comparable situations. When discussing the absence of allied unity on the Siberian policy, Balfour noted that 'whenever President Wilson sent over anyone from the United States to represent him on affairs of international importance, should that person take a view which supported one of the Allies and not the President in any particular matter that might arise, the President immediately thought that his emissary had been "got at" by the Ally concerned'.[62] Lockhart was particularly vulnerable on this score because the Bolsheviks also distrusted his attempts to improve relations.[63]

Not all decision-makers were willing to establish a model of reality which sustained cognitive consistency by the mechanism of differentiation. Lloyd

George, for example, was favourably inclined towards the Bolsheviks. It was even more difficult for the Labour Party. In the Labour Party Advisory Committee on Foreign Questions, however, a consensus was also achieved which supported a policy of intervention. Opposition to intervention in the absence of a Soviet invitation was overcome by the argument that the Bolsheviks, however unintentionally, were giving aid and comfort to the Germans and their removal, therefore, became a legitimate object of state policy. According to Graubard, the argument gained favour 'simply because prosecution of the war transcended all issues'.[64] Although not identical with the mechanism of transcendence, this cognition displays many similarities. It permitted the creation of a false consensus. In the next chapter, there will be a discussion about the effect on the false consensus when the war ended and the source of the transcendent cognition was eliminated.

DISSONANCE REDUCTION DURING THE UNILATERAL NONINTERVENTION RESPONSE

The nonintervention response implemented during the civil war in Spain reflected a bargained consensus within Britain which involved the suppression of individual interest specificity. The principal areas of compromise, reflected in the political bargain which allowed the formation of a consensus, concerned the non-recognition of Franco and the refusal to supply the incumbent government with war material. Such a compromise created a basic inconsistency within Britain's policy. Either Franco should have been recognized as an insurgent government, or the supply of war material to the incumbent government should not have been terminated. As international lawyers pointed out, within the framework of international law the two policies were mutually exclusive. The dissociative relationship which existed between these two points of cognition established an imbalanced triad. It was not possible to invert the relationship by differentiation; the mechanism of bolstering was employed to reinforce the two cognitions.

Failure to offer support to the incumbent government was bolstered primarily by the attitude which was developed towards the Republican regime. At the initial stage of the crisis, Mounsey commented: 'It seems to be growing daily more evident that the existing Spanish Government is powerless to exercise any control over anarchists and extreme communist elements in the country, who are its supporters, but who would at once overthrow it if it got the better of the rebel forces.'[65] Even before there was any suggestion that the Soviets were involved in the situation, therefore, it was felt that if the incumbent government recovered control it would be taken over by communists or anarchists.

Within a month, the rationale for not going to support the incumbent regime was extended and Mounsey indicated that

> ... while it is true that from the legal point of view the Spanish Government have a strong case, it is undeniable that in fact, even though not in theory, they were, long before the outbreak occurred, a Government that was failing to govern; they were merely giving way, in one direction after another, to the extreme demands of labour let loose, and were unable to keep order unless these demands were met. It was moreover no encouragement to civilized powers to assist that, when the outbreak occurred, the Spanish Government at once proceeded to arm all the workers and rabble, including irresponsible young boys, with all the consequences we are now witnessing of savage brutality and counter-reprisal.[66]

Vansittart noted: 'Sir G. Mounsey is quite correct.' So decision-makers attributed the direction and ferocity of the civil war to the Republicans. When King, a resident in Barcelona, wrote to describe the horrors of living under the jurisdiction of the Republican regime and complaining to the Foreign Office about the favourable press which was given to the regime in England, Vansittart observed:

> Mr. King's account is that of an able man writing of that which he knows. It would be presumptuous for any of us here to differ from him in our comparative ignorance. He has seen and described the unspeakable horrors committed by the reds ... these horrors are entirely without excuse in Catalonia when, as he points out, there has been no fighting for over six months. It is simply a case of barbarous and calculated extremism.[67]

This component of the bolstering mechanism, designed to achieve cognitive consistency, was reinforced by the relationship which the British perceived between the Republicans and the Soviets. By mid-October, Vansittart was commenting on the naval reports about Soviet assistance.

> This is in the ensemble, a formidable list of intervention on a large scale. It may be matched on the other side, but here we have from our own official sources a most striking array of statements which lead inevitably to the supposition that, if they go on, non-intervention is likely to break down as quickly as perhaps the Russians desire. This in fact looks like the beginning of a free for all in reinforcements and may well spur the Italians and Germans to corresponding efforts. Are we really to sit on this knowledge for the benefit of the Soviets simply because the Admiralty are timorous?[68]

This view of the situation had not filtered down to the lower levels of the Foreign Office, however, and the next day when a despatch was received from Moscow which indicated that there was no reason to infer from the current activity that the Soviets were contemplating intervening in Spain, Shuckburgh minuted that it did appear the 'Soviets are exercising a certain restraint'.[69]

It was the image of the Soviet Union as the major 'culprit' which came to dominate the perception of many decision-makers. Eden commented in Parliament at the end of October that the Soviet Union was the 'chief complainant' about the working of nonintervention;[70] within two weeks he wished to 'state categorically that I think there are other Governments more to blame than those of Germany and Italy'.[71] The War Office expressed surprise at the remark because it was not consistent with the evidence which they had available. They were also concerned in case Germany and Italy used the statement to justify their policy.[72] When Eden was informed that the Foreign Office was keeping a country-by-country record of infringements of the nonintervention agreement he noted: 'Glad, for I may have to justify my scarcely veiled allusions to the House today.'[73]

The search for evidence which would substantiate this view continued. The following year, for example, the Foreign Office wished to make public information about large volumes of arms which were being flown from the Soviet Union to Spain. They were restrained by the military, who insisted that the reports came from an 'unreliable source'.[74] The predisposition to accept information about Soviet infringements reflected an intense suspicion of the Soviets. Eden told the United States ambassador in Britain that he believed that the Soviets wanted a war between Germany and Britain allied to France, to leave them with a free hand in the East.[75]

Suspicion of the Soviet Union was matched by a marked reluctance, in the initial stages of the conflict, to accept information concerning infringements by the Germans and the Italians. When the Spanish Government requested that the arms embargo should be lifted because it was working to the advantage of the insurgents, Pollock commented that:

> The Spanish Government's note to Mr. Ogilvie Forbes and its enclosures do not contain a single piece of clear evidence of the breach of the terms of the agreement by the three powers [Germany, Italy and Portugal]. There is a good deal of evidence of the Italian officers still being in the service of the rebels, but no proof that these officers are still on the Italian active lists.[76]

Another official agreed that the information did not constitute proof, but he did add that there was a secret report which 'proves conclusively that it [the agreement] has been broken at least by Italy and although the evidence does not establish a case against Germany, it is at least doubtful whether the Germans have kept their understanding'.[77]

When the extent of the assistance to Franco had to be acknowledged, an additional construct was added to maintain cognitive consistency and it was argued that the level of assistance was not likely to be maintained. Shuckburgh observed:

> There is still great doubt as to the attitude which Italy will now adopt. It is still possible to hope that she will endeavour to liquidate her com-

mitments in Spain, and thus, perhaps put a brake on Germany. If so, there might be a chance of effective nonintervention.[78]

But he was forced to admit that the new supply of Italian troops which had just arrived did not augur well for this interpretation. Vansittart observed some months later that he had a good deal of information which indicated that the 'Spanish adventure' was becoming increasingly unpopular in Italy. Eden thought this interesting and felt that Britain should 'do her best to adhere to the non-intervention agreement as a consequence'.[79]

Even the importance of very significant moves by Germany and Italy could be minimized. After they had recognized Franco as the *de jure* government of Spain, it was commented: 'I doubt if either the Germans or the Italians are at all clear about what their next step is going to be.'[80] There was also a tendency to assume that German policy was based on bluff. When Baron Neurath indicated that the German Government was determined not to tolerate a Soviet Government in Spain, Shuckburgh noted: 'It looks, as far as one can tell, as if the Germans were having to face the possibility of a withdrawal from their position in Spain; military support to Franco on a sufficient scale is difficult for them to supply and dangerous – it may well be that these brave words are intended to cover a retreat.'[81]

Later in 1937, when it was apparent that Germany had no intention of withdrawing and was displaying great unwillingness to participate in a new proposal to over-see the nonintervention agreement, Roberts argued that the German and Italian position was not unreasonable in view of the refusal of the British to recognize the Franco regime. The German and Italian intransigence, therefore, did not lead to the assumption that they wanted to break the nonintervention agreement.[82] When all else failed, the British maintained cognitive consistency by blaming themselves and referred to the original imbalance within the cognitive consistency model.

An attempt to reconcile the failure to recognize Franco with the implementation of a nonintervention policy was also performed by extending the frame of reference. It was argued:

> If we were merely to consider the interests of this country *vis à vis* the Iberian Peninsula every consideration would impel us to recognize this position and grant belligerent rights to both parties at the earliest possible moment. The international aspect of the matter undoubtedly complicates matters. By granting belligerent rights to Franco under pressure we should undoubtedly be regarded in Europe as recognizing the success not of him, but of Italy and Germany. This is why it seems of the first importance that any grant of such rights should be preceded by the withdrawal of Italian and German forces.[83]

Eden, in particular, was opposed to any attempt to provide Franco with a degree of informal recognition. When resisting pressure in the Cabinet on this point, he insisted 'we should be held to be taking a preliminary step towards helping his cause . . . it would be represented as following the lead of Germany and Italy'.[84]

There was an important element of reactance[85] in the British position and in order to maintain cognitive consistency when this argument was used, explanations had to be offered for the failure to support the Republicans. The mechanism of denial was employed. Eden indicated in Parliament that 'there is not in this country an immediate surplus of arms ready for export'. It was also denied that a supply of weapons to the Republicans would have 'an important bearing on the subject'.[86] Later in life, he argued that 'the dictator powers could supply arms much more readily to the insurgents than the democracies could to the Spanish Government'.[87] There was an even more important argument which was employed to justify continued support of the nonintervention agreement in the face of repeated infringements by other states. Baldwin told the House of Commons, 'If there are some leaks in the dam it may at any rate keep the water out for the time being, and you may stop the leaks. It is a very different thing from sweeping the dam away altogether.' The French used a different metaphor, but the sentiment was similar. They compared nonintervention to a brake which 'undoubtedly slips but which nevertheless has the great merit of serving to keep the situation from plunging precipitously towards a catastrophe'.[88]

In the confines of the Cabinet, it was admitted that the nonintervention agreement was constantly being violated. Some went so far as to consider the scheme a farce. A new bolstering argument was brought forward when it was suggested that the scheme helped to keep the French neutral. If it disappeared, they 'would hardly be able to escape from allowing the exportation of arms to the Spanish Government'.[89] When the infringements of the agreement were discussed in Parliament, the government argued that the nonintervention agreement was not designed to prevent arms from getting into Spain. In order to explain this apparent contradiction, the government spokesmen began to employ the mechanism of transcendence. Eden stipulated, 'our purpose is not to help one side or another, but to prevent civil war . . . from passing the boundaries of Spain and involving the whole of Europe in its orbit'.[90] The Labour Party also adhered to this argument. Bevin believed that 'without the general embargo more arms would go to the insurgents than to the Government; and that with Germany and Italy actively supporting the insurrection, the war in Spain would almost inevitably become a general European war.'[91]

The central inconsistency in the model of reality which was adopted during the civil war in Spain created the need for a number of bolstering cognitions, some of which were contradictory. It was the transcendent cognition which permitted a resolution of these inherent contradictions, and also helped to establish the basis for the consensus which contained incompatible individual interest specificities. In a later chapter there will be a discussion of how these cognitions changed when decision-makers felt unable to continue their support for a policy which reflected group interest specificity.

DISSONANCE REDUCTION AND GROUP SPECIFICITY

There appear to be significant variations in the levels of dissonance experienced by decision-makers following the implementation of a response to an intervention stimulus. It is possible to attribute the variations to the divergence between individual and group interest articulation. When individual interests are diffuse and the response reflects group interest specificity, as in the case of a collective nonintervention response, then the level of dissonance experienced by decision-makers will be very low for all decision-makers. Variations begin to occur between decision-makers when individual and group interest specificity conflict. Two types of situation developed in the cases studied. In the cases of intervention, the response closely corresponded to the interest specificities of some decision-makers, but diverged markedly from others; while in the case of unilateral nonintervention, the response failed to correspond to the interest specificities of any of the decision-makers. All were aware of the essential inconsistency in the response but it was not possible to establish a consensus on any alternative line of action.

Different patterns of dissonance reduction were reflected in the two types of response. Decision-makers experienced a higher level of dissonance when the response reflected their interest specificity. It was Canning, not Wellington, who initiated the intervention response and he seemed to experience a much higher level of dissonance and a greater need to establish the cognitive consistency of his model of reality. In the Russian case, Balfour, rather than Lloyd George, favoured an intervention response, and he seemed to be more concerned about rationalizing the situation. When the interest specificity of a decision-maker is not reflected by the response, he appears to feel less pressure to defend the consistency and rationality of his model of reality. This is not true in the second type of response where there is a bargained consensus and the interest specificities of all decision-makers are compromised. Here, all decision-makers appear to be under pressure to rationalize, in an attempt to maintain cognitive consistency.

Once a response is implemented, costs begin to be incurred. The costs rise as time passes. In a rational decision-making model, it is possible to calculate the costs of a policy and the value of an outcome; a policy is implemented and maintained when the utility of the outcome exceeds the costs of implementation. Operating within the perspective of bounded rationality, calculations of this sort are not meaningful because decision-makers employ a 'subjective utility' to assess the costs and outcome. An evaluation of the outcome's utility will alter as time passes. If a policy is failing to achieve its objective, therefore, it is not possible to use the initial cost criteria to assess when the policy will be reversed. The utility of the outcome may increase with the length of time that the policy is implemented.

In the following two chapters, there is an examination of this phenomenon, illustrating how a decision-maker's perception of a situation alters over time. The level of rationalization among decision-makers associated with the response varies and it is stipulated that this affects their definition of the changing situation. In the next chapter there is an analysis of how divergent predispositions affect a decision-maker's evaluation of change and the impact which this has on the nature of the initial consensus.

CHAPTER 8

The Process of Commitment

DISSONANT information does not always precipitate rationalization: frequently it corrects the existing conception of reality. In such cases, the dissonant information can be identified as negative feedback, helping to regulate the decision-making process by closing the gap between the operational milieu and the psycho-milieu. But when dissonant information is rationalized, then it can act as positive or amplifying feedback, distorting the image held by the decision-makers. Social psychologists have suggested that this will only happen when decision-makers have been behaviourally committed to a decision. The cases examined in the previous chapter indicate that this analysis is incorrect: the rationalization process can begin before a behavioural commitment is established. Recent literature in social psychology supports this contention. In this chapter it is stipulated that a sharp distinction must be made between behavioural and psychological commitment. The two types of commitment can develop quite independently and it is contended that an actor will only experience dissonance when there is a psychological commitment to a policy.

The discrepancy between psychological and behavioural commitment is very clear when decision-makers form a consensus which is false or projected. In these cases, some decision-makers will be psychologically committed to pursuing a policy; they will be responsible for generating a consensus among the decision-makers. Once the policy is activated, then all the decision-makers are behaviourally committed to the policy, but this may not create a psychological commitment. Without a psychological commitment there is less tendency to rationalize in-coming information. This difference precipitates a divergence in the definition of the situation held by the decision-makers. However, in the first instance all the decision-makers wish to derive some benefits from the policy which has been implemented. A concomitant feature of any behavioural commitment, therefore, is a willingness to escalate the commitment if that appears the only way the initial costs can be recovered. In this chapter, the concept of commitment is examined and illustrated by the cases of intervention response.

COMMITMENT AND DECISION-MAKING

Commitment is a broad ranging concept which has been employed exten-sively inside and outside the social sciences.[1] Anthropologists,[2] sociologists,[3] social psychologists[4] and international theorists[5] have used the concept, but it remains confused and imprecise. A sociologist indicates that there has been little formal analysis of commitments in his field,[6] and social psycho-logists have complained that the definition of commitment which has been employed for experimental purposes is 'vague and rather unsatisfactory'. Commitment was added as an essential component to the cognitive dis-sonance theory because of the objections raised to the assumption that dis-sonance is an inevitable consequence of decision-making.[7] The importance of commitment for the theory was first stressed by Brehm and Cohen[8] and the point has subsequently been accepted by Festinger.[9]

When the theory of cognitive dissonance was formulated, attention cen-tred on the cognitive processes associated with decision-making; the nature of the decision was not considered. It was stipulated that before any decision is taken, conflict exists between various options, and dissonance occurs after a decision is made. This formulation was criticized on the grounds that it takes insufficient account of the fundamental difference which exists between decisions which affect attitudes and decisions which affect behaviour. As Gerard put it: 'Only by distinguishing between behavioral commitment and attitudinal conviction can we ever hope to understand the way in which attitudes accommodate to behavior, which is the central problem originally spelled out by Festinger.'[10]

This statement represents a simplification of Festinger's views and the decision-making process, since part of the problem must also centre on the way in which behaviour accommodates to attitudes. The two are inter-dependent in many instances, although behaviour patterns do not always correspond to related attitudes.[11] But attention has centred on decisions which involve a modification of behaviour and a subsequent reorientation of attitudes. It was asserted that only these decisions carry commitment. In Festinger's terms: 'A decision carries commitment with it if the decision unequivocally affects subsequent behavior.'[12] 'Stating a preference', it is argued, does not affect subsequent behaviour.[13] It follows that it will not create commitment or dissonance; only decisions which carry commitment cause dissonance and precipitate the mechanisms of dissonance reduction.

When Festinger refers to 'subsequent behavior', it is implied that com-mitment only arises when the behaviour is activated. The decision must be irrevocable, and commitment is defined in these terms. Gerard also argues that 'commitments exist to the extent that a person is unable to reverse his decision'.[14] But Festinger has attempted to avoid this connota-tion of irrevocability, insisting that when he indicates a decision carries commitment, he does not mean to imply that it is irrevocable, 'but rather that the decision has clear implications for the subsequent unrolling of events as long as the person stays with the decision'.[15] This still ties commitment to behaviour, and excludes decisions which simply involve a change in attitude.

By formulating commitment in this way, and relating the concept to patterns of behaviour, it is not possible to argue that a commitment has been made to an anticipated action. According to this formulation, an individual only experiences commitment when an action is initiated. It can be asserted, however, that individuals do feel committed to anticipated future action, and their behaviour reflects this attitudinal conviction, even though the behavioural act has not been performed. Kiesler has attempted to cover this contingency by defining commitment as 'a pledging or binding of the individual to behavioural acts'.[16] However, he also concludes that it is 'still an open question whether the one concept, commitment, is adequate to describe both the effects of anticipated future interaction and commitment to consonant behavior'.[17]

Any attempt to define commitment in a way which incorporates the two effects encounters difficulties because it is not easy to identify the existence of a commitment which is not associated with a behavioural act. Who is to say that an individual does experience commitment to perform an action in the future? This, however, is a question of identification which confronts the decision-maker as well as the analyst. Schelling accepts that commitments can be related to anticipated action and examines the procedures which actors implement in order to establish the credibility of a commitment which they themselves experience.[18] The fact that it is difficult to identify commitments does not invalidate their existence.

Social psychologists have demonstrated the inadequacy of their conceptualization of commitment. Some experiments have shown that dissonance and the mechanism of dissonance reduction can precede the behavioural act which has been defined as creating commitment. These findings have caused considerable controversy and Miller has argued that the debate can be avoided because it is not necessary to state that dissonance must occur either before the behavioural act or after it. He concludes that this is 'probably another of those silly instances where theoretical preferences force polar predications'.[19] While this conclusion may be correct, it undermines the initial theoretical assumption, which was that dissonance is a post-decisional phenomenon. Moreover, if dissonance can precede or follow a decision, then it is no longer necessary to distinguish between decisions which reflect attitudinal conviction and those which activate behaviour.

There seem to be two major sources of confusion in the literature. The first arises from a failure to distinguish between psychological and behavioural commitment. The second occurs because of the attempt to locate a commitment at a particular point on a temporal dimension. Commitment must be viewed as a process rather than as an event. It follows that the psychological and behavioural aspects will develop independently over time. A behavioural commitment is initiated when options are closed, leaving no alternative but to follow one particular course of action. Commitments operate through time and can be measured in terms of the fluctuations in the resources which are expended to maintain them. However, when a behavioural commitment is initiated, it need not be accompanied by psychological commitment. As Becker points out, 'commitments are not necessarily made consciously and deliberately. Some commitments do result from conscious decisions, but others arise crescively; the person becomes aware that he is committed only at some point of change and seems to have made the commitment without realizing it.'[20]

Becker cites a number of situations which can develop in the social system where an individual will adopt an option in the belief that a second option remains open, only to find later that the alternative is foreclosed. The individual only realizes retrospectively that he has made a commitment. Organizations often use the technique of retrospective commitment. Almond cites an interview with an ex-communist which illustrates one way the process can operate:

> Typically a person comes into the party before becoming a communist – makes a commitment before realizing the basis for it – becomes something and then goes about learning what it is he is supposed to have become ... the party is set up for such people; it does not expect to receive Marxists. It accepts non-communists and gives them the title in order to make them what the title implies.[21]

But when a conscious behavioural commitment is made, it is normally preceded by a psychological commitment defined in terms of attitudinal conviction. The level of psychological commitment can also vary over time. According to McGuire, psychological commitments can originate in a number of ways which do not serve to activate the behavioural commitment immediately.[22] The first is a 'private decision', which, it is often assumed, is more difficult to reverse when accompanied by a 'public stand' – the second way psychological commitment can be initiated. This seems an over-simplified view. For example, when an individual announces an intention to commit suicide, it may carry much less conviction than the individual who makes the decision privately. The 'public stand' may be designed to ensure that the suicide attempt fails. The third way a psychological commitment can emerge is through 'active participation'. When an individual joins a society whose members decide to engage in ritualistic suicide he may find that by participating with the group, he becomes psychologically committed to the action. Finally, there is 'external commitment'. A soldier, for example, may be instructed to commit suicide when a battle is lost; his socialization into accepting orders may create a strong psychological commitment to follow this command.

As psychological commitment rises, a threshold point is crossed which precipitates behavioural commitment. In the suicide illustration, the threshold occurs when the individual takes the step which will induce death. The commitment will terminate on death. Before that point, it is possible that psychological commitment will fall to the point where there is a desire to reverse the decision. If an antidote is found, and is successful, commitment is reversed rather than terminated. But, of course, the declining psychological commitment may have no effect on the behavioural commitment.

The behavioural commitment is experienced by all the decision-makers. But the level of psychological commitment may vary. Experimental evidence substantiates this supposition. When Lewin carried out some early experiments designed to test levels of commitment, he found that the level of psychological commitment to a new viewpoint was much higher when it emerged in a discussion group than when it was presented in a persuasive lecture. He attributed the higher level of commitment to the act of participation.[23] Later research by Bennett modified this finding. She demonstrated that participation in a group discussion will not necessarily create a psychological commitment among all the members of the group to the decision which emerges.[24] It seems that the degree of consensus perceived to exist among the members of the group determines the level of commitment individuals experience for the group decision.

If these findings are accepted, it follows that when there is a false consensus, the consensus itself will not precipitate a psychological commitment among members which does not already exist. The level of psychological commitment is, therefore, likely to be very low for those decision-makers whose interest specificities are not reflected in the group decision. They will participate in the consensus because of the high costs incurred when a group cannot operate on the basis of a consensus. Other decision-makers participate in the consensus because the group decision is consonant with their own interest specificities. They consequently require no inducement to participate in the consensus. Kiesler has carried out experiments which indicate that 'the less inducement to perform some consonant behavior, the greater the commitment to that behavior'.[25] On the basis of this finding, it is suggested that the more closely the outcome of a consensus reflects the views of a decision-maker, the greater is his commitment to the group decision. The divergence in the psychological commitment to the policy among the decision-makers is thereby accentuated.

THE PROCESS OF PROGRESSIVE COMMITMENT

Once a behavioural commitment is established, the level of commitment, both behavioural and psychological, will increase over time. Frank calls the process 'blind commitment'[26] and Rapoport has described it as the 'blindness of involvement'.[27] This implies that the increase in commitment can be attributed to irrational forces. To some extent this may be true, but the strengthening of a commitment can also be explained in terms of cost-benefit analysis. For example, if an individual telephones the operator for some information, as each minute passes waiting for the operator, opportunity costs mount; in other words, the benefits of spending the time more profitably have been inextricably lost. The only way to recoup the loss, or some of it, is to ensure that the benefit of the policy is achieved. The commitment to the policy will, therefore, increase as time passes.[28]

An optimum point will quickly be reached in the example of waiting for a telephone operator to answer, but as situations become more complex, the optimum point may never be reached. This can be explained by a process which has been described as 'circular incremental magnification'.[29] As the costs of a commitment increase, the perception of the utility attached to the outcome of the commitment will also increase. As the value attached to the utility of the outcome increases, there will be a greater willingness to expand the resources which are being deployed on the commitment. This can develop into a progressive expansion of the commitment. Because the process is circular, the progression can be endless, but there is normally an optimum point, which will be discussed in the next chapter.

Opportunity costs and progressive commitments can be encompassed within the limits of bounded rationality, but there is an area of 'irrationality' which needs to be discussed. This can be seen in some experiments conducted by Deutsch and Krauss, who suggest that 'the meaning of time changed as time passed without the bargainers reaching an agreement. Initially, the passage of time seemed to pressure the players to come to an agreement before their costs mounted sufficiently to destroy their profit. With the continued passage of time, however, their mounting losses strengthened their resolution not to yield to the other player.'[30] Festinger has explained the 'irrational' increase in commitment in terms of dissonance. He has observed that when prophecies concerning the end of the world fail to materialize, there is renewed fervour and an increased commitment among the members of the groups which make the prophecies. The individuals develop high psychological and behavioural commitment before the prophecy fails; when the prediction is falsified, rather than admit failure, the dissonance is dispersed by a massive distortion of reality. Often it was argued that the world had been saved because of the costs which the committed individuals had sustained. In order to maintain the cognitive consonance achieved by this definition of the situation, it is necessary to increase the commitment to the group.[31]

A similar analysis, although not expressed in these terms, is found in Kornhauser's study of the level of commitment to a political cause displayed by radicals and liberals in the United States. A radical has to tolerate a large volume of information which is inconsistent with his definition of the situation. He is dedicated to the cause of revolution, yet all the overt signs around him indicate that a revolution is not going to materialize. Radical leaders admit that this is a prime reason why they lose members, but it serves to increase the level of commitment to the cause among the members who remain in the group. Liberals, on the other hand, experience very little dissonance between their views and the world which they see around them. This is reflected in their low level of commitment to political activity.[32]

COMMITMENT AND THE INTERVENTION RESPONSE

When an intervention stimulus occurs, a policy cleavage may develop among decision-makers in the nonbifurcated actor. Some decision-makers may develop a psychological commitment to an intervention response. These decision-makers experience a need to establish the cognitive consistency of a model of reality in order to avoid dissonance when the behavioural commitment is made. Other decision-makers will develop interest specificities which do not include an intervention response. When they participate in the consensus which prescribes an intervention response, they will not develop a psychological commitment to the policy and will not experience a need to develop a model of reality with which an intervention response is cognitively consistent. After a behavioural commitment is initiated it is proposed:

Proposition 7: When dissonant information is received, decision-makers who are psychologically committed to the intervention response will seek to increase the level of behavioural commitment; decision-makers who are only behaviourally committed will seek to prevent the increase.

Initially, after the intervention response is first introduced, all decision-makers give some level of support to the policy because of the opportunity costs which are incurred. But the divergence between the operational and psycho-milieus will give rise to a large volume of dissonant information which will have to be accommodated within the model of reality already established. Decision-makers who are not psychologically committed to the response will feel less pressure to maintain the cognitive consistency of the model. Those decision-makers who are psychologically committed will endeavour to prevent imbalance occurring within the model and as a result there will be a desire to increase the level of the commitment. As time passes, there will be growing divergence among decision-makers about the acceptability of the level of commitment. The psychologically committed will endeavour to increase the commitment; those who are not psychologically committed will endeavour to restrain this development. The effects of this divergence will be examined in the next chapter.

COMMITMENT DURING THE UNILATERAL INTERVENTION RESPONSE

Before the occurrence of the intervention stimulus in Portugal, Britain accepted that a commitment existed to defend Portugal in the event of an external attack. When Canning agreed to send the fleet to the Tagus, he recognized that the fleet acted as a symbol of Britain's commitment. It was an outward manifestation of a psychological commitment. The advantage of the fleet was that it could be easily removed and did not precipitate a behavioural commitment. It could also be used to symbolize Britain's definition of the situation in Portugal. Canning recognized that A Court could threaten to withdraw the fleet if he observed 'any symptoms of a disposition to go beyond what had been legally established or to excite sedition and revolt either in this country or in any neighbouring country'.[33]

As the crisis escalated, however, it became increasingly difficult to restrict the function of the fleet to a symbolic level. After the death of King John, A Court informed the Portuguese Government that they could 'look for every countenance and assistance which was in the power of the British authorities to offer for the maintenance of public tranquillity'. He explained to Canning that he 'did not think it possible to avoid some declaration of the sort in the peculiar situation which we were placed by the presence of the British squadron in the Tagus'.[34] The Portuguese Government were able to force a reconfirmation of this position the following month, when they asked if it was true that the British fleet was going to be withdrawn if two ministers were not dismissed from the Government. A Court denied the suggestion and again he had to indicate that the fleet was present simply to strengthen the position of the Portuguese Government.[35]

The deterioration of the internal situation in Portugal served to increase the vulnerability of the symbolic value of the fleet. A Court indicated that while all parties in Portugal believed that the presence of the British squadron was responsible for maintenance of peace within the political system, he recognized that this would:

> ... tend to render our position extremely embarrassing if Dom Miguel should assume the reins of power without demanding any confirmation of his right from the representatives of the nation assembled according to ancient form, and without any concession to public opinion. It may be a question whether we can continue to charge ourselves with the guardianship of the public peace under such circumstances.[36]

By mid-October, it was no longer possible to argue that the fleet was being maintained for its symbolic value. Following the mutiny of several Portuguese regiments who proclaimed Dom Miguel as king, most of the troops in Lisbon were sent to control the situation. The Portuguese Prime Minister requested A Court for assistance from the British troops. After consulting with Admiral Beauclerk, A Court refused. By the evening of 12 October there were to be no Portuguese troops in Lisbon and a new request was made for troops to protect the royal family. A Court acquiesced, and agreed to land troops each day 'for the *sole service* of the palace'. He was sure that the safety of the royal family was 'merely a pretext and the moral effect is the object aimed at. But as this can be given under so fair a colour, and without the risk of committing ourselves beyond our profession, I cannot think that HMG will disapprove of my having afforded this last assistance to what I fear is a sinking cause.'[37] Within a week, he had come to the conclusion that the object of the Portuguese Government was to secure the presence of a foreign auxiliary force 'permanently stationed in Portugal'.[38]

Despite the existence of the general psychological commitment to the defence of Portugal, Canning was still far from convinced at this point that the situation warranted the activation of the commitment. He possessed no psychological commitment to an intervention response. While he complimented A Court on his decision to land the troops, he adopted an extremely cautious attitude towards the auxiliary force:

> In what character and on what plea is the presence of the British army required? Is it an army of occupation; such as Austria has sent into Naples and France into Spain? We protested against the principles of those occupations, both of which were in their respective degrees direct interferences in the internal concerns of the occupied countries; and we cannot imitate what we have in the face of the world condemned.[39]

At this point he believed that sending troops to Portugal could serve to decrease the level of stability within the state and increase the possibility of an external attack.[40]

When Liverpool wrote to Canning and asked 'Suppose, however, Spain to become *the aggressor*, and Portugal *to call upon* us as her ally. What is to be done?', he suggested that the British could seize and detain all Spanish ships; or ask allied powers to use 'strenuous efforts in order to compel Spain to give necessary satisfaction'; or, if that should fail, to send Spanish patriots who were living in Britain to Gibraltar and Portugal, where they should 'spare no exhaustion to raise the standard of the Constitution in Spain'.[41] The possibility of sending British troops was not raised. Nor was it raised at the end of October when Canning was prepared to argue that the *casus foederis* had occurred.[42]

Nevertheless, there is evidence which indicates that Canning was becoming increasingly predisposed towards the liberal regime in Portugal. Canning accepted their interpretation of events in preference to the explanations put forward by the Spanish Government,[43] and he was prepared to take action in their favour at the expense of alienating his colleagues. For example, when he sent instructions to Lamb to withdraw from Madrid if the Spanish Government refused to hand over the arms which had been taken from the Portuguese deserters, Wellington argued that this would be taken as a 'signal of war throughout Europe, a war which will infallibly mix this country in this Portuguese dispute unless we depart from the course now adopted, and will therefore involve this country in a war without any of the Ministers being aware of the existence even of discussion.'[44]

It is possible that the decision to reduce the size of the fleet in the Tagus, which followed this incident, represented an attempt by Canning and Liverpool to assuage Wellington.[45] Wellington clearly felt that Canning was looking for an opportunity to activate Britain's commitment to Portugal. During November, Canning's general psychological commitment to the defence of Portugal was transformed into a specific psychological commitment to an intervention response. The transformation was completed when the Portuguese soldiers crossed the frontier. A rigid model of reality was imposed which allowed the situation to be defined in terms of external aggression. The course of developments made it difficult for other decision-makers not to support Canning's request for a behavioural commitment.

Only after the decision to send troops to Portugal had been made was there any serious discussion about the implications of this behavioural commitment. Following the departure of the troops, Wellington received letters from Beresford which indicated that the Portuguese Government was in danger of imminent collapse.[46] Wellington immediately began to postulate alternative definitions of the situation which might arise and which would eliminate the need for the British troops.

> The discretion of whether the troops shall be landed or not will rest with Sir Wm. A Court, who, it is hoped, will exercise it wisely and will not allow them to be landed even upon the requisition of the Regent to involve them in a hopeless revolutionary contest at the very moment of their disembarkation. On the other hand, he will not allow them to land if a Provisional Government be in the exercise of authority of the state.[47]

The instructions which had been sent to A Court were not compatible with these alternative definitions of the situation, but Liverpool felt that it would be inappropriate at this stage to send fresh instructions. 'He has certainly an awful responsibility, but the decision, whatever it may be, must be taken by this time, and we can place him and ourselves in a very difficult situation by writing before we know what that decision has been.'[48]

Within a few days it had been established that the regime in Lisbon had not collapsed and this news was followed by a discussion between Wellington and Bathurst about the function which the British troops should fulfil in Portugal. Wellington had indicated that they could be employed to fight the 'enemy',[49] but as Bathurst inquired, who was the enemy? 'It clearly will not be French or Spanish troops, but deserters from the Portuguese population.' He maintained that it was not the task of British troops to 'hunt down' Portuguese deserters and he asserted that if the deserters did not have the support of the local population, it would be easy for the Portuguese troops to control the situation.[50]

Despite the absence of a psychological commitment to the intervention response, both Bathurst and Wellington did support the policy during the initial stages of the intervention and were determined to derive the benefits which could be gained from the policy. Although it was apparent that the danger of an external attack had subsided before the British troops had arrived in Portugal, both Bathurst and Wellington felt that the troops should not be withdrawn, but left in Lisbon. Bathurst argued that 'the opposition to the Portuguese authorities must be strong indeed, and they miserably weak, if with the capital secure, and all their forces free, they cannot drive out the enemy'.[51] It was felt that the British should attempt to bind up the wounds, and it was desirable that a general amnesty should be achieved. In this event, Britain would appear 'not simply the supporters of one party, but the protector of the rest'. In order to achieve this end, Bathurst felt that it would be necessary to maintain the troops in Lisbon. 'To this end I confess I have not the slightest objection.'[52]

At the same time, there was a very strong desire to prevent any escalation of the initial behavioural commitment. In his instructions to the commanding officer, Wellington stipulated that 'If there be any Portuguese deserters from Spain, or Spanish troops, to use his discretion whether to march to attack these troops if desired by Portugal or to remain in Lisbon.' But it was clearly indicated: 'If Portuguese deserters have been driven out but insurrection still continues, the officer commanding British divisions is not to move from Lisbon or the neighbourhood unless ordered by the King or the Ambassador.'[53] Even this allowed too much latitude for Bathurst, who felt it gave the commanding officer

> ... more discretionary power than will be convenient even for his own sake that he should be furnished with. If it be known that he has the power of marching into the interior, you may be quite sure that he will be earnestly pressed to do so, and he will be exposed to the choice either of hazarding an advance in compliance with a demand earnestly made, or false information that it may not be in his power to correct, or incurring the ill-will of the Portuguese for declining what they well know he can do, and which they may think he had no sufficient reason for declining.[54]

Wellington did not alter his instruction because he could not see any way of relieving the commanding officer of this responsibility. A Court was never made aware of the debate and acted on the assumption that the object was to repel the Portuguese deserters. On 1 January 1827, he received a request to repel the 'invaders'. Noting that it was vital to end the conflict at the earliest possible moment, A Court felt that it was important that the British troops should participate in the process.[55] There was never any serious discussion in Lisbon, therefore, about restricting the troops to the capital. Wellington accepted this expansion of the initial commitment, believing that 'our affair is now to put an end to this warfare in Portugal as soon, and with as high hand as possible.'[56] He considered that this was the only way to prevent war with Spain, from which 'no man can foresee the consequences'.[57]

Once the British troops had moved into the interior of Portugal, they were requested to form an observation corps. Bathurst noted: 'The Cabinet could not have foreseen that there would have risen such an occasion for a demand for our troops and accordingly there is no instruction which meets that case.'[58] In the new instructions which had to be sent to Clinton to deal with the evolving situation, Wellington clearly reveals the extent to which the nature and function of the British troops had escalated since they had arrived.

> In some military cases, *honour* and *safety* may be synonymous terms; but in this warfare, and in its existing state, complete success, and that at no distant period, is necessary, not for the safety of our troops, as they will be quite safe at all events, but for our military honour, and for our safety from the extension of the war.[59]

Nevertheless, elements of the extension continued to disturb Wellington and Bathurst. They were particularly concerned about the possibility that the Portuguese authorities might suddenly order their troops, which were acting in conjunction with the British troops, into another area, and the British would find themselves fighting the Portuguese deserters without Portuguese assistance.[60] Then in February it was learned that Clinton was employing Portuguese staff officers. Wellington observed: 'Lord Liverpool is not sufficiently alive to the inconveniences of mixing the command of the British and Portuguese armies. It must lead to our becoming principals in what is going on there in spite of ourselves.'[61]

In fact, Liverpool was well aware of how the situation was developing and he was becoming increasingly concerned. It was difficult to sustain the image of an external attack, and he felt that it was desirable that the troops should be withdrawn. Canning also accepted that the danger of an external attack had been eliminated but his psychological commitment to the policy was undiminished and as a consequence, and in order to maintain cognitive consistency, it was necessary to extend the behavioural commitment. The extension was sustained by the model of reality which he had imposed upon the situation.

The original aim of the behavioural commitment was to repel the foreign invaders; it was now extended as far as Canning was concerned, 'to obtain from Spain atonement for the past by the establishment of direct political relations with Portugal and security for the future by satisfactory assurances and engagements'. It was now necessary for Britain 'to watch over the full performance of such engagements and assurances', and he felt that this aim would be left 'miserably incomplete if we were to withdraw our force from Portugal'. He was convinced that Dom Miguel intended to carry out a counter-revolution and he argued that 'The attempt to effect this object by a foreign force, after our own had been withdrawn, would replunge us in all the difficulties from which we have so happily extricated ourselves on the present occasion.' Logically, this analysis led to the conclusion that Britain would have to maintain a permanent military force in Portugal. Before he had become psychologically committed to the policy, Canning had insisted that British troops could never perform such a function. Now he indicated that this reason for maintaining the troops must not be given in public.[62]

Liverpool was disturbed by this analysis. He replied to Canning:

> I admit that until the *whole question* connected with Dom Miguel is determined, Portugal will be subject to internal convulsion. But can we remain with a military force in Portugal, during such convulsion, without taking some decided part? And is it most for our interest to take such part, or to retire when satisfied as to the proceedings of Spain, declaring that the Portuguese must be left to themselves, and that we will not suffer Spain, or any other country, to interfere in their internal concerns?[63]

Liverpool was certain that the majority of the British people would prefer a withdrawal, and this was clearly his preference. He died shortly afterwards and Canning became Prime Minister. His policy prevailed. In the next chapter there will be an examination of the effect which an increasing volume of dissonant information had on Canning, and an analysis of the factors which ended the intervention response.

COMMITMENT DURING THE COLLECTIVE INTERVENTION RESPONSE

The necessity for working in cooperation with the United States in any venture in Russia complicated the commitment process. Although there was a consensus among British decision-makers in favour of an intervention response, they were unable to implement the policy because of the reticence of the United States. For some British decision-makers, psychological commitment to an intervention response steadily increased during the period before the intervention. After the initiation of the behavioural commitment, the British were unable to recognize that the decision-makers in the United States experienced no psychological commitment for the policy. As a result, from the moment that the behavioural commitment was initiated, the decision-makers in the United States concentrated their efforts on preventing any escalation of the commitment. Although the objective of the original commitment was quickly fulfilled, the British decision-makers extended the objective, allowing themselves to expand rather than retract the behavioural commitment.

During the months which preceded the behavioural commitment, British decision-makers expended considerable effort attempting to circumvent American opposition to intervention in Russia. The tone of the minutes indicates the existence of a high level of psychological commitment to the policy. Cecil wrote to Clemenceau,

> I ask myself, can nothing be done to impede the German progress and prevent our enemies, while over-running Russia with third-rate troops, from continuing to send their better divisions to fight us on the West. Is there no way of creating a division in the East if the Japanese and Americans combine to delay matters?

He proposed the use of the Czech troops which were in Russia, for he was sure that once action was initiated, there was 'little doubt that the Japanese would move and the Americans would find it impossible to hold back'.[64]

At that moment, however, it was believed that the Americans were 'too pro-Bolshevik' to consider any coordination of policy,[65] although it was hoped that this mood would change, and Lockhart was instructed to 'use encouraging language about intervention which is highly probable but until the United States actually agrees to it we must not pledge ourselves to anything'.[66]

Throughout this period, the British were under the impression that it was possible to create an American commitment and they supported any move which anticipated a future commitment. When the Americans suggested that an economic commission should be sent to Siberia, Wiseman advised the British to support the move, because he did not believe that it was possible to persuade the President 'to agree to armed intervention without some preliminary movement'.[67] By the end of June, British officials in Washington concluded that the President felt that the economic commission would be useless unless protected by a military force. Reading stated that 'it is the accompaniment by a military force which to my mind is of such importance to this new proposal. It is obvious that once that military force has entered Siberia it must be supplemented as and when necessities arise, as they assuredly will.'[68] The British were anxious that the United States should not foreclose this option. Balfour noted that 'it would be a serious blow if the President were to commit himself publicly' against intervention. Reading was instructed to request the United States administration to delay such a move.[69]

The United States and Britain made independent behavioural commitments. There was a marked divergence among British decision-makers in their reaction to the situation. Lloyd George possessed no psychological commitment for the policy. During the previous period, when many British decision-makers were devising schemes to initiate some kind of commitment, Lloyd George cautioned, 'Still we can go slow and not be precipitate so as to give time for developments which will probably all prove the necessity for action.'[70] Once the behavioural commitment was made, however, his analysis of the situation was influenced by an assessment of the opportunity costs. He was irritated by the conditions imposed by the United States. 'If we are to act in Siberia at all, surely what matters is that we should send a force which can make sure that the Czecho-Slovaks will not have their throats cut by German and Austrian prisoners . . . . In present circumstances, therefore, a proposal to send an expedition confined arbitrarily to 14,000 without reference to the military need is really preposterous.'[71]

Milner, the Colonial Secretary, who was psychologically committed to a policy of re-establishing an Eastern front, had a very different assessment. He believed that it was better 'to go slow to begin with than to suggest that no start at all was possible without a large military force'.[72] Lloyd George and Milner were getting contrary information on this issue from the United States. Wiseman cabled Milner: 'I feel the President is now committed to intervention on a small scale and that this will eventually lead to what we want. We must now work to the end that he shall commit himself finally and irrevocably, when I think that we will find the whole matter will go through in entire accordance with our wishes.'[73] Reading wrote to Lloyd George: 'The President is still opposed to intervention and somewhat apprehensive lest the step he is now willing to take should lead him into a much more extended policy.'[74] It is argued by Fowler that Wiseman also accepted this interpretation of the situation and his message to Milner was simply designed to please him.[75] The tendency to impart information which is acceptable to the receiver is a well-known phenomenon and a source of misperception in the decision-making process.

On this occasion, there was ample evidence that the Americans were concerned about the possibility that their initial behavioural commitment would be extended. It was recognized that the United States felt that Britain was only 'too ready to snatch at the first chance of committing the United States more deeply than the latter are willing to do'.[76] Wiseman warned that President Wilson was 'beginning to feel that the Allies are trying to rush, even trick him into a policy which he has refused to accept. He is well aware that he is committed to the task of rescuing the Czechs, but he thinks that the Allies are trying to change the character of the expedition into a full-fledged intervention with the object of reconstituting the Eastern front.'[77]

The French were very sensitive about the need to placate the Americans on this issue; when they agreed to establish a behavioural commitment with the British, they insisted that 'nothing should be done that would make the President of the United States think that we are forcing his hand'. The French Foreign Minister was 'very nervous lest the President should be irritated by the movement of troops and begs you therefore to take every step to explain to him how the necessity for immediate action arose'.[78] The British did, in fact, give the Americans an assurance that the move must not be interpreted as an intervention,[79] which the Americans officially accepted. But they still felt it necessary the next day to issue an *aide-memoire* which indicated that the United States would not take part in an 'organised intervention' and would feel free to withdraw its troops if the character of the allied involvement in Siberia developed beyond the original 'modest and experimental' plan.[80]

Despite this explicit statement, the British insisted on working upon the assumption that the Americans would be willing to increase the level of the behavioural commitment. When a cable was received from Tokyo which discussed Japanese concern about the American reaction to the Japanese decision to send a division to the Trans-Baikel, a Foreign Office official observed that 'If the Japanese go ahead, it seems doubtful whether the Americans will go so far as to protest against a *fait accompli*.'[81] The British failed to realize that their attempts to get the Japanese to increase the number of troops which they had in Siberia[82] would cause anger in the United States.[83] Balfour noted to the Japanese ambassador, 'that while the desire of the Japanese Government to work in perfect harmony with the Government of the United States had our warm approval, this in no way precluded the most vigorous and rapid action in favour of the limited objectives on which all Allied Powers were at one'.[84]

Britain's policy was completely counter-productive. While the Japanese were able to increase the number of troops which they had in Russia from 12,000 to 70,000 in three months, without censure from the Americans,[85] the British decision-makers completely failed to increase the level of the American commitment. They also failed to recognize that the Japanese had no intention of extending the nature of their commitment, by moving West of the Urals and establishing an Eastern front. The Japanese ambassador informed the British in July that their position on this issue was 'categorical and final'.[86] Nevertheless, in October, Balfour was still wondering 'if the Japanese might refuse to operate beyond the Urals since this was the limit to which Wilson would go'.[87] And despite categorical statements to the contrary, he 'always cherished the hope that President Wilson might eventually subscribe to their larger policy'.[88]

Policies pursued by the British decision-makers caused the Americans increasing irritation. By September, conflict between the two sets of officials came to a head. A request was brought forward by the British at Versailles for more assistance in Northern Russia. General Bliss noted: 'I think the British possibly feel that they have bitten off more than they can chew and want to throw the responsibility elsewhere. This they cannot do if I have anything to say about it.'[89] A week later it was learned in Washington that General Poole at Archangel had threatened to arrest anyone issuing Bolshevik propaganda. The United States threatened to withdraw their contingents if he continued with these 'high handed actions'.[90] Finally, towards the end of September, Lansing wrote a strong memorandum to the allied governments in which he called the military operations at Murmansk a failure and the allied hopes of establishing an Eastern front were described as 'impossible'. Consequently, he insisted that the United States would send no more troops to Murmansk and would request that the Czechs retire to a position East of the Urals, and he stipulated that the United States must postpone indefinitely its wish to 'bring succor' to the Russian people.[91]

While the American desire to terminate the behavioural commitment increased with time, Britain's psychological commitment to the intervention response was consolidated. At a Cabinet meeting in August, Lord Curzon insisted that the position of the Czech troops was more than precarious, and that 'the refusal of President Wilson to allow the Japanese to increase their forces threw upon him a very great moral responsibility if the Czechoslovaks were exterminated'.[92] But even before the American troops arrived, the position of the Czech troops had been secured, and it was in accordance with their initial position that the Americans began to call for the withdrawal of the Czech troops. The psychological commitment which many British decision-makers possessed for the intervention response made it difficult for them to accept the withdrawal. The commitment was, therefore, extended in a way which was consistent with the model of reality which had defined the initial commitment.

It was indicated to the United States that the British were 'honourably bound' to stand by their friends in European Russia and that, as a consequence, the British Government 'would not ask the Czechs to withdraw from the East'.[93] The British Government explained that they recognized this reasoning did not apply to the United States but that it did apply to the Czechs and while it was appreciated that the Americans would not wish to take a more active part, it was hoped that they would condone the action of other Allies who performed this task.[94] While the initial commitment was being extended in the East, a similar change was being initiated in the North. The War Office recognized that the Germans were in no position to launch an attack on Archangel and Murmansk and it was suggested that the troops located in this vicinity should maintain forward bases for operations against the Bolsheviks. Ullman comments: 'In matter-of-fact orders like this, intervention was transformed from an anti-German to an anti-Bolshevik venture.'[95]

Minutes by officials written at that time indicate that the transformation was quite self-conscious. Carr argued that in the event of an armistice, it would be necessary to answer two questions, '(a) whether a serious attempt in force to save Russia from herself and the Bolsheviks is politically desirable. (b) If so whether it is militarily feasible assuming that we cannot count on any effective allied support.' Another official commented, 'An attempt to save Russia from herself is scarcely within the range of practical politics at the moment.'[96] An official in Archangel warned that a military operation would 'inevitably commit the British Government to ever-increasing obligations from which they would not be able to free themselves without discredit and great loss of prestige'.[97] But it was the view which favoured an extension of the commitment which prevailed. As one official put it, 'One factor stands out: we cannot desert and hand over to the vengeance of the Bolsheviks the population which we have taken under our protection.'[98]

Memoranda increasingly referred to the Bolsheviks rather than to the Germans as the enemy. An official noted in mid-October:

> We are almost at a crisis as regards Russia. Intervention is temporarily at a stand-still. The non-Bolshevik Russians are for once showing a certain cohesion. They have set up a Government which embraces all parties and conflicting personalities. It seems of the first importance to give them all the external support that is possible. If we do so, and they collapse, nevertheless we have done no harm and we can but try again. We shall have gained the goodwill of all the non-Bolsheviks from one end of the country to the other.[99]

Another went even further. 'So long as Russia is ruled by the Bolsheviks, Russia will not be able to enter a League of Nations and without Russia any such League would be inadequate. The first duty of the League would be to settle the Russian problem and to declare war on the Bolsheviks.'[100]

By extending the commitment in this way, the termination of the war had no effect on the importance of maintaining the commitment. Without an extension of the commitment, it would have terminated with the war. The extended commitment was also perfectly compatible with the model of reality which had been established to define the behavioural commitment. It was on the basis of this model that the psychological commitment had developed. The model undermined the position of the Bolsheviks as a legitimate *de facto* government and by maintaining this cognitive construct, it was possible to adhere to the commitment after the war without fearing that established norms were being violated. But this was only possible for decision-makers who accepted the credibility of the model. In the next chapter there will be an examination of how doubtful decision-makers coped with the extended commitment and the factors which precipitated a policy reversal.

COMMITMENT AND GOAL DISPLACEMENT

Great difficulty is experienced in reversing a behavioural commitment when it is accompanied by a psychological commitment. In the Russian and

Portuguese cases, information was quickly received which disconfirmed the validity of the assumptions on which the commitment was based. The invasion across the Spanish border was not of major significance and the Government forces were capable of handling the situation. Similarly the Czech troops in Russia proved to be more than adequately equipped to defend themselves. In neither case was there any attempt to modify the model of reality on which the intervention response was based. Before Canning allowed the situation to crystallize, he was prepared to admit that the activities of the Portuguese could provoke an attack; after the introduction of the behavioural commitment, he came to insist that only a British presence could serve to defend the Portuguese from external attack. But the events which followed the incident which precipitated the British commitment seemed to disconfirm this model of reality which Canning accepted. It proved to be an isolated event which did not significantly alter the situation. Canning did not modify the model; instead, he based the extension of the commitment on its assumptions.

Similarly, in the Russian case, the invulnerability of the Czech troops disconfirmed the belief that they would be overwhelmed by German soldiers armed by the Bolsheviks. The incident served to increase the distrust felt for the Bolsheviks and since an attack on the Bolsheviks was cognitively consistent with the model of reality which was established, the commitment was extended in this direction. This process whereby the objective of a commitment is transformed, allowing the commitment to be continued when circumstances have changed, can be compared to the process of goal displacement which is found in organization theory.

The idea of goal displacement must be distinguished from the escalation which can be precipitated by a behavioural commitment. In the Portuguese case, even Wellington and Bathurst found it necessary to tolerate a steady expansion of the functions which were to be performed by the troops. The process was even more clearly demonstrated in the Russian case. After the withdrawal from Russia, it was observed in a memorandum to the Cabinet:

> It began with the landing of 150 marines at Murmansk in April 1918. These were reinforced by 370 more at the end of May, which were in turn reinforced by 600 infantry and machine-gunners on the 23rd June. From that time onwards demands for reinforcements followed each other without intermission and our commitments steadily grew without our being able to resist them until the British contingent numbered 18,400. I think the moral of this is easy to point. It is that once a military force is involved in operations on land it is almost impossible to limit the magnitude of the commitment.[101]

The type of arguments which were used to induce the increased commitment can be gauged by a Foreign Office official's comment on a request by General Poole for 5,000 men at Archangel:

The enterprise is undoubtedly a gamble and might commit us to even larger military enterprise later on. We risk undertaking hostile operations in a semi-friendly country which may resist them; we and our allies hazard losing prestige and some 6,000 men who may be completely annihilated. But if success is achieved and General Poole has reasonable faith in this possibility, the diversion might have very far reaching effects.[102]

It is not intuitively obvious, accepting the assumptions which underlie the preceding analysis, when the extension and escalation of commitments will be reversed or terminated. The processes will be examined in the next chapter.

CHAPTER 9

The Process of Decommitment

WHEN decision-makers initiate a policy, they frequently fail to specify the conditions for policy termination or reversal. There are good reasons for the reluctance. The international environment is perceived to be extremely fluid and uncertain; as a consequence, decision-makers recognize that their conception of a situation may change over time and it is important to leave their options open. Declarations of intent and the stated objectives of an activated commitment are ambiguously worded in order to prevent a possible foreclosure of future options when it may be desired to expand or contract a commitment. Decision-makers know that the utility attached to a commitment may change over time and the costs they are willing to sustain may increase or diminish. This process is often not subjected to close scrutiny and decision-makers frequently deny that commitments have changed over time.

Because of the changing utility which can be attached to a commitment, it is very difficult to formulate an analytical distinction between the reversal and the termination of a commitment in anything other than a static framework and analysts have shown a marked reluctance to examine either aspect of decommitment. However, decision-makers are sensitive about the distinction and when decommitment occurs, they try to demonstrate that a commitment has been fulfilled. In this chapter, it is stipulated that when there is decommitment in an interventionary situation, there is a concomitant redefinition of the situation. Not all decision-makers will redefine the situation at the same time, or in the same way. Decision-makers are always confronted by conflicting and ambiguous information and this complicates the task of redefinition. The cases indicate, however, that the redefinition policy is initiated by those decision-makers who do not have a psychological commitment to the initial response.

ANALYSIS OF DECOMMITMENT

Commitments can be reversed or terminated. Both kinds of decommitment possess distinguishable defining characteristics. Termination occurs in a 'rational model' when decision-makers observe that the goal associated with the commitment is achieved; reversal takes place when the costs outweigh the potential benefits of the commitment. If rationality is 'bounded', these conditions are more difficult to evaluate. As costs rise, goal displacement may occur, extending or contracting the commitment; or the assessment of the commitment's utility may rise or fall. The fulfilment of an objective, therefore, may not lead to policy termination, while escalating costs do not necessarily precipitate policy reversal. Nevertheless, decision-makers, aware of the difference, always endeavour to ensure that decommitment is defined in terms of termination rather than reversal.

The ability or willingness to terminate or reverse a commitment is influenced by a number of related factors. At the behavioural level, the possibilities for decommitment will, of course, vary with the nature of the environment. Roby has postulated two models to describe divergent environments which can confront the decision-maker.[1] The first is characterized by a tree maze, where each branch represents an irrevocable decision. At every stage of decision-making, therefore, the actor is confronted by options which involve total commitment. Once the option is taken, there is no possibility of decommitment. The second model is described by a diamond maze where a measure of retrieval is possible after every decision juncture has been passed, although there is never complete retrieval. For example, when an individual waits for a bus, despite the commitment which will build up as the result of rising opportunity costs, the potential for retrieval exists because of the availability of alternative means of transport.

The second model has more general applicability, because while it is true that in an absolute sense, 'the activation of any response changes the environment once and for all',[2] in practice there is normally some means whereby a commitment can be terminated or reversed. The willingness to decommit, however, will often depend to a large extent upon the opportunity costs which have been forgone and the current costs decommitment entails. Decommitment becomes more probable if an opportunity cost can be retrieved. A boy may be more willing to break an engagement if he knows that a former girlfriend is still waiting on the sidelines. Here, retrieval can accompany reversal and opportunity costs associated with the broken commitment can be recovered. Often, however, opportunity costs have to be carried, as well as the costs associated with breaking the commitment.

The ability to recover opportunity costs has to be balanced against the costs associated with breaking the commitment. Schelling has argued that once a commitment exists, in terms of bargaining theory, it is extremely difficult to reverse with 'cheap words'. Jervis believes that this conclusion must be modified and he demonstrates that when commitments are ambiguously defined, decommitment is possible with relatively low costs.[3] Weinstein adopts a compromise position and accepts that some commitments can be reversed because the costs of maintaining a commitment outweigh the costs of breaking it. However, there are other occasions when the commitment will be maintained no matter how high the cost because its form is more important than the content. It becomes impossible to reverse these commitments because they constitute a 'symbolic demonstration of a country's dedication to principles'. The cost of reversing the commitment must, therefore, be higher than the cost of maintaining it. He argues that 'the primary impetus for a commitment's fulfilment comes not from a continuing reassessment of the national interests in the situation but from a conviction that a government must keep all its commitments, even though, if it could reverse the clock, it would not so commit itself again'.[4] Commitments of this sort are designated as 'nonsituational'.

The irreversibility of these kinds of commitments need not be absolute: decommitment can be arranged on the basis of a mutual agreement. Of course, such situations are more complex than when the individual unilaterally decides, for example, to walk home instead of waiting for the bus, but it extends the possibility of decommitment. However, when the commitment involves interaction, reciprocity must be taken into consideration. Even in conflict situations, it has been observed that 'termination involves reciprocal activity and cannot be understood simply as a unilateral imposition of the will of the stronger on the weaker'.[5]

In social situations, therefore, decision-makers must endeavour to operate a policy of decommitment on the basis of reciprocity. Failure to achieve mutual understanding normally increases the cost of decommitment. In a marriage situation, for example, decommitment is more difficult if the desire for the reversal of the commitment is one-sided. Within the context of strategic interaction, diachronic exchange is always potentially possible when the decommitment process takes the form of a reversal. But in cases of commitment termination, synchronic adjustment may be forced on an actor. When a partner dies in a marriage, the remaining party has no choice but to make a synchronic adjustment to the situation.

Not all termination points are so clearly defined. Even in the absence of a commitment provision, the ending of any social process may be difficult and complex, if there is no specified point of termination. As Coser puts it, social processes may 'follow a law of inertia insofar as they continue to operate if no explicit provision for stopping their course is made by the participants'.[6] In an analysis of how wars end, for example, Ikle has shown how infrequently governments think about the conditions under which they will agree to terminate the conflict, and, of course, a government 'rarely reverses itself after the first campaigns of a war, treating the decision to fight as a mistaken choice which ought to be rectified'.[7] Policies often persist simply because no real thought has been given to the nature of the point of termination.

Even when an attempt has been made to define a termination point, the commitment can be prolonged because decision-makers are unable to identify if the point has arrived and wait in the hope that future events will clarify the situation. When the British sent troops into Egypt, for example, it has been suggested that 'in spite of the possible developments of a constantly changing situation, the hope and intention of the British Government, both in 1882 and for many years, was a speedy withdrawal, subject only to the fulfilment of a given purpose. This was simply to "secure that the order of things to be established shall be of a satisfactory character and possess the elements of stability and permanence".'[8] Identifying when a situation reflects 'stability and permanence' is a matter of judgement, and as far as the British decision-makers were concerned, the point of termination never occurred.

In the Vietnam situation American decision-makers were confronted by a more complex problem. As the war persisted, the decision-makers were placed under strong domestic and international pressure to stipulate the conditions which would describe a point of policy termination. In April 1971 President Nixon gave a very clear indication. He stipulated that he would continue to use American air power in Vietnam, and retain residual ground forces, for as long as 'there's one American prisoner being held in North Vietnam'. This created the impression that there was a clear point at which termination would take place. But decision-makers are often unwilling to make unambiguous statements of their position, and this was no exception. While Nixon insisted that he was not aiming at a 'permanent residual force' on the North Korean model, and that his goal was total American withdrawal, he went on to insist that the American withdrawal was also dependent upon the ability of the South Vietnamese to defend themselves against a communist takeover. Again, he attempted to give the impression that this provision was contained within the approaching point of termination when he insisted that this was 'a capacity they are rapidly developing'.[9] But the provision creates ambiguity. It is possible to identify if a last prisoner has been returned, but it is not so easy to identify if the South Vietnamese are capable of defending themselves.

Despite the constraints, decommitment does take place. The first stage of the process occurs when the cognitions which supported the initial response begin to unfreeze. Those decision-makers who are not psychologically committed to the response may modify their cognitions as new information is received. The extent to which their model of reality is modified depends upon the degree of divergence between the operational and psycho-milieus. Decision-makers who are psychologically committed to the model of reality use it to rationalize any dissonant information which is received. Those who are not psychologically committed will be more likely to modify the model.

Festinger argues, however, that there is a limit to the volume of dissonant information which can be rationalized. Once this threshold has been crossed, the decision-makers avoid information which reduces the dissonance and actively look for information which increases the dissonance. The 'step function' reflected in this change can occur, for example, if the information received indicates that the policy is counter-productive. Self-defeating policies are often unintentionally introduced by actors. It was realized after the Second World War that centre-city bombing served to promote what it was intended to deter. The bombing destroyed the tertiary industries of a city, and expanded the number of people who were available to assist in the war industries. Centre-city bombing, therefore, increased, rather than decreased, the level of war production.[10] The rationalization process makes it difficult to appreciate the self-defeating aspects of policy.

Nevertheless rationalization does break down at some point and established cognitions are unfrozen. When this happens the original consensus is undermined; attitudes change and consensus on a new model of reality is established which dictates the introduction of a policy of decommitment. A process of refreezing will take place when decommitment is activated.[11] In the case of an interventionary situation, it is stipulated that:

Proposition 8: Decommitment occurs when the intervention stimulus is redefined to activate the nonintervention norm and restore a dyadic interaction system.

The proposition implies that in the case of an intervention response, redefinition occurs when the persistence of conflict is attributed to conditions within the target actor. Decision-makers apply the nonintervention norm and activate a decommitment process. Redefinition occurs in the case of a nonintervention response when the decision-makers no longer identify the conditions of bifurcation. The metanorm of nonintervention is replaced by the nonintervention norm and decommitment occurs. In each case the dyadic interaction system is restored.

DECOMMITMENT FROM THE UNILATERAL INTERVENTION RESPONSE

By the middle of March 1827, despatches to England indicated that the rebels appeared to have been finally defeated and Britain need only remain as a 'spectator'.[12] *The Times* reported: 'The Constitutional troops have in all encounters beaten the insurgents and succeeded in obliging their regular troops to re-enter Spain by a single corner of the frontier without the aid of British bayonets or British officers.'[13] Dudley, who became Foreign Secretary when Canning became Prime Minister, wrote to A Court that 'the danger from foreign aggression has nearly passed' and that the Spanish Government had listened to Britain's representatives 'in a conciliatory spirit, and with a strong desire of giving complete satisfaction to the British Government. In fact, hostilities upon the frontier, if they still deserve that name, have dwindled down to mere acts of individual fanaticism.' This analysis meant that 'the reasons that entitled Portugal, under the faith of treaties, to call upon us for an armed interposition in her favour, have proportionately lost their efficacy, and it must, therefore, soon become our duty to consider withdrawing from the country'. It was at this point in the account that the conception of goal displacement was introduced. It was stressed that 'to retire instantly and before we have a reasonable assurance that our sudden disappearance from the scene of contest would not instantly provoke a renewal of those aggressions which we have just succeeded in checking, would undoubtedly be as harsh as impolitic'.[14]

Opponents of the policy were very critical of the delay. Ellenborough noted in a memorandum, 'The *casus foederis* has ended and the troops remain for some other purpose than that for which they were sent.'[15] Canning was very sensitive to criticism of this kind. In May it was stated that an adequate assurance had been received from Spain concerning the possibility of a future invasion, and, therefore, 'to retain, indefinitely, possession of the country when our presence is no longer required to defend it from foreign enemies would be directly contrary to the maxim which England has long professed and by which she has hitherto been guided'. October was chosen as the date for withdrawal because the French had agreed to withdraw from Spain then, and the question of the regency in Portugal was also to be settled. Dudley advised that 'the Portuguese Government must prepare to depend upon its own political and military resources and not expect to be upheld for an indefinite period against its domestic as well as foreign enemies by the presence of British power'.[16]

But the troops were not withdrawn in October and it is clear that this eventuality was anticipated. Dudley wrote to Granville:

> You may assure the French Ministry that the same unremitting attention will continue to be paid by HM Government to repress by its advice and its influence any conduct on the part of Portugal that may justly give umbrage to Spain – and that we may look forward with impatience for that period when sufficiently continued abstinence from provocation on the part of Spain shall justify HMG in considering the recall of his troops from the Peninsula. As Damas remarks – that period has not yet arrived, nor can we come away leaving anything to hazard without connecting our departure by an express or implied condition with that of the French in Spain. It is quite obvious that the same state of things which would justify us in leaving Portugal would also justify France in leaving Spain itself.

Dudley added that Britain's withdrawal was also dependent on a 'permanent arrangement of the Portuguese regency. Toward that arrangement no step can be taken until the ultimate destination of Dom Miguel be known'.[17]

The following month it became necessary to request Parliament for half a million pounds to sustain the troops in Portugal, and a major debate was held, during which Dudley admitted further conditions which had to be fulfilled before the troops could be withdrawn. Although the conditions which necessitated sending the troops now existed in a 'much more mitigated degree', they had not 'entirely ceased to exist'. He indicated that negotiations were being conducted between Spain and Portugal which were likely to bring about an accommodation. 'Such an accommodation will relieve us from the necessity of maintaining troops in Portugal; but in the meantime we ask for the means of maintaining them there as long as the honour and security of our allies may render it necessary.'[18] When the question of withdrawal was discussed, there was a marked reluctance to specify a time. Dudley insisted it was not a 'thing capable of accurate and precise specification'. He also suggested that the

> ... circumstances which might not be sufficient to induce us to send troops to Portugal, would be sufficient not to induce us to withdraw them. We ought, in prudence, to have a reasonable assurance – and I trust the period is not far distant when we shall have that assurance – that the troops may be withdrawn, without the recurrence of those circumstances which originally obliged us to send them thither. How long it may be before we can have that reasonable assurance, whether for a long or a short period it is not possible precisely to determine.[19]

The assumptions of this analysis reflected the model of reality used to define the intervention response. The model stressed the culpability of Spain and the inability of the Portuguese to withstand the attack. From the moment the troops landed, information was received which disconfirmed this definition of the situation. Before accepting the model, Canning had always recognized that an intervention of troops could be counterproductive since they could accentuate the divisions which were already present. As soon as the troops arrived, A Court had to report on their unpopularity. There was a great reluctance to billet British officers, and when the troops moved out of Lisbon, he indicated that it was like 'making war in enemy country'.[20] *The Times* reported that this must be expected, for while in 1808 the entire population greeted the British troops, that was a 'war against hostile aggressors', while the present situation was 'in some degree' a civil war.[21]

Dissonance caused by reports of this nature was reduced by a constant reiteration of Britain's adherence to the nonintervention norm. Towards the end of the crisis, Dudley could state to the ambassador in Lisbon, 'His Majesty has so often and sincerely declared his intention not to interfere in the internal concerns of Portugal, that it is unnecessary for me to restate a principle of your Government with which YE must be already so familiar.'[22] Despite the evidence to the contrary, Canning always asserted that it was possible to define the situation at the systemic level. He wrote to A Court:

The account which you have given of the torpid, if not unfriendly disposition of the Northern provinces tends rather to discourage than to invite the employment of British forces in a part of the country where it would have to deal not so much with foreign invaders, or with insurgents identified as foreign invaders, as with the sullen and discontented but genuinely Portuguese population. The line of discrimination must necessarily be difficult to draw in practice, but the principle must never be lost sight of that we are in Portugal to repel foreign aggression, not to repress internal discontent – to give the Portuguese nation free scope of action in its internal concerns, not to direct that action nor control it.[23]

Attempts to reduce dissonance in this way were made more difficult by internal critics. Lord Grey, for example, remarked:

By some singular fatality, however, it is found necessary by the French to continue an army in Spain for the support of the absolute monarchy to which the people are so attached; while we are supposed to maintain an army in Portugal, under the apprehension that if it were withdrawn, the Constitutional Government, of which the people are so fond, would be immediately overthrown.[24]

Another major inconsistency between the model of reality and the information received, related to the attitude of the Portuguese Government. The model dictated that the responsibility for the conflict rested with Spain. Soon after the response was initiated, Canning recognized that while the British were anxious to terminate the *casus foederis*, it was in the interests of Portugal to prolong the conflict as a means of retaining the British troops.[25] Information was received which supported this supposition. The British ambassador in Madrid complained that the Portuguese were threatening to subvert Spain if certain officers were not dismissed. He commented, 'If Portugal thinks she can carry these points by herself she is welcome to do so, but she can hardly be justified in turning round afterwards and looking to us to obtain them when her inconsiderate steps shall have doubled the difficulty.'[26]

The British decision-makers were forced to acknowledge that it was the Portuguese who were presenting the difficulties about reaching an accommodation with Spain. Discussing the 'serious and important step' taken by the Spaniards to restore 'good understanding' between Spain and Portugal, Dudley went on, 'unluckily it seems that just at that moment when the dispositions of Spain become more conciliatory, the Government of Lisbon has grown less tractable; so that the distance between the two parties remains as wide as ever'. This argument served to maintain the veracity of the model when it was originally applied, but suggested the need to unfreeze the cognitions which described the model. As always, it was the nonintervention norm which was used to resolve any inconsistency which might be caused by this admission. Dudley insisted that A Court must explain the principle of nonintervention to the Portuguese Government again, so as 'to prevent the possibility of even pretended misunderstanding – still less any imputation of bad faith upon us for adhering to those principles we have uniformly avowed'.[27]

The greatest source of dissonance for committed British decision-makers stemmed from the position of Miguel in relation to the conflict. Canning argued:

> It is a matter of indifference to the British Government whether the Regency be finally confided to the hands of Dom Miguel. But what is not indifferent to us is that Dom Miguel, if he is to be Regent, should arrive at the Regency through legitimate means and not be imposed upon Portugal by a combination of foreign powers.[28]

In a series of private letters to Canning, dating from September 1826, A Court indicated, however, that Portugal was as 'unfit for a constitution as Spain' and the only possible way of saving the constitution and maintaining stability was by ensuring the return of Miguel.[29] But it was also believed that if Miguel did return to Portugal by the constitutional processes, which seemed to be the only alternative to a counter-revolution, then the Apostolicals in Spain would foment revolution in Portugal.[30]

Canning's solution to the Portuguese problem was to gain Continental acceptance for a plan which would separate Brazil from Portugal, leaving Dom Miguel as Regent operating under the dictates of the constitution. In August, Esterhazy and Dudley worked out a plan along these lines[31] which Pedro accepted the following month.[32] It was also decided that Miguel should pass through London and Paris on his way to Lisbon from Vienna. According to the French, this would 'indicate to the world, the concurrence of the Court of the Tuileries and St. James in the arrangements under which Miguel took possession of the Portuguese Government'.[33] There was a strong desire to ensure that there was systemic support for any agreed solution. The implication of the solution was that having sent troops to Portugal to prevent Miguel taking the throne by force, they were being retained to ensure that he should be allowed to take control through constitutional channels. Palmerston felt, however, that if the plan could be implemented 'the state of Europe will be as satisfactory as it can ever be expected to be; for when Portugal is put to rights the French *must* quit Spain.'[34]

Decision-makers who were not psychologically committed to the intervention response were convinced that the British troops would not be withdrawn from Portugal until the French had left Spain. Wellington believed that when the Spanish army of observation moved away from the border, the *casus foederis* had come to an end and the troops should have been withdrawn. He believed that the government were waiting to see 'whether they could induce the French to withdraw their army simultaneously from Spain'.[35] Bathurst agreed:

There will, I suspect, be great exertion made to get the French to evacuate Spain; not only to enable Mr. Canning to boast that he has succeeded in his Portuguese expedition by procuring the evacuation of Spain, but also as a means of conciliating Lord Grey who laid great stress on the occupation of Spain by France.[36]

There was truth in this contention. It was maintained that since

... occupation of Spain by French troops and the aid lent to Portugal by England stand upon completely different grounds we cannot require France to treat the one as a counterpart of the other. On the other hand, if we have some reason to suppose the French Minister is desirous to withdraw the French troops from Spain, he may not improbably wish to avail himself of the simultaneous evacuation of Portugal by those of England.[37]

As the settlement with Austria concerning Miguel was being reached, Dudley observed that 'one of the advantages which we think may result from a settlement of the affair in Portugal is the evacuation of the whole Peninsula by foreign armies'.[38] By November, Dudley was anticipating no difficulty in arranging a simultaneous evacuation[39] and the announcement of the withdrawal was made by France and Great Britain at the end of January 1828.[40]

By the time this agreement was reached, the decision to withdraw had already been made; the agreement with Austria redefined the situation at the subsystemic level. Canning died during the period when the redefinition of the situation took place and an inability to reduce the dissonance experienced at that time can be inferred from the extreme agitation displayed by Canning. One friend attributed his death to the developments in Portugal.[41] The redefinition of the situation was based on a new model of reality. It dictated the need to withdraw the troops. Wellington noted: 'Huskisson told me yesterday that he intended to get the troops out of Portugal as soon as he could',[42] and at the beginning of November, Huskisson sent a letter to Clinton stating that 'should the arrangements with Dom Miguel meet with no hitch or delay, I have every reason to think that by the end of the month, I shall have to send you instructions to hold the army in immediate readiness to return to England'.[43]

The defining characteristics of the new model of reality which was established can be observed through the despatches sent at that time. Dudley observed:

It is very desirable for us to exempt ourselves even from the suspicion of wishing to interfere forcibly in the internal affairs of the country under its new sovereign. The external circumstances are all favourable to the recall of our troops – though it is difficult at present to form an opinion as to the turn the domestic affairs of Spain are likely to take. Still no disposition has appeared to resume hostile practices against Portugal; and the French by consenting to evacuate Barcelona have given a pledge of their intention not to remain in that country.

As a consequence, Dudley felt that withdrawal would resolve what would otherwise be a 'very embarrassing question'.[44] It was also observed that it was generally agreed that there was 'every reason to hope that Portugal can be considered as secure from danger as that which necessitated our sending there a British military force for the protection of our ally'.[45] Moreover, since the French had agreed in June that 'the same state of things which would justify us in leaving Portugal would justify France in withdrawing the army from Spain',[46] and relations between the two countries were so good, the British merely wanted an assurance from France that they were going to withdraw 'to calm any uneasiness that may exist in this country upon a point of so much importance and delicacy'.[47] It was also stressed that all the accounts from Spain and Portugal 'tend to place us completely at ease as to the fate of Portugal so far as it depends upon the conduct of neighbouring powers'.[48]

As events turned out, withdrawal proved to be more complex than was anticipated. Miguel arrived at Lisbon on 22 February, and within a month Lamb, the new ambassador, was reporting that Miguel was under pressure to declare himself king and eliminate the constitution.[49] At the request of Miguel, British troops were to have been retained in Portugal for some weeks after his arrival, so that his arrival and the British departure did not coincide.[50] Lamb advocated immediate withdrawal as the 'plainest and most unequivocal sign' that Britain was dissociated from Miguel's actions.[51] Four days later he countermanded his order to despatch the troops to England. In the interim, he had learned that there was a plan to send back armed Portuguese refugees from Spain. Lamb felt that such an event 'would be a revival of revolution instead of a conclusion, and might in its results expose the Peninsula to a renewal of the military occupation which we are on the point of getting rid of'.

Lamb hoped that the retention of the troops would deter the Spanish Government from activating their decision to allow the Portuguese refugees back into Portugal. In a long despatch to Dudley, he justified the decision:

> Enough has already been done to separate our occupation from the measures of the Government. It is not necessary that we should hastily relinquish our power of action in case it should appear to HMG that we are called upon . . . to interfere in averting the country from the fresh round of Revolutions with which it is menaced . . . . We have been deceived into bringing on the situation which led to this lamentable result. Should we withdraw ourselves from the scene without an effort to save the victims we have made I know not what can restore our credit or our character in Europe.[52]

Since Canning's death, Wellington had become Prime Minister. It was his Cabinet which discussed Lamb's postponement of the troops' withdrawal. Many of the decision-makers were actively hostile to the initial response and were determined to see the troops withdrawn. Few Canningites remained. Huskisson, after many 'conflicting feelings', agreed to stay in the Cabinet. He believed it would afford him 'a better chance of doing justice to Mr. Canning's memory'.[53] When he entered the discussion about the troop delay, he 'endeavoured to persuade us to keep them there. He said we should do so for the protection of the *constitutionalists to whom we had promised our support* and for the security of British property.'[54] No-one agreed. A rigid model of reality was imposed upon the situation which permitted a rationalization of all dissonant information.

The elimination of the constitution was not taken seriously, because the Charter was considered 'foolish'.[55] Lamb's advice was ignored because he had 'fallen into the hands of the Constitutionalists'.[56] The opposition maintained by Huskisson was simply an 'insidious attempt to obtain a continuance of Canning's policy'.[57] Wellington and Dudley insisted that the withdrawal was the only policy which was consistent with the nonintervention norm. Wellington indicated in Parliament that the only reason the troops had not been withdrawn before Miguel's arrival was 'in order that he might have the appearance of receiving the countenance of the British Government. But the moment his conduct was known, these troops were withdrawn.'[58] Dudley accepted that if Miguel permitted the Portuguese rebels to 'return in arms', the decision must be seen as 'actually making war upon the institution which, only a few days before, he swore to maintain'. But while the model of reality which defined the initial intervention response interpreted this behaviour as foreign aggression, the new model of reality depicted the event in terms of internal conflict. The conflict was defined at the subsystemic level, and as a consequence 'whatever might be the changes in the internal government of Portugal, however much to be deplored might be the consequences ensuing from them – it would be contradictory to the principles upon which we have throughout acted to interfere by force.'[59]

DECOMMITMENT FROM THE COLLECTIVE INTERVENTION RESPONSE

Before the end of the First World War, goal displacement took place among British decision-makers with respect to the Russian Civil War. Without this change, the response to the civil war would have been ended when the armistice with Germany was signed. After this point, however, the deep cleavage which divided British decision-makers reappeared and the two sectors began to work on increasingly divergent images of the situation. Immediately after the end of the First World War, the Cabinet agreed to maintain the intervention response.[60] The point at which the commitment would terminate, however, was never established. As far as Lloyd George was concerned, the only implication that he could draw from the revised commitment was that it would operate 'so long as there was any doubt about the local Governments being able to maintain their own standing'. For Lloyd George, this meant that there was 'no limit to the length of time for which we have to maintain troops at the place in question'. He endeavoured to establish a Cabinet position on the issue, but after some discussion and a failure to achieve any consensus, the question was postponed.[61] At the end of the war, it was still possible to maintain that 'it would be fatal to let it be thought we were committed to an anti-Bolshevik campaign',[62] while after the end of the war, those decision-makers who were psychologically committed to an intervention response could agree with Lord Curzon that 'The local Governments were doing their best to make good their position against the Bolsheviks, and as soon as they could stand alone, we could withdraw our troops.'[63]

Although the original consensus which favoured the intervention response dissolved at the end of the war, it was not possible to establish a consensus in favour of an alternative policy. This policy hiatus was reflected at all levels when the question of policy definition arose. At the end of the European war, despatches were sent from Russia enquiring about the position of the troops which were stationed there. From Archangel, Lindley felt that all his efforts aimed at creating goodwill were handicapped in the absence of a definite policy. He was told that although the allied occupation would not terminate immediately, it could not endure indefinitely, and it was stipulated that it was undesirable that he should enter into any explanation of allied policy.[64] Two months after the armistice was signed, a Foreign Office official minuted that 'The motives for our intervention may change – indeed must change, if continued intervention is decided upon.'[65] Curzon complained in the Cabinet that the growing success of the Bolsheviks could largely be attributed to the 'lack of decision and uncertainty of the Allied policy',[66] while in the House of Commons, members complained that they had still not been given an explanation for the presence of the British troops in Russia.[67]

In the absence of a consensus in favour of withdrawal, operations continued on the basis of the original consensus. Commitments escalated, partially as the result of the exigencies of the situation, partially because decision-makers who were psychologically committed to the response took advantage of the situation. When the Eastern Committee became aware that British troops seemed to be engaged in an occupation of Georgia, they asked the War Office to instruct the commander to restrict his operations. Ullman comments: 'Such distinctions, so easily drawn in London, seemed less obvious in the field. Once on the scene, as so often occurs when military forces are committed in distant lands among alien people, their involvement created demands which shaped the course of future policy just as surely as resolutions by committees in London.'[68]

The escalation in Northern Russia was more a reflection of an idiosyncratic policy established in London. In February, the Cabinet agreed to evacuate this area, and Churchill was asked to ensure that the necessary measures were taken to maintain the safety of the troops until the evacuation took place. The measures involved the immediate despatch of 40,000 troops, to be followed by a similar complement at a later date. Thompson has remarked: 'The first step in evacuation was, therefore, the increase by almost one third of the Allied force in North Russia.'[69] The War Office issued a statement to *The Times*, indicating that the troops in Northern Russia were in grave danger.[70] It was hoped that this would circumvent domestic criticism of the troop increase. Simultaneously, the War Office decided to use the troops against the Bolsheviks. Only by acting offensively, it was argued, would it be possible to carry out the 'delicate and difficult operation of withdrawal'.[71] Despite its decision to withdraw, the Cabinet sanctioned the attack on the Bolsheviks.[72] The sanction was largely retrospective, since the War Office had already authorized the commander in Northern Russia 'to make all preparations to strike a heavy blow against the Bolsheviks'.[73]

When there is a hiatus in the definition of policy, it seems that the idiosyncratic variable becomes critical in the formulation of foreign policy.[74] Churchill's ability to counteract the Cabinet decision to withdraw from Northern Russia was not an isolated incident. The composition of the Cabinet was always of crucial importance. At the beginning of 1920, for example, the Cabinet decided to withdraw the British troops from Batoum 'with all convenient speed'.[75] The decision was made in the absence of Curzon, who was at the Paris Peace Conference; as soon as he learned of the situation, he attempted to refocus the definition of the situation at the systemic level. He argued that the Paris Peace Conference had considered converting Batoum into a free port, with a zone about it which would be placed under the guarantee of the League of Nations. This was the only way in which Batoum could be guaranteed from becoming a 'cockpit not only of fratricidal struggles between the Caucasian States, but of revived rivalries between larger and more dangerous powers, Turkey, Germany and Russia'.[76] It was agreed in the Cabinet that the troops should stay after all.[77]

It is possible to extend the importance of the idiosyncratic variable to interactions at the inter-allied level. Lloyd George and Wilson were very influential in the Paris Peace Conference. They were able to divert any attempt to expand the intervention response. At a meeting of the Council of Ten, when pressure was being applied to develop a full-scale policy of intervention into Russia with an allied volunteer force, 'Lloyd George turned to the Heads of Government and asked of them how many troops their respective countries would contribute to such a volunteer army. President Wilson said none from the United States, Clemenceau said none from France, Orlando ruefully admitted Italy could not contribute.'[78]

Lloyd George pressed for a negotiated settlement. It is apparent that Lloyd George hoped to curb Churchill's enthusiasm (later Lloyd George called it an obsession[79]), by confronting him with the united opposition of the Allies. Lloyd George sent Churchill to Paris when under pressure to pursue a more active policy. Churchill confronted the Council of Ten on 15 February, and when he had finished, they all agreed that they were not happy with a plan to negotiate with the Bolsheviks. Hankey noted: 'They were all very brave and downright in the absence of Lloyd George and President Wilson.'[80]

Divergent images of the Russian situation were reflected by the policy cleavage. One side accepted that the Bolsheviks could count on 80% of the population,[81] while the other maintained that the Bolsheviks represented only a 'fraction of the population' and would be swept away at the next election.[82] At the end of September, Curzon indicated that it was necessary to prepare for the collapse of the anti-Bolshevik front as far south as the Ukraine.[83] But Churchill claimed:

> Out of all this Russian tangle it is, I think, now possible to see very definite decisions emerging. The Bolsheviks are failing and perhaps the end is not distant. Not only their system but their regime is doomed. Their military effort is collapsing at every point on the whole immense circle of their front, while communication, food, fuel and popular support are all falling within that circle.[84]

Divergent reports from Russia helped to bolster either image. One indicated that the morale of the Bolsheviks was steadily deteriorating. 'Five years of ill-treatment and deprivation of all decencies of life has reduced them in many cases to the level of animals.'[85] But on the basis of other reports, Fisher noted that it appeared as if the internal situation in Russia was undergoing a change, and that the Bolshevik Government was losing some of its 'more objectionable features'.[86] But by this point, decision-makers were beginning to take account of this phenomenon, and Curzon observed that it was possible to view the Bolsheviks from 'two sharply contrasted aspects'.[87]

Alternative policy options were discussed in the Foreign Office, but the different images of the situation made it difficult to establish a consensus. Opponents of the Bolsheviks wished to fight in Russia and 'stamp out the embers', others wished to 'draw a cordon around the conflagration and leave it to burn itself out'.[88] Cecil felt it would be 'painful' to desert those Russians who had remained loyal to the allied cause, but he asked: 'What is the alternative?' He advocated enclosing the Bolsheviks in 'a ringed fence'. Other officials, like Graham, strongly deprecated any idea of coming to an arrangement with the Bolsheviks.[89] It was believed that this would be 'exploited by the Bolsheviks to the full, both internally and externally. It will increase their moral strength, discourage our friends and influence the attitude of neutral neighbours'.[90] The most extreme line was adopted by Churchill, who believed that the more the Allies attempted to get away from the problem, 'the more it would stick with them'; and the problem would only be solved when it was realized 'we had the power and the will to enforce our views'. He predicted that if the Allies ignored Russia, they would celebrate a 'victory which was no victory – a peace that was no peace' and it would be necessary to 'march our armies again' in a few months.[91]

As the intervention response persisted through time, Lloyd George and Wilson made strenuous efforts to redefine the situation at the subsystemic level. Lloyd George insisted that it would be 'an outrage on every British principle of freedom that we should use foreign armies to force upon Russia a Government which is repugnant to its people'.[92] Wilson also maintained that there was a 'latent force behind Bolshevism which attracted as much sympathy as its brutal aspects caused general disgust'. He believed that Lloyd George's proposal for a peace conference was the only suggestion that 'led anywhere'.[93] A proclamation was drafted to all Russian factions which stated that the Allies 'recognized the revolution without reservation and will in no way and in no circumstance aid or give countenance to an attempt at counter-revolution'.[94]

Opponents of this view attempted to maintain the definition of the situation at the systemic level. In the House of Commons it was declared that the Bolsheviks were a 'blood-thirsty gang' who had 'declared war on civilization'.[95] Churchill also accepted this interpretation and he projected an image of the world sinking into 'Bolshevik anarchy' which seems to carry the same connotations as the later 'domino theory':

> I dare say honourable members recall the sinking of the Titanic. The state of Europe seems to me to have many points of sinister comparison with that event. That great vessel had compartment after compartment invaded by the sea. She remained almost motionless upon the water as each new bulkhead filled, or as each new compartment was flooded. She gradually took a more pronounced list. Finally, when the decisive compartments which regulated the flotation of the ship filled, the whole brilliant structure of science and civilization foundered in the ocean, leaving those on board . . . swimming in the icy waters of the sea.[96]

Many accepted the need to interpret events in Russia at this systemic level and when Lloyd George returned from Paris, having proposed a scheme to come to terms with the Bolsheviks, 'he found that Lord Northcliffe, acting through Mr. Wickham Steed, the editor of *The Times*, and Mr. Winston Churchill, British Secretary for War, had rigged the Conservative majority in the House of Commons against him, and that they were ready to slay him then and there if he attempted to speak his own opinion at the moment on Russian policies.'[97]

Continuing success by the Bolshevik forces, however, made it increasingly difficult to maintain that the intervention response was not contravening 'a cardinal axiom of the Allied and Associated Powers to avoid interference in the internal affairs of Russia',[98] and Lloyd George came under less pressure to dissociate himself from his conciliatory line towards the Bolsheviks.[99] The views of men like Carr and General Wilson became more acceptable. Carr argued: 'It may be said that the Bolsheviks would not keep to any terms which may be arrived at. This is possible. In this case, no harm will have been done by an attempt to arrive at an understanding';[100] while Wilson maintained that Bolshevism, 'like all cults, if radically unsound, as we think it is, cannot long survive the re-establishment of normal conditions in the rest of the world. If, however, it is better than we are prepared to admit, it will gradually develop into a higher organism and we cannot permanently stifle it by military action.'[101] It was arguments of this sort which constituted the cognitive constructs of the newly established model of reality.

Not all the decision-makers who were psychologically committed to the intervention response accepted the new model of reality, although even Churchill, who was actively opposed to withdrawal, found it necessary to argue: 'The Russians at Archangel knew perfectly well that we intended to withdraw, and they must now realize that when we went, they must endeavour to make the best terms with the Bolsheviks.'[102] But the most effective way of maintaining cognitive consistency by the psychologically committed decision-makers was to transfer the responsibility during the withdrawal. When decommitment occurred in the Caucasus, for example, Balfour accepted that the Italians were going to assume Britain's position in the area. Curzon was sceptical and called the idea 'downright madness' and he could only assume that the Italians had 'little idea what they were in for'.[103] Balfour later wrote to Curzon indicating doubt about the willingness of the Italians to move troops into the area.[104]

Balfour diffused the responsibility for the situation. 'I doubt the expediency of explaining at length to representatives of Allied and Associated Powers how incompetent they have been. Although each may comfort himself that the fault was with the other four the consolation may prove insufficient.'[105] Later, responsibility for the situation was completely transferred. 'As usual it is the Italians who have got us into this mess. Ever since April they have said they were going to the Caucasus and now they say they cannot.'[106] The British then attempted to apply pressure on the Americans, in the hope that they would provide assistance. Bonar Law argued that the situation in the Caucasus 'is, if I may be permitted to say so, an American problem rather than a British. They are in a position to deal with it.'[107] A different perspective was used by the Americans. They appealed to the British not to withdraw because of the 'chaos' and 'massacre of the Christian population' which would follow if the troops departed. The American ambassador further argued that 'although the United States fully realized the difficulty of HMG in the matter, the latter would be held responsible in the eyes of the civilized world'.[108] Japan also argued that without allied assistance, they had no alternative but to withdraw from Siberia.[109] As each state withdrew, responsibility was transferred to the other states.

After the war ended, attempts to formulate policy with regard to Russia were either postponed or transferred. When Lloyd George was asked in the House of Commons to explain British policy, it was always possible to reply 'this is a question which will be under discussion, in the next two or three days, in Paris and I do not wish to interfere in the least with the progress of these discussions'.[110] But as Crowe explained to Hardinge:

> You will remember that whenever the Russian question has come before the conference, it has always created differences. These in the last resort have generally been due to the absence of any well-defined policy on which all the allies are agreed and which has been thought out by them in all its bearings. For some time the affairs of Russia have been dealt with outside the conference and I was under the impression that so far as our government was concerned, this was deliberate and intentional.[111]

By diversifying the *loci* of decision-making it was relatively easy to transfer and postpone the enunciation of policy. It was the inexorable progression of events in Russia which precipitated the decommitment. As the cost of sustaining the anti-Bolsheviks rose, an increasing number of decision-makers preferred to define the situation at the subsystemic level, viewing the Bolsheviks as an indigenous and potentially legitimate government. Decommitment maintained the cognitive consistency of this new model of reality.

DECOMMITMENT FROM THE COLLECTIVE NONINTERVENTION RESPONSE

Nonintervention always contains the possibility of system transformation. But from the beginning of the American Civil War, Britain refused to specify the conditions under which system transformation could occur. Russell reported to Dallas, who was then the American ambassador in London, that Britain was in no hurry to recognize the separation of North and South as 'complete and final. But on the other hand, I could not bind HMG nor tell how or when circumstances might arise which would make a decision necessary.'[112] Both Russell and Palmerston felt a desire to bring 'the necessary and injurious civil war to a speedy and satisfactory conclusion',[113] but Palmerston declared in Parliament that mediation was out of the question because 'the two parties seemed animated with the most bitter feeling in angry resentment against each other'. But the possibility of mediation was not eliminated. 'If, however, at any time, a different state of things should arise, and a fair opening appear for any step which might be likely to meet with the acquiescence of the two parties, it would be not only our duty to offer our services, but would afford HMG the greatest possible pleasure to do so.'[114]

Some Members of Parliament were less circumspect, and Forster, a Northern supporter, was very critical of a suggestion made in the House of Commons that 'an offer of mediation should be accompanied by a threat'.[115] By September 1862, however, Palmerston also began to ponder the possibility of imposing a settlement, following the 'complete smashing' of the Northern forces. He raised the possibility of threatening to recognize the Southern States, thereby bringing about a system transformation, if the North should 'refuse to negotiate'.[116] Russell supported this move, but felt the Cabinet must be called 'for the purpose of taking so important a step'. If the Cabinet agreed, he thought it would be necessary to approach the French, Russians and others, and also make Canada 'safe' by concentrating troops in strategic positions.[117]

Gladstone was another Cabinet member who favoured mediation. He feared that if violence broke out in Lancashire as the result of the Civil War, then Britain's position 'in the face of America, and our influence for good might be seriously affected; we might then seem to be interfering with less dignity on the grounds of our immediate interests and rather in the attitude of parties than as representing the general interests of humanity and peace.'[118] Palmerston's position was prompted by a practical consideration. He felt that since the two sides were 'pretty equally balanced and that neither side are likely soon to overpower the other', then this was the right time 'for the stepping-in of friends'.[119] Russell was also convinced: 'Proceedings about mediation between the Federals and the Confederates seem to be excellent'; his major concern was how to proceed. The principal difficulty was that while he felt Russian participation was essential because 'her part in the offer might render the North more willing to accept it', Russian participation would reduce the impartiality of the mediation 'because she would be too favourable to the North'.[120]

Events in the United States had allowed the commitment to the non-intervention response to unfreeze, but Palmerston's original conviction was almost immediately re-established. He was taken aback by the alacrity with which Russell had taken up his suggestion for mediation; to call the Cabinet he considered premature and he now felt that it was likely, at this stage, that the Federal forces would refuse to negotiate.[121] Soon after, news began to indicate that the Southern advance had been checked,[122] and Palmerston began to temporize his suggested mediation. Negotiations, he now indicated, could only be contemplated in the event of Southern military successes; in any event, the first communication of Britain and France 'might be not an absolute offer of mediation but a friendly suggestion', opening the way to an agreement based on the 'principle of separation'.[123]

Within a day, however, Palmerston had come to the conclusion that any form of mediation would be rejected by the North.[124] Since Palmerston was opposed to any form of temporary settlement, which he saw as 'breathing time allowed to boxers between the rounds of a fight to enable them to get fresh wind', inclining them to think 'less of the past and to be more buoyed up by hopes of the future', he was convinced that the North required 'a good deal more pummelling by the South' before mediation was likely to be successful.[125]

On 22 September 1862, Lincoln made his Emancipation Proclamation; from that moment, the freedom of the slaves was associated with the success of the Union cause.[126] For Palmerston, any possibility of mediation was eliminated by this development. In June, Adams, the American ambassador in London, had threatened a servile war in the event of foreign intervention[127] and Russell observed that 'the prospect of a servile war will only make other nations more desirous to see an end of this desolating and destructive conflict';[128] but the Proclamation eliminated any possibility of British involvement. It meant, according to Palmerston, that the military struggle was now accompanied by a 'political struggle'; although he considered that 'The slavery question was from the beginning the obvious difficulty in our way as mediators.'[129] To be acceptable to the South, for example, a mediated settlement would have included a provision to return fugitive slaves. Palmerston felt that Britain could 'hardly frame a proposal which the South would accept and the people of England would approve of';[130] so, in the final analysis, Palmerston agreed with Lyons that it would be preferable if Britain did not play any 'prominent part in the final settlement of the quarrel'.[131]

Palmerston cancelled a meeting which was due to discuss the question of mediation, and when Gladstone made his controversial speech at Newcastle on 7 October 1862, in which he stated that the Southern States had formed an army, and more important, a nation, Palmerston, while agreeing with the sentiment,[132] threatened to resign if the Cabinet did not repudiate this position.[133] Despite the lack of encouragement, Russell continued to hanker for mediation, arguing that if a friend is going to cut his throat 'you do not refuse to give advice on the grounds that it might be ignored'.[134] While he was not disposed 'in any case to take up arms to settle the American war by force', he did feel that 'if the Great Powers of Europe were to offer their good offices and those were rejected by the North we should be fairly entitled to choose our own time to recognize the Southern States'.[135] This point of view was strenuously denied by Lewis, another Cabinet member, who believed that Britain could only recognize the independence of the Southern States after the Northern States had done so.[136] Palmerston adopted a compromise position; the Lewis doctrine, he felt, was not consistent with historical events, but he was sure 'the pugilists must fight a few more rounds before the bystanders can decide that the States should be divided between them'.[137]

The French were also anxious to mediate, but when their proposal for joint mediation was brought before the Cabinet in November, it was rejected by almost all members. Only Russell and Gladstone proffered support. Later in life, Russell denied this fact,[138] while Gladstone came to regret the stand which he took during the Civil War.[139] Once the non-intervention response was implemented, the possibility of reversing the policy was remote. These discussions about mediation constituted no more than a brief interlude; not only do they reflect the difficulty of modifying a nonintervention system once it is established, but also the extreme caution with which decision-makers approach the task of mediation. It was only with the elimination of the intervention stimulus that the response was terminated.

DECOMMITMENT FROM THE UNILATERAL NONINTERVENTION RESPONSE

From the moment that it was acknowledged in Britain that the Italian Government was extensively involved in Spain, it was accepted that any agreement with Italy must be preceded by a settlement of the Spanish question. Opinion varied as to the nature of the settlement. In Parliament Halifax maintained: 'Probably everyone felt that the only effective remedy in this matter was to bring the war to an end.'[140] But privately, there were extensive discussions about the issue. Mounsey accepted that public statements indicated that troops must be withdrawn before there could be any question of a settlement. He then postulated the situation where the Italians were not responsible for any delay in a settlement, and he questioned Britain's position in that event.[141] Halifax saw the dilemma; it was necessary to choose an interpretation of what was meant by a 'settlement'. Either the interpretation must be liberal so as 'to permit us to exonerate the Italians if the delay is not their fault', or restrictive, exposing the negotiations to a long delay until 'the actual liquidation of Spain, in the sense that volunteers are actually being withdrawn'.[142]

When the Prime Minister discussed the question in the Cabinet, he intimated that it was never his intention that, irrespective of what other countries were doing, withdrawal from Spain should be seen as a *sine qua non* for an agreement with Italy; any difficulty on this point, however, was likely to be avoided, because he believed the Italian Government was anxious to withdraw.[143] A Foreign Office official was asked to see if any clear statement had been made on what was meant by a 'settlement of the Spanish question'. None existed. 'The search has been made more difficult by the fact that in recent months we have deliberately avoided defining what we meant by this expression.' For example, the Prime Minister had stated in the House of Commons on 2 May 1938 that 'At this stage it would be wrong to define circumstances in which one could say that a settlement had been arrived at. It may be that later on we shall get nearer the time when we can give a definition.' The only occasions when the nature of a settlement was clearly articulated occurred before the talks for an Anglo-Italian agreement. Eden had stated in May 1937 that the objective of the Nonintervention Committee would only be realized when the 'last foreigner' had been withdrawn from Spain and 'that unhappy country has been allowed to settle her own destiny in her own way'.[144]

In answer to Attlee's request for an articulation of the conditions which would define a settlement in Spain, Chamberlain stated in July 1938: 'I would like to see what happens when the volunteers are withdrawn. If HMG think that Spain has ceased to be a menace to the peace of Europe, I think we shall regard that as a settlement of the Spanish question.'[145] Many decision-makers did not share Chamberlain's optimism. Plymouth observed that he could not see what would 'satisfy British public opinion in this regard after recent events except perhaps the complete withdrawal of all Italian troops from Spain – and that can only come when the war is over'.[146]

The interest in a termination point was accompanied by an interest in the reversal of the commitment to the Nonintervention Committee, and during 1937 there were discussions about the conditions which would permit Britain to withdraw. Mounsey believed that the parties in Spain were not going to use the situation to 'precipitate a European conflagration'; consequently Britain should prepare to follow a more independent policy, threatening to leave the Committee, for example, if Italy and Germany failed to agree with the proposals which it put forward. Sargent added that such a threat could only be successfully employed at a point before the Committee began to disintegrate. This approach to the problem was strongly opposed by Cranborne, who felt: 'To take the initiative in breaking an agreement which has the overwhelming support of public opinion in this country and has after all fulfilled its main purpose of stabilizing a dangerous situation would be a great gamble.'[147] Vansittart agreed that while every effort should be made to get the Italians out of Spain, if this failed, 'we must be very careful to take stock of our whole position before we take any further steps'.[148] The Prime Minister preferred to avoid discussion of the eventuality of a breakdown and desired to concentrate on finding ways to avoid such a contingency.[149]

Any possibility of the British withdrawing from the Nonintervention Committee was very slight, but the prospect of coming to an agreement with Italy improved with time. From the beginning of the crisis, it was Britain's relations with Germany and Italy which served as a point of potential friction within the Cabinet. By 1937, Eden felt that Spain had become an international battleground and that the 'character of the future Government of Spain has now become less important to the peace of Europe than that the dictators should not be victorious in that country'.[150]

But Halifax reduced Spain to a 'tactical situation' where it was important not to 'loose sight of the main *"desideratum"* of not allowing our relations with Italy and Germany to deteriorate'.[151] At this point, the Italians were occupying the Balearic Islands. According to Eden, future relations with Germany could be conducted 'with very much greater advantage to ourselves if we had demonstrated beyond all possible doubt that in the Mediterranean there is a point beyond which the United Kingdom cannot be drawn by sapping and mining or by bluster and threats'.[152]

In the first instance, Eden accepted the model of reality on which the definition of the Spanish situation was based, but as time passed, the model of reality which he accepted began, by degrees, to diverge from that accepted by the majority of other decision-makers. The growing disparity between Eden and his advisers is apparent from his minutes on reports which he received. In November 1937, Mounsey noted that there were indications that the situation in the Far East was making it impossible for the Russians to continue assistance to Spain. 'This has been the origin of the whole trouble: and if this ceases, the Spanish situation internationally may resolve itself.' Eden asked 'Is this really fair? Did Russia really begin it?' And while Mounsey felt that it was necessary to 'go slow' on the 'expensive measures' which the Nonintervention Committee were contemplating, Eden noted, 'we should not go slow'.[153]

The argument continued the following month when Mounsey maintained that the Spanish Government depended 'practically entirely on support from Moscow' and that this was granted or withheld 'according to the extent to which Moscow's orders are obeyed'. Eden wondered 'whether so much material is in fact arriving from Moscow?' and he was informed that there was no evidence that much material had recently arrived from Moscow.[154] Later that month, Mounsey commented: 'Instead of trying to wean General Franco away from the increasing German and Italian influence they have under the cover of non-intervention thrown him more and more into their arms'; to which Eden replied: 'There are others who think that the democracies should have done more to help the Government, thus obviating this danger'.[155] It can be inferred from these remarks that Eden was exposing himself to an increasing volume of dissonant information. The policy which was being pursued was totally inconsistent with the model of reality which he had now accepted, and the only way in which he could maintain cognitive consistency was by resigning, which he did in February 1938.[156]

Although there was perceived to be a danger that Mussolini's policy could not be changed because the 'present German display of force is overwhelming', it was hoped that an Anglo-Italian agreement would 'wean Mussolini from Berlin'.[157] It was argued in the Cabinet that the government should be prepared to inform the House of Commons of a willingness to separate the issue of Spain from an Anglo-Italian agreement '*if and when* convincing proof can be adduced that the delay is not due to Italian obstruction'.[158] However, there was also the realization that 'we can only make progress with the conclusion of the Anglo-Italian conversations if we can persuade, cajole or bargain with Italy to make some gesture of withdrawal of her help to Spain'.[159]

Information which would substantiate the claim that Italy was willing to reduce the commitment to Spain was actively sought, and it became part of the government's policy to define the actions of Italy in a favourable light. The Prime Minister decided that it was important to reassure the general public that the Italians were 'playing the game' and were not sending more troops to Spain. While the Foreign Secretary did not disagree, he advocated caution, since it was known that the Italians were assisting in the bombardment of Barcelona.[160] On 24 March, however, the Prime Minister announced that the Italians had given assurances that they would not send additional troops to Spain. When the Italian Government indicated that they had no record of such assurances, the British Foreign Office agreed that they also had been unable to ascertain any records 'and we have in fact been somewhat embarrassed by the lack of suitable Italian assurances to quote in Parliament'; in order to answer a question on the issue they 'had to fall back on the Prime Minister's statement of 24 March'.[161]

An agreement with Italy was reached in April, pending a settlement of the Spanish question.[162] When the Foreign Office was informed at the beginning of October that the Italians were preparing to evacuate 10,000 Legionnaires from Spain, it was felt that the ratification of the agreement should be discussed immediately.[163] Opinion was divided in the Foreign Office. Some felt that 'unprejudiced opinion' would not consider that the move eliminated Spain as 'a source of international friction'; others argued that the Cabinet must decide what public opinion would 'stand for' and that it was 'imperative to bring the Italo-Anglo agreement into force now'. Mounsey added that the conflict was 'losing, if it has not already lost, its importance as a European powder magazine'.[164]

This proved to be a critical argument. Halifax referred to Chamberlain's statement that the Spanish question would be considered settled 'when it ceased to be a menace to the peace of Europe'; ignoring the reference to troop withdrawal, he insisted that when he looked at 'the facts of the case and at public opinion' it appeared that the Spanish question was now 'of much less importance and was far less likely to be a cause of any major international complications'. Chamberlain agreed and argued that it was on these grounds that the ratification of the Anglo-Italian agreement should be defended.[165] Subsequent accounts of the situation in Spain by the British Government evoked immediate response by the Republican Government, who complained that the British description of events was 'tendentious and partial'. Halifax promised to attempt to rectify any false impressions which may have been given.[166] But when the Republicans attacked the argument that Spain was no longer a threat to the peace of Europe, Mounsey observed:

> I am afraid we cannot drop this argument just to please the Spanish Government. It is of great importance to put the Spanish conflict back into its proper proportions, and we cannot be deterred merely by the consideration that it has far too long been engrossing too much of the limelight. Spain is at heart already tired of her war. If only Europe will get tired of it too and shake herself out of the habit of thought which she has adopted about it, it may possibly fizzle out.[167]

Cadogan expressed irritation because the French would not allow the conflict to 'fizzle out'. It was felt that since Franco was certain to win, such a policy 'merely prolongs the fighting – allowing Mussolini to dig further in'.[168]

By this time, the model of reality had changed. Although Franco's victory was not yet conclusive, and although foreign troops were still present in Spain, as far as the British decision-makers were concerned, the issue was settled. Effectively, the situation was no longer being defined as a civil war; there was a desire to restore a dyadic interaction system.

REDEFINITION AND LEARNING

Although decommitment occurred in the cases examined, they do illustrate that, once established, commitments have a tendency to be self-perpetuating. Once the intervention responses were implemented, goal displacement took place before decommitment: rather than decommit when the conditions initially specified materialized, the decision-makers extended the established goal. Similarly, in the cases of nonintervention response, despite a strong desire among some decision-makers to alter the orientation of the commitment, the established policy persisted. But in each case, decommitment was achieved by the same process; the model of reality used to introduce the response was taken out of focus and replaced by a new model of reality. The new model down-graded the international importance of the events in the target state and dictated the reassertion of the nonintervention norm; the diminished significance of the situation perceived by the decision-makers was accompanied by a desire to restore normal relations. The ability of the decision-makers to redefine the situation by altering the model of reality ensured that the decommitment was not inconsistent with the decision to initiate the commitment, and decision-makers consequently felt that the commitment had been terminated rather than reversed.

The juxtaposition of the two models of reality reinforced adherence to the norm which proscribes intervention into civil wars. The response provided a learning experience both for the decision-makers involved and subsequent decision-makers. When the British decision-makers wrestled with the conflict in Spain, for example, reference was often made to the response implemented during the American Civil War. Similarly, during the collective intervention response there were frequent references to the European intervention into the French Revolution and attention was drawn to the unsuccessful nature of the policy.[169] Decision-makers do appear to 'learn' from the experience of other decision-makers, and with the benefit of hindsight, the pressure to 'rationalize' information declines. Campbell has described this process in terms of 'the economy of cognition', whereby 'the trial and error explorations of one member serve to save others the trouble of entering the same blind alleys'.[170] The Spanish Civil War, however, does not provide a case which neatly fits into this pattern of vicarious learning. On this occasion, it seems in retrospect that the decision-makers who were most responsible for violating the nonintervention norm gained substantial rewards, while those decision-makers who observed the norm were punished. The ramifications of this development will be explored further in the conclusion.

CHAPTER 10

An Evaluation of the Model and the Approach

When this study was first started, it was intended to establish a model of intervention. However, it is apparent from the way the propositions have now been formulated that the model which has emerged is as much concerned with nonintervention as it is with intervention. The change in emphasis was necessitated after the analysis of the cases and it constitutes the major divergence between the preliminary model, on the basis of which comparative data about the four cases were collected, and the reformulated model which has now been presented. Originally, the two cases of nonintervention were included in the study to act as 'controls' to see how decision-makers behave when they do observe the nonintervention norm, especially when it is apparent that all states are not adhering to the norm. The cases demonstrated that the analysis of interventionary situations is much more complex than was originally supposed and that many aspects of the decision-making process which operated in the cases of intervention response could also be observed when nonintervention occurred. Provision was made for the nonintervention response in the reformulated model.

Although the cases have been used as illustrative material, it was on the basis of this information that the preliminary model was revised, so the reformulated model conforms with the information collected. It was not a question of selecting information which supported an established model; rather, the model was used to select information which could be used to compare each case. The final structure of the reformulated model, therefore, was dictated by those aspects of the cases discrepant with the original model. Establishing and testing a model with the same body of information has been termed retroduction, and it was on the basis of this approach that the present study was conducted.

So far, there has been no attempt to elaborate how the interventionary situation was first conceived. The original model was itself based on earlier studies of intervention, and it is assumed that with further empirical studies of interventionary situations additional refinements would be necessary. It is possible to argue that the original model should have been presented in the introduction, or during the course of the exposition; but it was decided that this would confuse the analysis. Now that the reformulation has been completed, it is possible in this concluding section to show where the two models diverge.

In addition to describing the modifications which have been made during the process of reformulating the model of an interventionary situation, this concluding chapter will also evaluate the relevance of the model for other cases, and discuss the advantages and disadvantages of the approach which has been adopted. It is apparent that there is an intimate connection between the model and the approach: the accuracy of the model is largely dependent upon the validity of the approach. On the basis of the experience derived during the course of this study, it does seem that the approach can fruitfully be employed in order to develop models which allow processes in international relations to be compared and theories to be constructed.

A COMPARISON OF THE PRELIMINARY AND REFORMULATED MODELS[1]

The eight propositions, constituting the model of an interventionary situation, which have been established in this study, diverge considerably from the propositions which formed the preliminary model. The comparative data generated by the preliminary model made it necessary not only to alter and supplement the original propositions, but also to refine the way in which critical concepts were defined. Initially, intervention was self-defined, occurring when an external actor perceived that it was committed to one side of a conflict within the bifurcated target actor. It was assumed that there was a norm which proscribed intervention into civil wars and that actors in the international system accepted the norm. From this it followed that when an actor implemented an intervention response, the response would be perceived as deviant.

When the case studies were analysed, a very different picture emerged. The external actor failed to identify the intervention stimulus and the intervention response was defined in terms of systemic interaction. The response, therefore, was not considered to violate the nonintervention norm. But not only did the external actor fail to consider the behaviour deviant, the non-intervention norm was reaffirmed throughout the duration of the response. This fact could not be reconciled with the preliminary model and so the self-definition of intervention was eliminated. The concept of intervention could not be defined in terms of the perceptions of the decision-makers; to have done so would have eliminated the cases of intervention response. An analytical definition was formulated.

This development precipitated alterations in subsequent propositions. In the preliminary model, the first proposition simply stipulated that there was a norm which proscribed intervention into civil wars. Since the decision-makers considered that they were adhering to the norm, a distinction was drawn between prescribed and behavioural norms. The difference was incorporated into the reformulated model: the prescriptive norm described the stated beliefs of decision-makers, while the behavioural norm reflected patterns of behaviour.

This distinction created the need for a new proposition in the reformulated model; the new proposition reflected the decision-makers' failure to observe the discrepancy between their stated attitudes and their observable behaviour during an intervention response. It was proposed that a disparity between the operational and psycho-milieus develops when an intervention response is implemented; such a disparity does not emerge during a non-intervention response. Although the second proposition was limited in the context of the model to troop intervention into civil war situations, it is possible that it can be more widely applied.

This new proposition, concerning the operational and psycho-milieus, replaced the original proposition which assumed that decision-makers would perceive an intervention response as deviant. The earlier proposition stipulated that when an actor implements an intervention response, the motive would reflect a desire to eliminate the perceived bifurcation. It was the writings of Simmel and Coser which had stimulated the formation of this proposition. Simmel maintains that when one party is unified, it will often prefer a conflicting party to be equally unified. Coser has modified this hypothesis and proposes that it is only applicable 'in so far as there exists a level of struggle in which the contending parties have reached a rough equality of strength'.[2] It was assumed that actors which intervene would express a desire to confront unified actors within the international system. But the contention in the reformulated model, that intervening actors will fail to perceive the bifurcated system, or consider the response unrelated to the bifurcation, made this proposition redundant.

The examination of the cases also eliminated the subsequent proposition in the preliminary model, which defined the circumstances which activate intervention. Originally, it was postulated that as the definition of a situation becomes more ambiguous, the possibility of norm violation increases. The proposition reflected the Parsonian concept of pattern-maintenance. According to Devereux: 'The problem of pattern maintenance is essentially that faced by an actor in reconciling the various norms and demands imposed by his participation in any particular social system with those of other systems in which he also participates, or with the more general norm of broader culture.'[3] In the case of an intervention response, it was hypothesised that the need to clarify an ambiguous situation conflicts with the nonintervention norm. So as the situation in the target state becomes increasingly confused and anarchic, the chances of an intervention response occurring become greater.

After an analysis of the cases, it was apparent that an inversion of this process occurs. As time passed, the decision-makers' image of the situation, which preceded an intervention response, became progressively less ambiguous. Confronted by ambiguity, the decision-makers eventually established a clear and simple model of reality which allowed them to define the conflict at the systemic rather than the subsystemic level of analysis. Only in the cases of a nonintervention response did the decision-makers establish a model of reality which defined the situation at the subsystemic level. The model used in these cases of nonintervention response was complex. The dyadic interaction system which exists between two states in a systemic, or billiard-ball, form of analysis was never entirely eliminated. Instead, a triadic interaction system which incorporated the external actor and the two halves of the bifurcated actor was superimposed on the established dyad. Because the dyadic structure was maintained, the external actor operated on the assumption that there had been system change, but not system transformation.

Perceived deviance was an essential element of the preliminary model. Because of the costs associated with deviance, it was assumed, therefore, that decision-makers would always endeavour to legitimize an intervention response, in order to reduce these costs. It was possible to retain this proposition in the reformulated model because the ambiguity in the situation which precipitated an intervention response in the cases examined permitted the formation of a series of divergent images. One of these images did define an intervention stimulus. Although this image was not accepted when the intervention response was implemented, it did affect behaviour. Conscious of this image, decision-makers in the external actor recognized the need to legitimize the intervention response. In the reformulated model, however, this proposition was also extended to the nonintervention response. Because decision-makers perceived that nonintervention precipitated system change, both intervention and nonintervention created a need for legitimization.

At this point in the analysis, an important new proposition was introduced into the reformulated model. Originally it was assumed that because the intervention response was perceived to be deviant, there must be wide support for the response before it could be introduced. In a sense this contention was supported by an examination of the cases, but a detailed analysis indicated that the nature of the consensus differed in each case. Only in the case of the collective nonintervention response did the consensus flow from a common conception of the situation. In all the other cases, the consensus appeared to mask substantial differences between the decision-makers. The consensus contained divergent definitions of the situation. Eulau's typology of different modes of consensus formation was used in the construction of the new proposition.

Subsequent propositions were affected by this addition. Provision was made in the original model for the process of rationalization which decision-makers employed to reduce any dissonance experienced after introducing the deviant intervention response. After the proposition concerning consensus was incorporated into the reformulated model, the rationalization provision had to be extended. It now stipulated that when a consensus fails to reflect the individual's interest specificity, the need to rationalize the decision diminishes.

The next proposition in the preliminary model also had to be modified in order to accommodate the refinements made to the previous propositions. Before the analysis of the cases, it was proposed that the processes of legitimization and rationalization create a commitment to the intervention response. It was necessary to change this proposition to take account of the variations which occur among decision-makers in their propensity for rationalization. In the cases examined, the decision-makers were not a unified group; their definitions of the situation diverged and so did their levels of rationalization. In the reformulated model, it was accepted that once a response is introduced, all decision-makers are equally committed in behavioural terms, but distinctions must be drawn between behavioural and psychological commitment. The level of psychological commitment is related to the degree of rationalization employed by a decision-maker.

When the preliminary model of an interventionary situation was first established, it was assumed that there was a perception of deviance and an equal level of commitment to the intervention response among all decision-makers. It followed that if there was no decisive outcome to the intervention response, the response would persist because of the commitment. Policy reversal would not occur unless it was perceived that the response was proving to be counter-productive. For example, if decision-makers intervened in order to eliminate bifurcation in the target state and it was later found that the bifurcation was only persisting because of the intervention, then the policy would be reversed. Failure to achieve a policy objective was not sufficient to induce a reversal of the commitment.

In the light of the revisions which had already been made, it was necessary to modify this proposition. There was no perception of deviance among those who implemented the intervention response in the reformulated model, and not all decision-makers experienced a commitment to the intervention response. It was proposed, therefore, that once information began to be received which was dissonant with the original definition of the situation, those decision-makers who were not committed to the response would work towards establishing a new consensus to redefine the situation. If a new consensus formed, defining the situation at a subsystemic level, then the nonintervention norm would come into operation. A violation of the norm could only be prevented by withdrawing the troops. The proposition also indicated that a nonintervention response would terminate as soon as the triadic structure was eliminated and it was possible to perceive the situation in systemic rather than subsystemic terms.

This comparison reveals that the preliminary model did not simply generate comparative data which substantiated the model. Major modifications were necessary in order to accommodate some of the information collected. Although the reformulated model remains similar in general outline, some critical differences did evolve. But despite these modifications, the universality of the model cannot be asserted because it has only been established and tested on the basis of four cases. Given the detailed analysis which is required by a decision-making model, it was not practical to extend the number of cases; only by changing the nature of the model is it feasible to enlarge significantly the sample of cases. If a macro-model had been formulated, for example, a different approach could have been adopted. A macro-model would have contained propositions concerning the frequency, duration and distribution of intervention responses. After collecting information from all known intervention responses on these factors, the propositions could have been formed.

If an analogy is drawn with criminology, it is possible to argue that the development of a macro-model should precede the formation of a micro-model. Early attempts to explain crime in terms of genetics were discarded when it was demonstrated that crime rates remained high in certain areas despite the changing composition of the population.[4] It is doubtful, however, if the analogy ought to be applied. In international relations, research should proceed simultaneously at several different levels of analysis. A macro-model of an interventionary situation will complement and also supplement a micro-model of an interventionary situation. Only by proceeding at different levels of analysis is it possible to move towards a general theory.

AN EVALUATION OF THE APPROACH

The approach adopted in this study was largely dictated by the way in which the preliminary model was formulated. Since the propositions concerned the nature of decision-making in an interventionary situation, it was necessary to have access to detailed information about the way in which the decisions were made. The original model indicated that in order to understand the processes involved in an interventionary situation, information about the perceptions and motivations of the actors involved is required. It was on the basis of similar reasoning that Burton established the idea of 'controlled communication', an idea which reflected

... a belief that official, historical, journalistic and even analytically des-
criptive accounts written up after a crisis cannot provide answers to many
of the questions which are prompted by contemporary inter-disciplinary
studies of world politics. These can be answered only by analyzing perceptions and misperceptions, interactions and features of state decision-
making, which are best observed when the parties in conflict are in an
interacting situation.[5]

It was hoped to gain a greater insight into conflict situations by having
'representatives who could reflect the views of their governments to take
part in discussions in the presence of a panel of political and social scientists'. The purpose of this controlled communication was to 'lead to insights
and hypotheses, and perhaps to means of testing propositions'.[6] Here was
a means, therefore, of analysing the motivations and perceptions of decision-
makers, in a context where 'the intervention of foreign states in a local
conflict cannot readily be justified in terms usually employed in public
statements'.[7]

Without entering into a discussion about the merits of this approach, it
is obviously a method which is not readily available. Analysis of historical
cases, where access to information about interactions, perceptions and
motivations can be acquired, offers an alternative and more accessible
method. This approach to theory-building is becoming increasingly attrac-
tive, although, as Holsti and North point out, it is not without its problems:

Social science approaches to historical situations are based upon the
fundamental assumption that there are patterns, repetitions and close
analogies throughout the history of human affairs. The circumstances
and paraphernalia will differ between the Peloponnesian War and the
Wars of the Roses or between World War I and World War II, but the
patterns of human fears and anxieties and perceptions of threat and
injury may not be dissimilar. A fundamental part of the problem lies
in identifying the levels of abstraction where likenesses can be found
between problems or events that are widely separated in time and also
in space.[8]

Finding the right level of abstraction obviously poses problems. Taking
several cases from different points of time, as was done in this study, does
increase confidence in the generality of the model. On the other hand, all
the cases in this study centre on Britain, and it may be that the resultant
model does no more than reflect aspects of decision-making which are
peculiar to Britain. During the analysis of these case studies, however,
the attitudes of other states to an interventionary situation did emerge and
they were not inconsistent with the reformulated model.

The ability to test and generate hypotheses about a concept, on a comparative basis, constitutes the major advantage of the approach adopted
in this study. The primary sources available in historical cases also provide
the sort of data which can be used to develop a behavioural model. If the
importance of relating the behavioural sciences to international relations

is accepted, then access to data of this kind is essential. Primary source material will not give completely reliable information concerning the way in which decision-makers interact and perceive situations, but the information is certainly not any less accurate than the information gained using techniques like controlled communication. The major disadvantage of the approach stems from the limited number of case studies which can be examined. Any generalizations made on the basis of the propositions which constitute the model must be treated with caution. Moreover, because the model reflects historical case studies, any attempt to apply it to the contemporary international system may be particularly suspect.

INTERVENTION IN THE CONTEMPORARY INTERNATIONAL SYSTEM

A model of an interventionary situation which has been based on four cases drawn from the nineteenth and early twentieth century may have very little relevance when applied to an international system which has been characterized by bipolarity and the emergence of nuclear weapons. Both of these factors have, for example, been cited as reasons which have dictated violations of the norm of nonintervention. In a review of two works which examined the role of norms in the international system, Hoffman notes: 'The disregard of the old rules regarding intervention, the collapse of many of the assumptions on which they were based, the emergence of internal war with outside interference as a kind of low-level substitute for the kind of interstate violence that nuclear arsenals have made too risky, lead both writers to gloomy thoughts about the present state of international law in this respect.'[9] Tucker has also argued: 'The weakening of the traditional restraints upon intervention in the present period is due as much to the revolutionary character of the international system as it is to the distribution of power marking this system.'[10]

If the distinction between prescriptive and behavioural norms is accepted, however, there must be a distinction drawn between deviance from the norm and a rejection of the prescribed norm. The model clearly takes account of deviance, but the validity of the model is dependent upon an acceptance of the prescribed norm. Some writers insist that, in fact, it is not a question of the norm being violated, but rather that the norm is no longer accepted. Barnet has argued that:

> States with global ideologies have devoted energy to the encouragement of world-wide revolution or the suppression of revolutionary movements. Indeed, all major powers now regard it as their right or even duty to help transform the economy and social structure of other states... Thus the old rules of nonintervention seem so at odds with universal practice that despite their long history and continued reaffirmation, they do not elicit wide acceptance.[11]

If this assessment is accurate, then it follows that the model established in this study cannot be applied to the contemporary international system. There is some indication, however, that Barnet's analysis needs to be modified. The importance attributed to the norm can be observed in those situations where states prefer to pursue the policy prescribed by the norm. When the United Nations became involved in the Congo situation both France and Britain were strongly opposed to the action, and their reserve reflected their traditional concern with the nonintervention norm. According to Lefever, the French felt that:

> Armed intervention in an internal struggle served to encourage conflict and to prevent the state from settling its own problems in its own ways and in its own time. French spokesmen contended that the U.N. Mission might lead to interference in the Congo's domestic affairs. The French wanted to avert civil war in the Congo in which the United States would support one camp and the Soviet Union the other, and insisted that U.N. intervention would increase rather than decrease the probability of such a confrontation.[12]

Both the French and the British said that they would invalidate the passport of any national who acted as a mercenary. The British were even more concerned about the effect of the United Nations action on the nonintervention norm than the French. It has been noted that:

> Britain's insistence on noninterference of the UNF in the Congo's internal conflict reflected a concern that such interference would create a dangerous precedent which would place the Organization 'at the beck and call of any state with the problem of a dissident minority within its own borders'.[13]

It can also be argued that if the acceptance of the norm of nonintervention has been eroded, then there should be no divergence between the operational and psycho-milieus when external actors pursue intervention responses. It seems, however, that the divergence still occurs. Scott has noted that:

> The doctrine of non-intervention has served to hamper the development of effective aid administration, to slow the evolution of ideas and techniques for dealing with problems of development, and it has stood in the way of a candid recognition by American officials of what they have, in fact, been doing for two decades.[14]

Specific examples suggest that on occasions the discrepancy between the operational and psycho-milieus of the external actor has been substantial. For example, the American administration did believe that Castro was an unpopular dictator who would be overthrown at the first opportunity. Evidence which contradicted this image was ignored.[15] Similarly, it was believed that North Vietnam was invading the South at a time when the conflict was almost entirely attributable to internal unrest.[16] It is more difficult to verify the existence of similar distortions among Soviet decision-makers, but it is likely that they accepted the statement in *Pravda* issued after the invasion of Czechoslovakia, that the Russian soldiers 'do not interfere in the internal affairs of the country, they are fighting for the principle of self-determination of the people of Czechoslovakia not in words but in deeds'.[17]

It is also worth noting that criticism of the nonintervention norm in situations of ideological struggle is not a new phenomenon. Mill argued over a hundred years ago that:

The doctrine of non-intervention, to be a legitimate principle of morality, must be accepted by all governments. The despots must consent to be bound by it as well as the free states. Unless they do, the profession of it by free countries comes to this miserable issue, that the wrong side may help the wrong, but the right side must not help the right.[18]

This tendency to discuss norms in terms of morality ignores the sociological argument that norms evolve in order to permit actors to relate more easily to their environment. Many writers simply do not take account of the fact that the nonintervention norm may be self-sustaining because of the costs associated with an intervention response. There is an element of confusion among writers on this issue, particularly when the norm is related to international law. It is noted on the one hand that 'the traditional rule of non-interference is incompatible with the revolutionary ideology of Communist nations and the anticolonial commitments of the Afro-Asians',[19] and on the other, that:

The time is ripe for defining a norm prohibiting overt assistance by armed personnel in a civil war. Certainly all recent practice indicates that states have paid, in either political or military terms, very heavily for direct participation; and that their decisions to send forces would not be lightly repeated. One thinks of the American experience in Vietnam, the British in East Africa, and the Egyptians in Yemen.[20]

The same point has been made in an analysis of local conflict, where it is argued that

... on the record, internal struggles have tended to be harder to control than inter-state conflicts. Considerable great-power partiality has usually been a feature of those conflicts that have proven hard to control. The more intense that partiality has been, the more the conflicts have resisted prevention, moderation, or termination of hostilities.[21]

Hammarskjold came to a similar conclusion after the experience of the United Nations in Suez, Lebanon and Jordan. He felt that the United Nations could operate in a Suez-type situation, where the force 'would be interposed between regular, national military forces which were subject to a cease-fire agreed to by the opposing parties'. The same argument did not apply in cases of domestic conflict, and he believed: 'Neither in Lebanon nor in Jordan would it have been possible in either of these situations to preserve a natural distinction between the presence and functions in various areas of any United Nations force and the presence and functions of government troops.'[22]

It is not just in international relations that the significance of this aspect of the norm of nonintervention has been noted. When the Labour Government in Britain put forward legislation for dealing with the trade unions, an analysis of Government intervention into conflict between labour and management propounded similar arguments, and it was observed, 'the fact is that such a procedure can only be used sparingly. If it is kept for only the most extreme cases, these are precisely the ones in which it is least likely to have the intended effect.'[23] There are, in other words, very real difficulties associated with becoming involved in internal conflict.

The advantages of nonintervention, therefore, have persisted through time. In a theoretical analysis, Burton suggests that when governments are faced with internal unrest, but have an expectation of external assistance, it is possible that they 'are less inclined to meet demands upon them, and that conflict is ultimately promoted and not avoided by expectations of foreign intervention'.[24] Metternich held to the same view. 'The very nature of my thesis excluded all idea of foreign interference for France as for other countries. No one can govern for a government, and there are cases where the appearance of support does more than feebleness itself.'[25] Temperley assumes that, because Metternich subsequently sent troops to suppress revolution in Naples and Piedmont, he must have 'executed a complete change of position and principle'.[26] This line of argument corresponds with Barnet's belief that because interventions occur, the norm of nonintervention must not 'elicit wide acceptance'.

By drawing the distinction between prescribed and behavioural norms it is not necessary to assume that principles have been completely changed whenever behaviour deviates from a prescribed norm. But in line with the model which has been established it does indicate that the behaviour will be accompanied by perceptual distortion. This is not to suggest, however, that prescribed norms are not subject to change. Although it is unusual for norms to be changed suddenly, or rejected, norms can change over time. According to Ferguson:

> In the last analysis, norms change because the behavior of men and their governments changes as they both shape their choices and find them circumscribed by the world in which they live. Norms usually change slowly because the environment is relatively stable, with significant changes customarily occurring so gradually that they are almost imperceptible for a period of years.[27]

But in one perceptive analysis of the norm of nonintervention it has been suggested that the prescriptive element of nonintervention is undiminished. Norms are defined in terms of 'system symbols' and it is argued:

> If indeed states care deeply about the authoritative formulation of the principle of nonintervention because of its symbolic position in a chang-

ing system, we could further ask whether states – since they consist of men – need the psychic support of favourable symbols or myths, particularly as a means of easing the transition from one social reality to another, or whether they feel that the manipulation of symbols and myths is a key to promoting or impeding such a transition.[28]

It is not possible to examine this issue without direct access to the relevant decision-makers. In the historical context, the cases indicate that decision-makers are not conscious of manipulating norms, but rather they modify their perception so that their behaviour is perceived to conform with the norms. The same analysis may also apply in the contemporary international system.

It is possible that the incidence of intervention is now greater than during earlier periods, although only systematic research could justify this assertion. Provided that the prescribed norm of nonintervention is accepted, then the model which has been established in this study has relevance. It cannot, however, explain why the distribution of intervention responses may vary with time. It is possible that the current generation of decision-makers in the international system are still reacting to the events which surrounded the appeasement policy, of which the Spanish Civil War formed a part. The victory of the Fascists in Spain may have taught other members of the international system to be wary of attempting to maintain the nonintervention norm when not all actors observe the norm. The lesson may be inappropriate for the contemporary international system. It is possible that a future generation of decision-makers will use images of Vietnam as the basis of perception, reinforcing the nonintervention norm. Whether the images will be particularly relevant or useful in the new context remains to be seen.

Appendix 1

THE PORTUGUESE CIVIL WAR

The emergence of Portugal as an independent state, separate from Spain, can be viewed as an accident of history, the result of battles of independence fought in the twelfth century. Conflicts with the Spaniards and the Mohammedans at that time gave rise to myths and legends and a national heritage which sustained later attempts to unite Portugal with Spain. By the end of the thirteenth century commercial treaties were signed with Britain and the relationship developed with time. After a war with Castile, Portugal signed a permanent treaty of friendship with Britain, in 1386, and, thereafter, the alliance with Britain remained a crucial element in Portugal's foreign policy. On several occasions British troops were employed to assist the Portuguese in their continuous struggle to maintain independence.

It was on the basis of these ancient ties that Britain was called upon for assistance during the period which followed the Napoleonic Wars. Events which directly impinge on the British intervention in 1826 can be traced back to 1807 when Napoleon invaded Portugal and Dom John, who was Regent, was forced to escape to Brazil, a Portuguese colony, leaving a Council of Regency to govern the country. With the help of the British, the French were forced to leave Portugal the following year, but the situation remained insecure until the defeat of Napoleon. British troops remained after 1815 and were employed to suppress the discontented population. Dom John was now King of Portugal but he refused requests from Britain and Portugal to return from Brazil. In 1820 a new regency was established, following a major revolt, and the British were expelled. It was demanded that John return and in 1822 he agreed. He left his elder son Pedro to govern Brazil and he adhered to a new constitution when he arrived in Lisbon.

Under pressure from his younger son, Miguel, he abrogated the constitution the following June, although he insisted that another must be introduced. At the same time, the French were invading Spain in order to remove its Constitutional Government. Canning gave an assurance that Britain would provide assistance if a similar attack was made on Portugal.

When a formal request was made by the Portuguese Government for assistance to control the reactionaries in the country, Canning refused, on the grounds that Britain's treaty with Portugal related only to an external attack. But he did agree to send a fleet into the Tagus. The following year Miguel again placed pressure on his father to adopt a more reactionary stance. From the safety of the British fleet, the King ordered Miguel to travel abroad. Miguel left and eventually resided in Vienna.

Later in the year, a further request was made for British troops, but this time the request had the support of the British ambassador, who was endeavouring to counteract the influence of the French. Canning was extremely embarrassed by the request. To accept would open Britain to the charge of following the principles of the Neo-Holy Alliance states; to refuse would be interpreted as an agreement to French occupation. The dilemma was resolved by a decision to send Hanoverian troops, but following a French undertaking not to invade Portugal, Canning rescinded the order. Soon after, the ambassador was replaced by Sir William A Court.

The crisis in 1826 was precipitated by the death of King John on 16 March, leaving the Council of Regency to govern. His successor, Dom Pedro, decided to remain in Brazil. He renounced the throne in favour of his young daughter, whom he proposed should marry Miguel. This meant first, that the Council of Regency would remain in control until Pedro's daughter came of age, and second, that in 1827 when Miguel became twenty-five, he would become regent. Pedro also granted Portugal a constitution, a move which was completely unacceptable to many European statesmen. This news reached Europe on 22 June. Metternich offered help to the Spanish King, if he should decide that the constitution would threaten his security. He also called a Conference of Ambassadors, representatives of the Neo-Holy Alliance.

The reaction of the European statesmen ensured that Canning gave the constitution his support. He warned that any threat to Portugal would activate Britain's ancient treaties. On 31 July, the constitution was formally accepted in Portugal; early in August, supporters of Miguel deserted from the army and crossed into Spain. The regency demanded that these deserters should be dispersed, but there were continual incursions into Portugal. At the same time, the Portuguese were assisting dissident Spaniards in a similar fashion. However, at the beginning of December, Canning received information about a concerted attack by the Portuguese deserters which had taken place at the end of the previous month. With the acquiescence of Parliament, it was agreed to send 4000–5000 troops to Portugal. By the time the British troops arrived the situation was virtually under control, but Canning was unwilling to withdraw until a more permanent solution had been evolved.

A solution necessitated the withdrawal of French troops from Spain, and it proved exceedingly difficult to reach an accommodation on this issue. In the meantime, criticism about the delay in withdrawing the troops began to increase. Eventually, an agreement was reached with Austria, which was to allow Miguel to return to Portugal under the auspices of the constitution. On the basis of this agreement, Britain agreed to withdraw the troops. Shortly after this point, a final agreement was reached with France about the withdrawal from Spain. On his return as regent early in 1828, Miguel almost immediately broke with the constitution. Internal dissension broke out. The British ambassador informed the British Cabinet that Miguel was permitting the return of armed troops from Spain. He delayed the withdrawal of the troops in the hope that the Cabinet would permit them to stay and protect the Constitutionalists. Although this had been sufficient reason for Canning to send the troops in 1826, it was insufficient reason for Wellington to allow them to stay. The British troops left in April 1828.

THE AMERICAN CIVIL WAR

The issue of slavery divided the United States from the time of its independence. In the South, slavery was considered economically profitable, and its dissolution seemed likely to create grave problems. The Northern States, on the other hand, had few slaves, and by 1800, slavery was practically extinct. When the union was formed, the population of North and South was roughly equal, but by 1860, nearly two-thirds of the population lived in the North. The drive West, and the incorporation of new states into the Union, threatened the precarious balance which existed in the Senate between free and slave states, but in 1850 there was a compromise settlement. While California was established as a free state, it was accepted that before subsequent states were admitted into the Union, the issue of slavery should be settled on the basis of self-determination.

Although the compromise helped to maintain unity for a further decade, it did nothing to solve the underlying sources of conflict. Over the next ten years, changes in the political structure served to exacerbate the situation. In the Democratic party, the section of the party which favoured slavery began to increase, while at the same time, the Republican party established itself on an anti-slavery platform. Its growth was dependent on the continued significance of the slavery issue. Attempts by the Southerners to extend slavery into new territory provided the necessary vehicle for the sort of political controversy which permitted the Republican party to flourish. The issue precipitated violent conflict in the new territory of Kansas.

As the controversy festered, the issue began to split the Northern and Southern Democrats. During the Convention in 1860, the Southerners walked out and elected their own Presidential Candidate. Lincoln won the election for the Republicans, not as the result of the Democratic schism, but because of the economic and political power which had accumulated in the North. Within three months of the election, eight Southern states had seceded. It was believed that they would get better terms from the North outside of the Union, and it was intended to return once satisfactory guarantees had been given. Lincoln, in his inaugural speech, insisted, however, that it was not possible to tolerate secession. Neither side was willing to compromise.

In April 1861 there was an attack on Fort Sumter. It was taken as a symbolic gesture by the South, and Lincoln called for volunteers. The Civil War was initiated not on the issue of slavery, but on the right of secession. Once the conflict began, however, many began to feel that the question of slavery must be settled permanently. Republican radicals began to demand that the war aims should be extended beyond the ending of secession. By September 1862, the pressure had increased to the point where Lincoln felt it expedient to issue the Emancipation Proclamation. The decision had major ramifications for European decision-makers.

From the beginning of the conflict, the Confederates had endeavoured to gain European support. They over-estimated the significance of cotton. It proved futile to withdraw this commodity from the European market in an attempt to apply pressure on the European decision-makers. At the high-point of the Southern victories, British decision-makers did briefly consider the possibility of mediating in the conflict, but the resurgence of the North and the Emancipation Proclamation eliminated the grounds on which a settlement could have been established. Neutrality was observed until 1865, when the South surrendered.

THE RUSSIAN CIVIL WAR

Unprepared for sustained conflict, Russia entered World War I in 1914, honouring earlier alliance commitments. Persistent military failure and economic hardship contributed to the declining morale of the population as the war progressed. In March 1917 soldiers refused to fire on a group of demonstrators, disobeying orders from the Emperor. Within a week, the situation had deteriorated so rapidly that the Emperor was forced to abdicate. Two separate authorities were established, both claiming to represent the population. One was the Provisional Government, the other was the Soviet of Workers' Deputies. The Provisional Government wanted to have free and comprehensive elections, but there was also a desire to prosecute the war successfully, and it was decided to delay the elections until after the war. The Provisional Government, therefore, failed to establish its own legitimacy.

During the next few months, observers were under the impression that the significant political conflict was between the conservatives and the moderate socialists, but throughout this period the Bolsheviks, under Lenin, gathered strength, and in November took control in Petrograd and Moscow, with little resistance. The first actions of the Bolsheviks were to call for a general peace and to abolish private ownership of land. When the call for peace and an end to the war was rejected, it was decided that it was essential to make a separate peace with Germany. In February the terms offered by the Germans were refused, but as the situation in Rusisa deteriorated, a punitive peace was signed at Brest Litovsk at the beginning of March.

Opposition to the Bolsheviks came from the right and from the non-Bolshevik left. Before the termination of the war in Europe, these sectors united. In September, as the result of a conference held in Ufa, an all-Russian Directory was established. At Omsk an anti-Bolshevik army formed under Kolchak, but a conflict between Kolchak and the Directory soon developed, reflecting the fundamental political cleavage which existed among the anti-Bolsheviks. In November 1918 Kolchak overthrew the Directory and established himself in a dictatorship. This development coincided with the end of the war in Europe, and many of the left-wing anti-Bolsheviks, who had been concerned about the Bolshevik decision to sign a separate peace with Germany, found it impossible now to sustain the alliance with the right wing, so they shifted camps.

From the moment the Bolsheviks gained control Western European countries gave support and assistance to the anti-Bolsheviks. Ostensibly, the assistance was given to forces in Russia which were prepared to continue the struggle against the Germans. But these forces were synonymous with the anti-Bolsheviks. In March 1918 a small British force landed at Murmansk and this initiated a troop commitment to a policy which was ambiguous from the start. The British were restrained by the Americans, who refused to take action without approval from the Bolsheviks. This position broke down, however, in July, when it appeared that the Czechoslovakian Legion was endangered. The Legion was made up of deserters from the Austro-Hungarian Army. After the Bolsheviks withdrew from the war, they agreed that the Legion could leave by the Far East, so that the Czechs could continue fighting on the Western front. During the evacuation conflict occurred, and Trotsky ordered the troops to be disarmed. The Czechs refused and took control of the Trans-Siberian Railway. It was this situation which precipitated American action. Wilson agreed that they and the Japanese should each send 7000 troops. Independently the British, with French support, decided to send two battalions. Soon after, more British troops were sent to Northern Russia. Eventually, there were more than 18,000 British troops in the North.

When the armistice was signed with Germany, the political difficulties associated with the support which was being given to the anti-Bolsheviks were accentuated. Many decision-makers in Europe were anxious to see the Bolsheviks eliminated, but they were not prepared to pay the financial and political costs associated with a continuation of the war. Half-hearted support for the anti-Bolsheviks continued, but their inability to counteract the growing strength of the Bolsheviks made this an increasingly dubious policy. On 25 July 1919 the British Cabinet decided that troops must be withdrawn from Archangel and Murmansk, Siberia and the Caucasus, as soon as possible. By the beginning of 1920, British troops were left only in Transcaucasia. The Eastern Committee decided to retain troops there, but it was insisted that they must be evacuated if there was any danger of them being cut off. As the position of the anti-Bolsheviks deteriorated, the British commitment was further reduced. In February, following the collapse of Kolchak's army, it was agreed to withdraw the military mission which had been left in Siberia. The next month, a similar decision was made to withdraw the British mission which was with Denikin's anti-Bolshevik troops in Southern Russia. Then, in June, all support for the anti-Bolsheviks under Wrangel was withdrawn, and in July, the last troops were removed from Batoum, marking the end of the military commitment to the anti-Bolsheviks.

THE SPANISH CIVIL WAR

Spain's first Republic was brought to an end by the army in 1875, and it was more than fifty years later before the next attempt was made to establish a second Republic. The regime took control in April 1931, without bloodshed, largely because the King had lost the support of the army. Nevertheless, the new regime was confronted by insuperable problems. The right-wing elements in society were prepared to tolerate a republic only so long as there was no attack on their own privileges, while the left-wing elements saw the emergence of the new regime as a stage in the overthrow of the established order of the society. During the next five years, power shifted from the left to the right, and there was growing violence within the state. The centre-right party, unable to hold on to power, called for an election on 16 February 1936.

A Popular Front Government emerged from the election. There followed a four month period which was beset by strikes and incidents of arson. The Fascist party, which had recently been established, came into open confrontation with the Government. In mid-July, there was an army mutiny in Morocco, which immediately spread to the mainland. The mutiny was successful almost everywhere, except Madrid and Barcelona, but on the basis of this support, it was possible for the Republican Government to transform a military coup into a civil war.

Britain had important economic interests in Spain, and decision-makers in Britain had little sympathy with the Republicans, but it was not possible to offer support to the Fascists. After some indecision it was decided to favour the French policy of a nonintervention agreement. The agreement was to have little effect on Germany, Italy and the Soviet Union, those states which were most responsible for supplying arms to the two sides engaged in civil war. For the next two years the British Government were instrumental in devising and taking measures designed to improve the efficacy of the nonintervention agreement. They were of little avail. In the absence of any other constructive policy British decision-makers persisted with this approach, until Franco eventually forced the Republicans into a total surrender, early in 1939.

Appendix 2

WHEN this study was initiated, the possibility of carrying out a quantitative analysis of intervention was considered. Such an analysis would have looked for indicators which were present when civil wars precipitated intervention responses. The preliminary model eventually took a form which precluded any possibility of analysing interventionary situations in terms of aggregate data. Before that point was reached, however, a preliminary list of interventions had been established. It was based on the data which can be found in L. F. Richardson's *The Statistics of Deadly Quarrels.* He used two criteria to order the 315 conflicts for which he gathered data. Firstly, he grouped the conflicts according to the number of people killed; he established five groups. Within these groups, the conflicts were classified according to the date of the armistice. At no point does he list the conflicts in terms of international or civil wars, although he does give the aggregate figures for some of the conflicts which he examined.

FATAL QUARRELS 1820–1945

Numbers of people killed	Numbers of fatal quarrels		
	Mainly internal	Mixed	Mainly external
3 mill—30 mill	0	0	2
300,000— 3 mill	3	2	0
30,000—300,000	10	4	10
3,000— 30,000	11	16	36
300— 3,000	> 88	>11	> 89
Totals	>112	>33	>137

While he does not list the conflicts which fall into the three categories, he gives an indication of the criteria which he employed to isolate those conflicts which he defines as 'mainly internal'. He argues that before a civil war, the insurgents possessed 'an allegiance to authority which they shared in common with those who remained loyal to the government. It is reasonable therefore to regard insurrection, revolt, rebellion, and mutiny as

together forming a subclass of civil war in which one belligerent had previously exercised authority over the other' (p. 187). He employs two
symbols to denote the difference; one indicates the 'exercise of authority'
and the other indicates 'common government'. Only the first symbol is
employed in the case of many colonial conflicts, but for most civil wars,
both symbols are employed. Both types of conflict are covered by the norm
of nonintervention.

Richardson considers that it is 'unsatisfactory' to have a class entitled
'mixed' and he does not discuss the criteria which he employed to select
the cases which fall into this class (p. 187). It has been assumed that these
cases correspond to behaviour which has been defined in this study in terms
of intervention response. When Richardson isolated those cases which he
defined as 'mixed', it would seem that he included cases where a third
party assisted one side of a civil war. It was on this basis that a list of
intervention responses was drawn up.

When it came to isolating the cases, however, the task proved to be difficult. For example, Richardson did not think that there was a common
government which exercised authority over the two parties prior to conflict
during the Spanish Civil War. As a consequence, the symbols which identify
civil wars are not presented. As such the Spanish Civil War appears to fall
in the 'mainly external' category. Richardson comments: 'This decision,
though unconventional, is in accord with the general policy throughout this
book, that of attending to strong motives and of ignoring any names which
denote mere conventions empty of psychological drive' (p. 188). Identification of the 'mixed' category is further complicated when he divides a conflict into a number of cases. The initial case may be defined as a civil war;
thereafter the symbol denoting common government is eliminated. It did
not seem possible to adhere strictly to Richardson's convention, and his
symbols, consequently, were only used as a guide in the selection of the
following cases:

INTERVENTION RESPONSES 1820–1945 (taken from Richardson)

		Numbers killed
1	Great War in La Plata: 1865–70	
*2	Sequel to Bolshevik Revolution: 1918–20	300,000–3 mill.
*3	Spanish Civil War: 1936–9	
4	The European Revolutions: 1848–9	
*5	First British Afghan War: 1838–42	
6	Russo–Turkish War: 1877	30,000–300,000
7	The Mexican Revolution: 1910–20	
8	War and Massacre in Anatolia: 1919–22	
9	Greek Civil War: 1946–9	

```
 *10   War of Greek Independence:  1821–9
 *11   Miguelite War:  1828–34
 *12   First Carlist War:  1833–40
 *13   War in Syria:  1839–41
 *14   War in La Plata:  1836–52
  15   War of Italian Unity:  1859
 *16   Mexican Intervention:  1861–7
 *17   The Revolt of the Mahdi:  1881–5               3,000–30,000
 *18   Sudanese Independence:  1885–95
 *19   The Chinese Boxer Rising:  1899–1900
 *20   War in Libya:  1911–17
  21   War in Finland:  1918
  22   Chinese Civil War:  1926–28
  23   Rebellion in Chinese Turkestan:  1931–4
 *24   Greek Civil War:  1944–5


  25   Spain:  1823
  26   Annam:  1833–9
  27   Chile:  1836
  28   Nicaragua:  1855–57
 *29   Montenegro:  1958
  30   Turkish Lebanon and Damascus:  1860
  31   Graeco–Turkish War:  1897                      300–3,000
 *32   British Somaliland:  1899–1904
  33   In Morocco:  1907–13
  34   In Middle Atlas Mountains:  1914–17
  35   In Hungary:  1919–20
  36   In Haiti:  1915–20
  37   Japanese Invasion of China:  1931–33
  38   In Morocco:  1929–33
```

*Denotes involvement by British Government or citizens.

The list does not correspond exactly with the figures given by Richardson, but it is very close. It is probable that the difference reflects the liberal interpretation given to the definition of civil wars in a few instances; since Richardson does not give a list of conflicts classified in this way, it is not possible to make a comparison. It can be seen that Britain was involved in almost half of the total number of interventions, and in terms of the numbers killed, British involvement is bunched in the range 3,000–30,000 killed. It can also be seen that the Portuguese case which is examined in this study is almost missed. Richardson does not consider the civil war in Portugal between 1826 and 1828, but starts the conflict in 1828. Although Richardson considered that his figures were fairly complete for the first four of his magnitudes, he acknowledged that his figures for the fifth range, number of deaths below 3,000, were not complete. Although the data collected represent a considerable achievement, the completeness of the figures must be questioned. A new attempt to gather a comprehensive list of conflicts is currently being carried out by the Hoover Institution of War, Revolution and Peace.

Appendix 3

The Definition

1   A potential interventionary situation exists when system A perceives the existence of open conflict within system B between the authority structure and a dissident subsystem.

2   Intervention takes place when system A takes action which it perceives as deviant in order to assist either the subsystem or the authority structure.

The Propositions

1   There is an international norm which proscribes military intervention into civil war situations.

2   In a conflict situation, a party will always desire to be confronted by a single opponent.

3   There is an inverse relationship between decision-makers' ability to predict events in an area and the probability of the norm proscribing intervention being violated.

4   The policy of intervention will always be preceded and accompanied by the processes of legitimization and rationalization.

5   The processes of legitimization and rationalization will increase the commitment to the policy of intervention.

6   A state will withdraw from a policy of intervention when the policy becomes counter-productive in terms of the initial frame of reference of the commitment.

THE REFORMULATED MODEL OF THE INTERVENTIONARY SITUATION

The Definition

An interventionary situation exists when an actor responds to an intervention stimulus. The stimulus emerges when conflict develops between the units in a bifurcated actor, creating a potential for system transformation. Maintaining a relationship with one side of a bifurcated actor constitutes an intervention response; maintaining a relationship with both sides of a bifurcated actor constitutes a nonintervention response.

The Propositions

1   There is a prescriptive norm in the international system which proscribes military intervention into civil wars and a behavioural norm which reflects the prescription.

2   In an interventionary situation, the operational milieu and the psycho-milieu of an actor will converge when a nonintervention response is implemented and diverge when an intervention response is implemented.

3   When an actor implements an intervention response, the interventionary situation is defined in terms of systemic conflict; when an actor implements a nonintervention response, the interventionary situation is defined in terms of subsystemic conflict.

4   When pursuing an intervention response or a nonintervention response, an actor will endeavour to gain international approval for its definition of the situation.

5   An intervention response reflects a false or projected consensus; a nonintervention response reflects an ancestral or bargained consensus.

6   In an interventionary situation, decision-makers will experience dissonance when there is either a false or projected consensus which reflects their interest specificity, or a bargained consensus which fails to reflect their interest specificity.

7   When dissonant information is received, decision-makers who are psychologically committed to the intervention response will seek to increase the level of behavioural commitment; decision-makers who are only behaviourally committed will seek to prevent the increase.

8   Decommitment occurs when the intervention stimulus is redefined, to activate the nonintervention norm and restore a dyadic interaction system.

References and Notes

In the notes which follow, full bibliographical details of any book or article cited are given in the first footnote in which it appears. Thereafter further citations are given in an abbreviated form, followed by the chapter and note number under which the complete citation can be found. For primary documents, generally, the date of the document is given, followed by the author and recipient of the document, then by the reference required to retrieve the document. The location of these documents is given below.

Unpublished Documents and Private Papers

The records of the **Cabinet Office** and the **Foreign Office** in the Public Record Office, London.
The **Russell Papers** in the Public Record Office, London.
The **Ellenborough Papers** in the Public Record Office, London.
The **Granville Papers** in the Public Record Office, London.
The **Huskisson Papers** in the British Museum, London.
The **Palmerston Papers** in the British Museum, London.

Introduction

1. J. N. Rosenau, ed. *The International Aspects of Civil Strife* Princeton, Princeton UP (1964) p.2
2. In 1972 E. M. Foreman was still referring to the 'tentative nature of the literature'. See 'Civil War as a Source of International Violence' *Journal of Politics*, 34 (1972) 1111–34, p. 1116. In addition to the Rosenau volume, he also cites C. R. Mitchell 'Civil Strife and the Involvement of External Parties' *International Studies Quarterly*, 14 (1970) 166–94.
3 The ramifications of this distinction have been explored by J. N. Rosenau 'Pre-theories and Theories of Foreign Policy' in R. B. Farrell, ed. *Approaches to Comparative and International Politics* Evanston, Northwestern UP (1966).
4. See, for example, J. N. Rosenau, ed. *Linkage Politics: Essays on the Convergence of National and International Systems* New York, Free Press (1969) and J. Wilkenfeld, ed. *Conflict Behavior and Linkage Politics* New York, McKay (1973).
5. The notion of a paradigm comes from T. S. Kuhn *The Structure of Scientific Revolutions*, Chicago, Chicago UP (1970). Despite criticism (see J. Stephens 'The Kuhnian Paradigm and Political Inquiry: An Appraisal' *American Journal of Political Science*, 17 (1973) 467–88), the idea has proved useful in international relations by drawing attention to the influence of power political assumptions in the

literature. See A. Lijphart 'The Structure of the Theoretical Revolution in International Relations' *International Studies Quarterly,* 18 (1974) 41–74; and J. R. Handelman, J. A. Vasquez, M. K. O'Leary and W. D. Coplin 'Color it Morgenthau: A Data-Based Assessment of Quantitative International Relations' (mimeo, I. R. Program, Maxwell School, Syracuse University).

6. R. H. Wagner makes a useful distinction between the state-centric model and the state-as-actor model. The first assumes that governments are the only important actors in international politics; the second assumes that states are unitary actors. He asserts that the two assumptions 'have been the most important starting-points for serious analysis in the field and that they underlie much, though certainly not all, of the empirical work done in it'. See 'Dissolving the State: Three Recent Perspectives on International Relations' *International Organization,* 28 (1974) 435–66.

7. See H. A. Hornstein *et al.,* eds *Social Intervention: A Behavioural Science Approach* New York, Free Press (1971).

8. A. M. Rosenthal *Thirty-Eight Witnesses* New York, McGraw–Hill (1964).

9. J. M. Darley and B. Latane 'Bystander Intervention in Emergencies: A Diffusion of Responsibility' in H. C. Lindgren *et al.,* eds *Current Research in Psychology* New York, Wiley (1971).

10. A. R. Beals and B. J. Siegel *Divisiveness and Social Conflict: An Anthropological Approach* Stanford, Stanford UP (1966) p. 18.

11. For a discussion of retroduction see N. R. Hanson *Patterns of Discovery: An Inquiry into the Conceptual Foundations of Science* Cambridge, Cambridge UP (1958).

12. For a good discussion of this point see M. W. Jackson 'The Application of Method in the Construction of Political Science Theory' *Canadian Journal of Political Science,* 5 (1972) 402–17.

13. See, for example, H. Bondi *Assumption and Myth in Physical Theory* Cambridge, Cambridge UP (1967) p. iii.

14. *Ibid.* ch. 2.

CHAPTER 1

1. I de Sola Pool *Symbols of Internationalism* Stanford, Stanford UP (1951) lists intervention and nonintervention as two of the fifty-six international political symbols which he identified. In an analysis of the most commonly counted symbols relevant to international relations, based on newspaper editorials, intervention appeared eleventh in French newspapers, twentieth in British newspapers and not at all in the American list. Since the publication of the study the importance of intervention has unquestionably increased.

2. See K. E. Boulding *Conflict and Defence: A General Theory* New York, Harper (1962) p. 2.

3. For a discussion of this issue see O. Thomas *Transformational Grammar and the Teacher of English* New York, Holt, Rinehart (1967) p. 27.

4. A. Kaplan *The Conduct of Inquiry* Scranton, Chandler (1964) p. 47.

5. J. N. Rosenau 'The Concept of Intervention' *Journal of International Affairs,* 21 (1967) 165–76, p. 167. See also J. N. Rosenau 'The Scientific Concept of Intervention' *Journal of Conflict Resolution,* 13 (1969) 149–71.

6. H. J. Morgenthau 'To Intervene or Not to Intervene' *Foreign Affairs,* 45 (1967) 425–46, p. 425.

7. Thucydides *History of the Peloponnesian War,* transl. by R. Warner, Harmondsworth, Penguin (1954) p. 208.

8. See A. M. Scott *The Revolution in Statecraft: Informal Penetration* New York, Random House (1965); and J. H. Herz *International Politics in the Atomic Age* New York, Columbia UP (1959).

9. See N. O. Berry 'The Management of Foreign Penetration' *Orbis,* 17 (1973)

598–619. The same point has been made about the influence of multinational companies; see L. Turner 'Multinational Companies and the Third World' *World Today*, 30 (1974) 394–402.

10. J. Russell *The Foreign Policy of England* London, Longman, Green (1871) p. 2; *Essay on the British Constitution* London, Longman, Green (1821) makes the same point.

11. If relationships with friends are affected by marital squabbles, this is an unintended consequence, whereas one objective of an insurgent regime may be to alter the international orientation of the state. For the distinction between first- and second-order consequences, see R. A. Bauer, ed. *Social Indicators* Cambridge, M.I.T. Press (1966).

12. See G. Modelski 'The International Relations of Internal War' in Rosenau *Civil Strife* [Intro: 1].

13. Taken from A. Etzioni *Political Unification: A Comparative Study of Forces and Leaders* New York, Holt, Rinehart (1965) p. 37.

14. See R. H. Ullman *Britain and the Russian Civil War* Princeton, Princeton UP (1968) pp. 353–6.

15. See D. Holden *Farewell to Arabia* New York, Walker (1967) pp. 58–63.

16. See J. H. de Rivera *The Psychological Dimension of Foreign Policy* Columbus, C. E. Merrill (1968) pp. 425–30.

17. See J. A. Swets 'Detection Theory and Psychophysics: A Review' in *Psychometrica*, 26 (1961) 49–63.

18. See A. Kalleberg 'Concept Formation in Normative and Empirical Studies' *American Political Science Review*, 63 (1969) 26–39.

19. Although there is nothing in principle to prevent an actor's definition of the situation being used in aggregate studies, in practice the analyst's definition of the situation is normally used. See Ch. 3.

20. See S. Hoffmann, ed. *Contemporary Theory and International Relations* Englewood Cliffs, Prentice-Hall (1960) p. 176.

21. See O. R. Holsti and R. C. North 'The History of Human Conflict' in E. B. McNeil *The Nature of Human Conflict* Englewood Cliffs, Prentice-Hall (1965) p. 156.

CHAPTER 2

1. Resolution 2131; see *International Organization*, 21 (1967) 367–72.

2. See O. R. Holsti 'The Study of International Politics Makes Strange Bedfellows: Theories of the Radical Right and the Radical Left' *American Political Science Review*, 68 (1974) 217–42.

3. See M. Sherif *Group Conflict and Cooperation: Their Social Psychology* London, Routledge (1967); and *The Psychology of Social Norms* New York, Harper (1966).

4. See R. A. Falk 'The Reality of International Law' *World Politics*, 14 (1962) 353–63.

5. M. Barkun *Law Without Sanctions: Order in Primitive Societies and the World Community* New Haven, Yale UP (1968).

6. See A. W. Gouldner 'The Norm of Reciprocity: A Preliminary Statement' *American Sociological Review*, 25 (1960) 161–78.

7. 30.6.1828, *Parliamentary Debates*, XIX, p. 1552 (speech given by Robert Peel).

8. 19.10.1918, memo by Robert Cecil, FO/371/3344/W175192.

9. *Lord Riddell's Intimate Diary of the Paris Peace Conference and After* London, Gollancz (1933) p. 249.

10. 29.1.1920, *Cabinet Papers*, 23/7

11. 21.8.1863, Russell to Lyons, FO/5/872.

12. J. H. Rose 'The Struggle with Revolutionary France' in A. W. Ward and G. P. Gooch *Cambridge History of British Foreign Policy*, 3 vols, Cambridge,

Cambridge UP (1922) 1, pp. 242–3.

13. A. G. Stapleton *Intervention and Nonintervention or the Foreign Policy of Great Britain from 1790–1865* London, Murray (1866) pp. 230–9.

14. Darley and Latane 'Bystander Intervention in Emergencies' in Lindgren *Research in Psychology* [**Intro: 9**].

15. H. C. F. Bell *Lord Palmerston* London, Cass (1966) II, p. 275.

16. J. L. Brierly *The Law of Nations*, 6th edn. revised by C. H. M. Waldock; Oxford, Clarendon Press (1963) p. 402.

17. *Ibid.* p. 142.

18. 12.12.1826, *Parliamentary Debates*, XVI, p. 388.

19. 12.12.1826, *Parliamentary Debates*, XVI, p. 360.

20. H. W. V. Temperley *Life of Canning* London, Finch (1905) p. 136.

21. 3.7.1827, Dudley to A Court, FO/63/318.

22. 10.3.1830, *Speech of Viscount Palmerston* London, James Ridgeway (1830) pp. 11–12.

23. 16.11.1919, *Parliamentary Debates*, CXIV, p. 2940.

24. R. H. Ullman *Intervention and the War* Princeton, Princeton UP (1961) pp. 185–6.

25. 17.2.1919, FO/371/3957/W31956.

26. 8.4.1918, FO/371/3290/W62043.

27. B. E. C. Dugdale *Arthur James Balfour* London, Hutchinson (1936) II, p. 191.

28. 6.3.1918, Balfour to Lockhart, FO/371/3285/W4133.

29. W. B. Fowler *British–American Relations 1917–18: The Role of Sir William Wiseman* Princeton, Princeton UP (1969) p. 166–7.

30. 22.12.1860, Admiralty to Admiral Milne; J. P. Baxter 'The British Government and Neutral Rights' *American Historical Review*, 34 (1928) 9–29, p. 10.

31. 5.1.1861, Russell to Lyons, FO/5/754.

32. 29.12.1860, Palmerston to Somerset *Palmerston Papers*, BM48582.

33. 18.10.1861, Palmerston to Russell, *Russell Papers*, PRO/30/22/14B.

34. 15.2.1859, Russell to Lyons, FO/5/708.

35. F. S. Northedge *The Troubled Giant: Britain Among the Great Powers* London, Bell (1966) p. 441.

36. 2.8.1936, Mounsey to Halifax, FO/371/20526/W7504.

37. 19.8.1936, Mounsey to Cadogan, FO/371/20573/W9717.

38. 12.8.1936, Washington to FO, FO/371/20530/W8459.

39. 12.8.1936, FO/371/20530/W8652.

40. 31.7.1936, *Documents on German Foreign Policy* London, H.M.S.O. (1951) p. 19.

41. W. K. Kleine-Ahlbrandt *The Policy of Simmering: A Study of British Policy During the Spanish Civil War* Hague, Martinus Hyoff (1962) p. 9.

42. *Speech of Viscount Palmerston* London, James Ridgeway (1830) pp. 11–12.

43. A. Wellesley, *Despatches, Correspondence and Memoranda of F. M. Arthur Duke of Wellington* 8 vols, ed. by R. A. Wellesley, London, Murray (1867–80) IV pp. 586–8. Hereafter cited as *WND* (Wellington's New Despatches).

44. E. Law *Earl of Ellenborough: A Political Diary* London, Bentley (1881) I, p. 152.

45. *Ibid.* I, p. 103.

46. Lord Salisbury 'Lord Castlereagh' *Quarterly Review*, 3 (1862) 201–32.

47. T. Parsons 'Polarization of the World' in Q. Wright *Preventing World War III: Some Proposals* New York, Simon & Schuster (1962) p. 320.

48. Modelski 'International Relations of Internal War' in Rosenau *Civil Strife* p. 40 [**Intro: 1**].

49. A. G. Stapleton *The Political Life of George Canning* 3 vols, London, Longman, Green (1831) 3, p. 140.

50. 28.5.1861, *Parliamentary Debates* CLXIII p. 191.

51. 18.7.1862, *Parliamentary Debates* CLXVIII, pp. 572–3.

52. Temperley *Life of Canning* p. 159 [**2:20**].

53. J. A. Rose 'The Struggle with Revolutionary France' in Ward and Gooch *British Foreign Policy*, 1, p. 216. [**2:12**].

54. 28.12.1860, Russell to Lyons, FO/5/733.
55. 22.2.1937, Pollock memo, FO/371/21284/W3124.
56. E. J. Stapleton, ed. *Some Official Correspondence of George Canning* London, Longman, Green (1887) 1, p. 86.
57. D. W. Miller and M. K. Starr *The Structure of Human Decisions* Englewood Cliffs, Prentice–Hall (1967) pp. 51–2.
58. J. G. March and H. A. Simon *Organizations* New York, Wiley (1958) p. 165.
59. H. A. Simon *Models of Man: Social and Rational. Mathematical Essays on Rational Behavior in a Social Setting* New York, Wiley (1957) p. 198–9.
60. 10.8.1936, memo by Malkin, FO/371/20529/W8234.

CHAPTER 3

1. 17.2.1938, Fitzmaurice memo, FO/371/22635/W738.
2. W. Buckley *Sociology and Modern Systems Theory* Englewood Cliffs, Prentice–Hall (1967) p. 67.
3. G. Liska 'Continuity and Change in International Systems' *World Politics,* 16 (1963) 118–36, pp. 122–3.
4. R. Jervis *The Logic of Images in International Relations* Princeton, Princeton UP (1970) p. 97.
5. O. R. Holsti 'The Belief System and National Images: A Case Study' *Journal of Conflict Resolution,* 6 (1962) 244–52.
6. For example, P. M. Burgess *Elites and Foreign Policy Outcomes* Columbus, Ohio State University Press (1967); and Jervis *Logic Of Images* [3:4].
7. H. and M. Sprout *The Ecological Perspective on Human Affairs: With Special Reference to International Affairs* Princeton, Princeton UP (1965).
8. Sprout *Ecological Perspective* p. 31 [3:7].
9. March and Simon *Organizations* p. 151 [2:58].
10. E. D. Adams *Great Britain and the American Civil War* 2 vols, London, Longman, Green (1925) 1, p. 53.
11. 10.1.1861, Russell to Lyons, C. F. Adams 'The British Proclamation of May 1861' *Massachusetts Historical Society Proceedings,* 49 (1915) p. 208.
12. H. E. Maxwell *Life and Letters of the Fourth Earl of Clarendon* 2 vols, London, Edward Arnold (1913) 2, p. 237.
13. 22.4.1861, Lyons to Russell, FO/5/762.
14. 20.5.1861, Lyons to Russell, FO/5/764.
15. 24.5.1861, *Palmerston Papers,* BM48582.
16. Baxter 'Neutral Rights' p. 14 [2:30].
17. 2.5.1861, Russell to Lyons, FO/5/754.
18. 15.4.1861, Lyons to Russell, FO/5/762.
19. 6.5.1861, Russell to Lyons, FO/5/754.
20. 21.5.1861, Russell to Lyons, FO/5/754.
21. 21.6.1861, Russell to Lyons, FO/5/754. For Canning's use of this phrase see H. W. V. Temperley *The Foreign Policy of Canning, 1822–27* London, Cass (1966) p. 326. This was a maxim which was to recur in the attack on Britain's policy towards Spain and it differs sharply from Malkin's argument that recognition is a pure act of grace. 10.8.1936, FO/371/20529/W8234.
22. Adams *Britain and the American Civil War,* 1, p. 58 [3:10].
23. 9.4.1861, Adams 'Proclamation of May 1861' p. 224 [3:11].
24. 26.3.1861, *Ibid.* p. 221–2.
25. 12.4.1861, *Ibid.* p. 226.
26. 4.5.1861, Adams *Britain and the American Civil War,* 1, p. 86 [3:10].
27. J. W. Foster *A Century of Diplomacy* New York, Houghton, Mifflin (1901) p. 367.
28. 23.7.1936, FO/371/20525/W7223.

29. 6.8.1936, Leigh Smith memo, FO/371/20526/W7601.
30. 14.8.1936, Pollock memo, FO/371/20530/W8509.
31. Ahlbrandt *Policy of Simmering* p. 73 [2:41].
32. 11.1.1937, Sargent memo, FO/371/21285/W3322.
33. 13.2.1937, FO/371/21285/W3300.
34. 28.10.1936, *Cabinet Papers,* 23/86.
35. 31.8.1936, *Cabinet Papers,* 24/264.
36. 21.7.1937, FO/371/21298/W14857.
37. 8.8.1936, FO/371/20527/W7918.
38. 21.10.1936, *Cabinet Papers,* 23/85.
39. 13.8.1936, FO/371/20530/W8554.
40. 10.8.1936, FO/371/20529/W8234.
41. 13.8.1936, FO/371/20530/W8554.
42. 17.8.1936, FO/371/20533/W9066.
43. 7.9.1936, FO/371/20575/W10779.
44. 23.8.1936, FO/371/21285/W4165.
45. 12.2.1937, FO/371/21283/W2390.
46. 17.2.1938, FO/371/22635/W738.
47. 9.11.1936, FO/371/20586/W16562.
48. 22.3.1938, FO/371/22641/W4211.
49. 28.6.1826, Canning to A Court, FO/63/305.
50. 18.5.1826, A Court to Canning, FO/63/307.
51. 2.6.1826, A Court to Canning, FO/63/308.
52. 5.7.1826, A Court to Canning, FO/63/308.
53. 17.7.1826, Canning to A Court, FO/63/305.
54. 2.8.1826, A Court to Canning, FO/63/308.
55. 8.9.1826, A Court to Canning, FO/63/309.
56. 11.10.1826, Canning to A Court, FO/63/306.
57. 17.7.1826, Granville to Canning, FO/27/351.
58. 14.7.1826, A Court to Canning, FO/63/308.
59. 31.10.1826, Canning to A Court, FO/63/306.
60. 13.5.1826, A Court to Canning, FO/63/307.
61. 4.11.1826, Canning to A Court, FO/63/306.
62. 7.7.1826, Lamb to Canning, FO/72/316.
63. E. J. Stapleton *Some Official Correspondence of George Canning,* 2 vols, London, Longman, Green (1887) II, pp. 125–7.
64. 14.7.1826, A Court to Canning, FO/63/308.
65. 11.11.1826, A Court to Canning, FO/63/310.
66. G. Edmundson 'Brazil and Portugal' in *The Cambridge Modern History,* X, p. 321.
67. 22.11.1826, A Court to Canning, FO/63/310.
68. 1.12.1826, *WND,* III, pp. 472–3 [2:43].
69. *WND,* III, pp. 474–5 [2:43].
70. A. G. Stapleton *George Canning and his Times* London, Parker (1859) p. 543.
71. Stapleton *Political Life of Canning,* 3, pp. 234–5 [2:49].
72. 12.12.1826, *Parliamentary Debates,* XVI, p. 360.
73. 24.7.1917, Lockhart to Buchanan, FO/371/2998/W159273.
74. 12.9.1917, FO to Buchanan, FO/371/2999/W178763.
75. 11.12.1917, Report from G. M. Young, FO/371/3018/W238609.
76. T. Jones *Whitehall Diary* London, Oxford UP (1969) 1, p. 51.
77. 18.12.1917, Buchanan to FO, FO/371/3017/W240433.
78. 23.11.1917, Buchanan to FO, FO/371/3017/W224699.
79. 19.12.1917, Buchanan to FO, FO/371/3017/W240797.
80. A. M. Gollin *Proconsul in Politics: A Study of Lord Milner in Opposition and in Power* Letchworth, Anthony Blond (1964) p. 557.
81. 17.3.1917, FO to Buchanan, FO/371/2995/W57143.
82. 21.11.1917, Buchanan to FO, FO/371/3017/W223644.
83. 27.11.1917, Buchanan to FO, FO/371/3017/W226991.
84. 23.12.1917, *Cabinet Papers,* WC/303.

85. 5.12.1917, Buchanan to FO, FO/371/3018/W232002.

86. 3.12.1917, Cabinet to Buchanan, FO/371/3018/W232002.

87. 5.12.1917, Buchanan to FO, FO/371/3018/W232002.

88. 5.12.1917, Buchanan to FO, FO/371/3018/W232002; the Cabinet came to share this concern, see Ullman *Intervention and the War* p. 53 [**2:24**].

89. 18.12.1917, Barclay (Jassy) to FO, FO/371/3019/W241264.

90. 8.1.1918, Dugdale *Balfour,* II, pp. 254–5 [**2:27**].

91. D. Lloyd George *The War Memoirs,* 6 vols, London, Nicholson & Watson (1936) 2, p. 1547.

92. 23.12.1917, Lord Bertie (Paris) to FO, FO/371/3018/W242080.

93. 29.12.1917, FO/371/3019/W245940.

94. 4.4.1918, Lyons memo, FO/371/3290/W59365.

95. 25.10.1919, E. L. Woodward and R. Butler *Documents on British Foreign Policy* London, HMSO (1947–) first series, III, p. 585.

96. Holsti 'Belief System and National Images' [**3:5**].

97. T. Shibutani *Improvised News: A Sociological Study of Rumor* New York, Bobbs–Merrill (1966) p. 23.

98. *Ibid.* p. 5, citing G. W. Allport and L. J. Postman 'The basic Psychology of Rumor' *Transactions of the New York Academy of Sciences* series 2, 8 (1945) 61–81.

CHAPTER 4

1. D. G. Pruitt discusses the idea that a system may contain two points of stable equilibrium. See 'Stability and Sudden Change in Interpersonal and International Affairs' *Journal of Conflict Resolution,* 13 (1969) 18–38.

2. H. Aldrich 'Organizational Boundaries and Inter-organizational Conflict' *Human Relations,* 24 (1971) 279–93.

3. K. W. Deutsch 'External Influences on the Internal Behavior of States' in Farrell *Comparative and International Politics* p. 5 [**Intro: 3**].

4. See M. B. Nicholson and P. A. Reynolds 'General Systems: The International System and Eastonian Analysis' *Political Studies,* 15 (1967) 12–31, p. 16.

5. See L. Thayer 'Communication and Organization' in F. E. X. Dance *Human Communication Theory* New York, Holt, Rinehart (1967). He argues that when two actors interact in a system: 'in some cases one or the other participant is a "sink" or terminal point for such an exchange, but in others there is a mutual modification. In the synchronic pattern, the objective is a satisfactory regulation of one to another; in the diachronic pattern, there is mutual regulation and something akin to progress through conceptual (and/or affective) space over time' p. 91. It can be seen that the terms have been modified here.

6. See O. R. Young *The Intermediaries* Princeton, Princeton UP (1967) p. 23.

7. 4.10.1860, Russell to Crompton, *Russell Papers,* 30/22/14A.

8. See W. T. Powers 'Feedback: Beyond Behaviorism' *Science,* 179 (1973) 351–5.

9. 30.3.1861, Lyons to Russell, FO/5/762.

10. 18.5.1861, H. W. Temple *W. H. Seward* New York, Knopf (1923) p. 53.

11. 20.4.1861, Russell to Lyons, FO/5/754.

12. 10.6.1861, Lyons to Russell, T. W. L. Newton *Life of Lord Lyons* 2 vols, London, E. Arnold (1913) 2, p. 37.

13. 4.11.1936, *Cabinet Papers,* 23/86.

14. 22.11.1936, *Cabinet Papers,* 24/265.

15. 18.1.1937, FO/371/21282/W1382.

16. 29.1.1937, FO/371/21283/W1665.

17. 16.3.1937, FO/371/21288/W6021.

18. 17.3.1937, *Cabinet Papers,* 23/87.

19. 25.8.1937, *Cabinet Papers,* 24/271.

20. 17.2.1938, Beckett memo, FO/371/22635/W738.

21. 24.7.1936, FO/371/20524/W6996.

22. 29.7.1936, FO/371/20525/W7400.
23. 12.8.1936, FO/371/20530/W8514.
24. 3.9.1936, FO/371/20574/W10476.
25. Such action constitutes an intervention response.
26. 3.10.1860, Palmerston to Lewis *Palmerston Papers* BM48582.
27. 14.9.1936, FO/371/20577/W11524.
28. 5.9.1936, FO/371/20575/W10515.
29. 5.9.1936, FO/371/20575/W10515.
30. 14.9.1936, FO/371/20577/W11524.
31. 28.9.1936, FO/371/20578/W12282.
32. 16.1.1937, FO/371/21319/W886.
33. 22.3.1937, FO/371/21287/W4970.
34. 21.5.1937, FO/371/21292/W10096.
35. 27.10.1826, Canning to Granville, Stapleton *Canning and his Times* p. 531 [**3:70**].
36. 31.10.1826, Canning to A Court, FO/63/306.
37. 31.10.1826, Canning to A Court, FO/63/306.
38. C. D. Yonge *Life and Administration of the 2nd Earl of Liverpool*, 3 vols London, Macmillan (1868) III, p. 407.
39. Temperley *Foreign Policy of Canning* p. 194 [**3:21**].
40. 19.8.1826, Canning to A Court, FO/63/306.
41. 18.8.1826, A Court to Canning, FO/63/308.
42. Temperley *Foreign Policy of Canning* p. 198 [**3:21**].
43. 18.8.1826, A Court to Canning, FO/63/308.
44. 11.10.1826, Canning to A Court, FO/63/306.
45. 13.11.1826, A Court to Canning, FO/63/309.
46. 15.11.1826, Canning to A Court, FO/63/306.
47. 18.8.1826, Granville to Canning, FO/27/351.
48. 9.9.1826, Canning to A Court FO/63/306.
49. 16.9.1826, A Court to Canning, FO/63/309.
50. 20.9.1826, A Court to Canning, FO/63/309.
51. 3.10.1826, A Court to Canning, FO/63/309.
52. 24.11.1826, A Court to Canning, FO/63/310.
53. 8.12.1826, Canning to Granville *Granville Papers*, PRO/30/29/18/12.
54. 4.10.1826, Canning to Lamb, FO/72/313.
55. 9.9.1826, A Court to Canning, FO/63/309.
56. 18.4.1826, Canning to Granville *Correspondence of Canning*, II, p. 31 [**3:63**].
57. 3.2.1826, Granville to Canning, FO/27/348.
58. 14.6.1826, Lamb to Canning, FO/72/316.
59. 14.6.1826, Lamb to Canning, FO/72/316.
60. 23.6.1826, Granville to Canning, FO/27/350.
61. 24.8.1826, Lamb to Canning, FO/27/351.
62. 29.9.1826, Lamb to Canning, FO/72/317.
63. 11.12.1826, *WND*, III, p. 484 [**2:43**].
64. This will be examined in Chapter 7.
65. 22.12.1826, Canning to Granville, Stapleton *Canning and his Times* [**3:70**].
66. 12.12.1826, *Parliamentary Debates*, XVI, p. 390.
67. 13.12.1826, L. J. Jennings, ed. *The Croker Papers* London, Murray (1884) p. 322.
68. 23.12.1826, Wellington to Bathurst, *WND*, III, pp. 503–4 [**2:43**].
69. Ullman *Intervention and the War* p. 211 [**2:24**].
70. 20.6.1918, Ullman *Intervention and the War* p. 211 [**2:24**].
71. A. J. Mayer *Political Origins of the New Diplomacy, 1917–18* New Haven, Yale UP (1959) p. 254.
72. Fowler *British–American Relations* p. 186 [**2:29**].
73. 31.10.1917, Bagge to Buchanan, FO/371/3000/W24331.
74. 11.11.1917, Greene to FO, FO/371/2999/W215977.
75. 15.2.1918, Lindley to FO, FO/371/3284/W30368.
76. 23.1.1918, Lockhart to FO, FO/371/3309/W36587.

77. 19.2.1918, Lindley to FO, Minute by Lyons, FO/371/3299/W31250.
78. 19.2.1918, Lindley to FO, FO/371/3299/W32015.
79. 2.1.1918, Buchanan to FO, FO/371/3296/W2004.
80. 7.2.1918, *Cabinet Papers,* 23/340.
81. 30.1.1918, Ullman *Intervention and the War* pp. 69–9 **[2:24]**.
82. 13.4.1918, FO to Lockhart, FO/371/3285/W64890.
83. 12.3.1918, Balfour memo, FO/371/3323/W46134.
84. 8.4.1918, Lockhart to FO, FO/371/3285/W64890.
85. 30.4.1918, FO to Jordan, FO/371/3291/W73788.
86. 20.4.1918, FO memo, FO/371/3291/W69189.
87. 4.5.1918, FO to Lockhart, FO/371/3309/W80028.
88. 9.5.1918, Lockhart to FO, FO/371/3285/W84749.
89. 6.4.1918, Lockhart to FO, FO/371/3285/W62282.
90. 8.4.1918, FO to Lockhart, FO/371/3285/W60446.
91. 13.4.1918, Cecil memo, FO/371/3285/W68677.
92. 17.4.1918, FO to Lockhart, FO/371/3307/W66525.
93. 6.5.1918, Lockhart to FO, FO/371/3307/W81518.
94. 27.5.1918, Lockhart to FO, FO/371/3307/W98208.
95. 23.5.1918, Ullman *Intervention and the War* p. 172 **[2:24]**.
96. Burgess *Elites and Foreign Policy Outcomes* p. 6 **[3:6]**.

CHAPTER 5

1. I. L. Claude 'Implications and Questions for the Future' *International Organiz-ation,* 19 (1965) 835–46, pp. 843–4.
2. D. Easton *A Systems Analysis of Political Life* New York, Wiley (1965) p. 285.
3. I. L. Claude 'Collective Legitimization as a Political Function of the United Nations' *International Organization,* 20 (1966) 367–79, p. 368.
4. See J. Slater 'The Limits of Legitimization in International Organizations: The O.A.S. and the Dominican Crisis' *International Organization,* 23 (1969) 48–72; and E. B. Haas 'Comparative Study of the United Nations' *World Politics,* 12 (1960) 298–322.
5. See J. D. Singer and M. Small 'National Alliance Commitments and War Involvement; 1818–1945' in J. N. Rosenau *International Politics and Foreign Policy* New York, Free Press (1969) p. 515.
6. See W. A. Phillips 'Great Britain and the Continental Alliance, 1816–1822' in Ward and Gooch *British Foreign Policy,* 2, p. 38 **[2:12]**.
7. See H. Nicolson *The Evolution of Diplomatic Method* London, Constable (1954) p. 74.
8. This reflects the idea of the 'collectivity-oriented pattern variable'. See E. C. Devereux 'Parsons' Sociological Theory' in M. Black, ed. *Social Theories of Talcott Parsons* Englewood Cliffs, Prentice–Hall (1961) pp. 38–44.
9. W. H. Dawson 'Forward Policy and Reaction' in Ward and Gooch *British Foreign Policy,* 3, pp. 171–2 **[2:12]**.
10. Newton *Life of Lord Lyons,* 1, p. 45 **[4:12]**.
11. S. Walpole *The Life of Lord John Russell* London, Longman, Green (1889) 2, p. 344.
12. 30.6.1862, *Parliamentary Debates,* CLXVII, p. 1214.
13. 17.9.1862, Russell to Palmerston *Russell Papers* 30/22/140.
14. M. B. Duberman *Charles Francis Adams 1807–1886* Stanford, Stanford UP (1968) p. 277.
15. 14.10.1861, Lyons to Russell, FO/5/772.
16. 14.10.1861, Lyons to Russell, FO/5/772.
17. 3.12.1861, Lyons to Russell, FO/5/776.
18. 6.12.1861, Lyons to Russell, FO/5/776.

19. Newton *Life of Lord Lyons,* 1, p. 64 [**4:12**].
20. The agent of legitimization took the form of a convention signed by the interested parties which stipulated that there would be no intervention in the internal affairs of Mexico. For a full account of the negotiations which surrounded the convention see C. H. Bock *Prelude to Tragedy: The Negotiation and Breakdown of the Tripartite Agreement* Pittsburgh, Pennsylvania UP (1966).
21. 29.7.1936, FO/371/20525/W7259.
22. 3.9.1936, Eden memo, FO/371/20537/W10351.
23. 2.8.1936, FO/371/20526/W7504.
24. 4.8.1936, FO/371/20526/W0649.
25. Ahlbrandt *Policy of Simmering* p. 12 [**2:41**].
26. *Ibid.* p. 13.
27. 3.9.1936, FO/371/20575/W10587.
28. R. K. Merton 'Manifest and Latent Functions' in *Social Theory and Social Structure* 3rd edn, New York, Free Press (1968).
29. 12.9.1936, FO/371/20576/W11301.
30. 14.9.1936, FO/371/20576/W10853.
31. 13.10.1936, FO/371/20580/W13608.
32. 21.10.1936, *Cabinet Papers,* 23/85.
33. 24.10.1936, FO/371/20582/W14335.
34. 4.12.1936, FO/371/20587/W16927.
35. 3.6.1937, FO/371/21334/W16518. A unanimous appeal was sent out on 18.6.1937. See FO/371/21337/W11943.
36. 9.7.1937, FO/371/21340/W12891.
37. 2.9.1936, FO/371/20537/W10314.
38. 29.9.1826, Lamb to Canning, FO/72/317.
39. 27.7.1826, Canning to A Court, FO/63/305.
40. *The Annual Register* (1827) p. 197.
41. T. C. Schelling *The Strategy of Conflict* New York, Oxford UP (1963) Ch. 2.
42. 27.7.1826, Canning to A Court, FO/63/305.
43. 17.12.1826, Canning to A Court, FO/63/306.
44. 11.12.1826, Canning to Wellington, *WND,* III, p. 484 [**2:43**].
45. *The Annual Register* (1827) p. 197.
46. 22.12.1826, Wellesley to Canning, FO/63/318.
47. 1.1.1918, Ullman *Intervention and the War* p. 90 [**2:24**].
48. 7.1.1918, *Cabinet Papers,* WC/316.
49. 1.1.1918, FO to House, FO/371/3296/W1397.
50. 29.5.1918, *Cabinet Papers,* WC/420.
51. 30.5.1918, Fowler *British–American Relations* p. 181 [**2:29**].
52. 12.6.1918, FO/371/3292/W104391.
53. 28.6.1918, Reading to FO, FO/371/3286/W114760.
54. 1.6.1918, Greene to FO, FO/371/3323/W97858.
55. 5.6.1918, Lockhart to FO, FO/371/3323/W107385.
56. 9.6.1918, FO/371/3323/W103431.
57. 14.6.1918, Lockhart to FO, FO/371/3324/W113393.
58. 21.6.1918, Balfour to Reading, FO/371/3324/W110145.
59. 25.6.1918, Derby to FO, FO/371/3324/W112629.
60. 5.7.1918, Ullman *Intervention and the War* pp. 213–4 [**2:24**].
61. *Ibid.* p. 215.
62. 20.6.1918, Lockhart to FO, FO/371/3286/W110971.
63. 11.7.1918, Jordan to FO, FO/371/3324/W122045.
64. 7.7.1918, FO/371/3324/W120020.
65. 10.7.1918, *Cabinet Papers,* WC/443.
66. 10.7.1918, FO to Reading, FO/371/3324/W119443.
67. 12.7.1918, Derby to FO, FO/371/3324/W122643.
68. 16.7.1918, Reading to FO, FO/371/3324/W124239.
69. 10.7.1918, FO to Reading, FO/371/3324/W120749.
70. 13.7.1918, FO/371/3324/W24082.
71. 13.8.1918, Greene to FO, FO/371/3287/W139947.

72. 5.8.1918, FO/371/3324/W134878.
73. 5.8.1918, FO/371/3324/W134878.
74. K. W. Deutsch 'The Commitment of National Legitimacy Symbols as a Verification Technique' *Journal of Conflict Resolution*, 7 (1963) 360–9, p. 360.

CHAPTER 6

1. Reification, of course, does not have to denote rationality.
2. R. Hilsman 'Congressional-Executive Relations and the Foreign Policy Consensus' *American Political Science Review*, 55 (1958) 725–44, p. 731.
3. See J. W. Prothro and C. W. Rigg 'Fundamental Principles of Democracy: Bases of Agreement and Disagreement' *Journal of Politics*, 22 (1960) 276–94.
4. H. Eulau 'Logic of Rationality in Unanimous Decision-Making' in *Macro–Micro Political Analysis: Accents of Inquiry* Chicago, Aldine (1969) p. 23.
5. See T. Newcombe 'The Study of Consensus' in R. K. Merton *et al.* eds. *Sociology Today: Problems and Prospects* New York, Basic Books (1959) p. 290.
6. Eulau 'Unanimous Decision-Making' p. 25 **[6:4]**.
7. J. M. Buchanan and G. Tullock *The Calculus of Consent: Logical Foundations of Constitutional Democracy* Ann Arbor, Michigan UP (1962) p. 88.
8. Eulau 'Unanimous Decision-Making' p. 29 **[6:4]**.
9. *Ibid.* p. 30.
10. *Ibid.* p. 39.
11. A complete version of Castlereagh's White Paper on Intervention can be found in Ward and Gooch *British Foreign Policy*, 2, pp. 622–32 **[2:12]**.
12. D. W. Rae and M. J. Taylor *The Analysis of Political Cleavages* New Haven, Yale UP (1970) pp. 1–4.
13. H. C. Kelman 'Patterns of Personal Involvement in the National System' in Rosenau *International Politics* pp. 279–80 **[5:5]**.
14. *Ibid.* pp. 280–1.
15. *Ibid.* p. 280.
16. Rae and Taylor *Political Cleavages* p. 4 **[6:12]**.
17. *Ibid.*
18. 12.12.1826, F. Bamford and Wellington, eds *The Journal of Mrs. Arbuthnot* London, Macmillan (1950) II, p. 63.
19. 12.8.1826, *Ibid.* p. 45.
20. 5.9.1826, Arbuthnot to Liverpool, in Yonge *Earl of Liverpool*, III, p. 395 **[4:38]**.
21. A. Aspinall 'The Correspondence of Charles Arbuthnot' *Camden Society* 3rd series, 65 (1941) p. 83.
22. 12.8.1826, *Journal of Mrs. Arbuthnot*, III, p. 45 **[6:18]**.
23. Canning modified his Greek policy to accommodate Wellington, see Stapleton *Correspondence of Canning*, II, p. 160 **[3:63]**; and also on the terms of reference for Beresford, who was sent out to reorganize the Portuguese army, see Yonge *Earl of Liverpool*, III, pp. 404–9 **[4:38]**.
24. *Journal of Mrs. Arbuthnot*, II, p. 45 **[6:18]**.
25. Aspinall 'Correspondence of Arbuthnot' p. 83 **[6:21]**.
26. 1.1.1827, Stapleton *Correspondence of Canning*, II, p. 241 **[3:63]**.
27. *Ibid.* p. 170.
28. 19.3.1828, E. Law *Earl of Ellenborough*, I, p. 64 **[2:44]**.
29. H. L. Bulwer *Life of Henry John Temple* London, Richard Bentley (1870) 1, p. 242.
30. 19.5.1827, Landsdowne memo, A. Aspinall 'The Formation of Canning's Ministry' *Camden Society* 3rd series, 54 (1937) p. 123.
31. *Ibid.* p. 28.
32. 1.8.1823, *Journal of Mrs. Arbuthnot*, I, pp. 247–8 **[6:18]**.

33.   8.8.1823, *Ibid.* p. 251.
34.   27.5.1824, *Ibid.* p. 315.
35.   16.7.1824, *Ibid.* pp. 327–8. Canning's explanation of the decision is contained in a letter to Sir Charles Bagot, 23.7.1824, see J. Bagot, ed. *George Canning and His Friends* 2 vols, London, Murray (1908) 1, p. 326.
36.   13.7.1824, *Journal of Mrs Arbuthnot,* I, p. 326 [**6:18**].
37.   12.12.1826, *Parliamentary Debates,* XVI, p. 347.
38.   *Ibid.* pp. 364–5.
39.   14.12.1826, Stapleton *Canning and his Times* pp. 546–7 [**3:70**].
40.   Stapleton *Correspondence of Canning,* II, p. 170 [**3:63**]. Wellington was not alone in his reaction. Mrs. Arbuthnot observed: 'In the House of Commons Mr. Canning made the most abominable speeches that ever were heard, I think . . . Mr. Canning was most loudly and vehemently cheered by the opposition, those on his own side were deadly silent.' *Journal of Mrs. Arbuthnot,* II, p. 64 [**6:18**]. The same point was made by Greville. 'Canning's speech the night before last most brilliant; much more cheered by the opposition than by his own friends.' G. L. Strachey and R. Fulford, eds *The Greville Memoirs,* 8 vols, Toronto, Macmillan (1938) 1, p. 161.
41.   24.1.1826, Stapleton *Canning and his Times* p. 493 [**3:70**].
42.   14.12.1826, Canning to Granville, Stapleton *Canning and his Times* pp. 546–7 [**3:70**].
43.   11.12.1826, *WND,* III, p. 484 [**2:43**].
44.   *Annual Register* (1827) p. 199.
45.   *Ibid.* pp. 199–200.
46.   15.12.1826, Granville to Canning, FO/27/352.
47.   19.12.1826, Canning to Granville, FO/27/347.
48.   22.12.1826, Granville to Canning, FO/27/352.
49.   26.12.1826, Canning to Granville, FO/27/347.
50.   12.12.1826, *Parliamentary Debates,* XVI, p. 395.
51.   Mayer *Origins of the New Diplomacy* p. 5 [**4:71**].
52.   22.12.1919, Hoare memo *DBFP,* 1st series, III, p. 738 [**3:95**].
53.   Jones *Whitehall Diary,* 1, p. 52 [**3:76**].
54.   Riddell *Lord Riddell's War Diary: 1914–18* London, Nicholson & Watson (1933) p. 308.
55.   30.5.1920, Riddell *Intimate Diary* p. 198 [**2:9**].
56.   26.1.1919, *Ibid.* p. 15.
57.   23.7.1920, *Ibid.* p. 224.
58.   R. R. James *Churchill: A Study in Failure 1900–39* London, Weidenfeld & Nicolson (1970) pp. 105–6.
59.   12.4.1918, Jones *Whitehall Diary,* 1, p. 59 [**3:76**].
60.   20.1.1918, Riddell *War Diary* p. 308 [**6:54**].
61.   C. Hardinge *Old Diplomacy* London, Murray (1947) p. 234.
62.   H. Nicolson *Curzon, The Last Phase: 1919–25,* London, Constable (1934) p. 57.
63.   J. M. Thompson *Russia, Bolshevism and the Versailles Peace* Princeton, Princeton UP (1962) p. 52.
64.   R. H. B. Lockhart *Memoirs of a British Agent* London, Putnum (1932) p. 198.
65.   Ullman *Intervention and the War* pp. 83–4 [**2:24**].
66.   6.11.1918, FO memo, FO/371/3344/W184126.
67.   Thompson *The Versailles Peace* p. 102 [**6:63**].
68.   20.7.1918, Jordon (Peking) to FO, FO/371/3324/W127058.
69.   15.11.1918, FO/371/3341/W189463.
70.   1.7.1918, FO/371/3286/W115514.
71.   4.6.1918, Wedgewood memo, FO/371/3297/W98763.
72.   Ullman gives a full account of Balfour's failure to accept the categorical statements by the Japanese to this effect. See *Britain and the Russian Civil War* pp. 202–6 [**1:14**].
73.   16.6.1918, FO/371/3286/W110740.
74.   Ullman *Intervention and the War* p. 211 [**2:24**].

75. Fowler *British–American Relations* p. 173 [**2:29**].

76. 18.8.1918, FO memo, FO/371/3324/W142775.

77. Mayer *Origins of the New Diplomacy* p. 252 [**4:71**].

78. *Ibid.* p. 252.

79. Adams *Great Britain and the American Civil War*, 1, p. 2 [**3:10**].

80. R. H. Jones 'Anglo-American Relations 1861–65 Reconsidered' *Mid-America*, 45 (1963) 36–49, p. 44.

81. C. P. Cullop *Confederate Propaganda in Europe 1861–65* Coral Gables, Miami UP (1971) p. 59.

82. L. B. Schmidt 'The Influence of Wheat and Cotton on Anglo-American Relations During the Civil War' *Iowa Journal of History and Politics,* 16 (1918) 401–39.

83. W. D. Jones 'The British Conservatives and the American Civil War' *American Historical Review,* 58 (1953) 527–43.

84. 15.8.1861, Newton *Lord Lyons,* 1, p. 48 [**4:12**].

85. 28.10.1862, *Russell Papers,* PRO/30/22/14D.

86. J. Morley *Life of William Ewart Gladstone* 3 vols, London, Macmillan (1904) 2, pp. 70–3.

87. R. Read *Cobden and Bright: A Victorian Political Partnership* London, Edward Arnold (1967) p. 219.

88. J. L. Hammond and M. R. D. Foot *Gladstone and Liberalism* 2nd edn, London, English UP (1966) p. 68.

89. A. C. Benson and Viscount Esher *Letters of Queen Victoria* 3 vols, London, Murray (1907) 3, p. 538.

90. Bell *Lord Palmerston* II, p. 275 [**2:15**].

91. 10.3.1862, *Parliamentary Debates,* CLXV, p. 1242.

92. Read *Cobden and Bright* p. 220 [**6:87**].

93. Jones 'Conservatives and the American Civil War' [**6:83**].

94. D. Southgate *The Most English Prime Minister: The Policies and Politics of Palmerston* London, Macmillan (1966) p. 455.

95. Duberman *Charles Francis Adams* p. 277 [**5:14**].

96. C. F. Adams 'A Crisis in Downing Street' *Massachusetts Historical Society Proceedings,* 48 (1914) 372–424, pp. 412–3.

97. *Ibid.* p. 418.

98. G. E. Buckle *The Life of Benjamin Disraeli,* 6 vols, London, Murray (1920) 4, p. 332.

99. 6.6.1861, *Parliamentary Debates,* CLXIII, p. 631.

100. Cited in Ahlbrandt *Policy of Simmering* p. 22 [**2:41**].

101. W. C. Churchill *The Gathering Storm* London, Cassell (1948) p. 166.

102. Northedge *The Troubled Giant* p. 439 [**2:35**].

103. 23.11.1936, FO/371/20586/W16391.

104. 23.11.1936, FO/371/20586/W16391.

105. 19.8.1936, FO/371/20533/W9717.

106. 11.4.1937, *Cabinet Papers,* 23/88.

107. K. W. Watkins *British Divided: The Effects of the Spanish Civil War and British Public Opinion* London, Nelson (1963).

108. 19.8.1936, FO/371/20533/W9717.

109. 30.6.1937, *Cabinet Papers,* 23/88.

110. Ahlbrandt *Policy of Simmering* p. 7 [**2:41**].

111. C. Attlee *As It Happened* London, Odhams (1954) p. 24.

112. This conception of individual interest specificity does not correspond to Eulau. He makes no provision for the situation where there are group and individual specific interests. Certainly, unanimity under such conditions is very precarious. In this instance, the Foreign Secretary eventually resigned.

113. Northedge *The Troubled Giant* p. 443 [**2:35**].

114. 6.8.1937, FO/371/21298/W15082.

115. 14.7.1937, FO/371/21341/W13250.

116. O. R. Holsti 'Individual Differences in the "Definition of the Situation"' *Journal of Conflict Resolution,* 14 (1971) 303–10, p. 303.

117. J. Coleman, R. R. Blake and J. Mouton 'Task Difficulty and Confronting Pressure' *Journal of Abnormal and Social Psychology*, 57 (1958) 120–2.

118. Different ways of aggregating articulated interests are discussed in G. Almond and J. S. Coleman *The Politics of Developing Areas* Princeton, Princeton UP (1960).

119. Rivera *Psychological Dimension of Foreign Policy* p. 27 [1:16].

CHAPTER 7

1. Simon *Models of Man* pp. 198–9 [2:59].

2. M. Deutsch and R. M. Krauss *Theories in Social Psychology* New York, Basic Books (1965) p. 70.

3. C. A. Kiesler, B. E. Collins and N. Miller *Attitude Change* New York, Wiley (1969) p. 201. Cognitive overlap means similarity.

4. Deutsch and Krauss *Social Psychology* p. 20 [7:2].

5. See L. Festinger *Conflict, Decision and Dissonance* Stanford, Stanford UP (1964).

6. Deutsch and Krauss *Social Psychology* pp. 70–1 [7:2].

7. L. Festinger *A Theory of Cognitive Dissonance* Stanford, Stanford UP (1962) p. 3.

8. M. Deutsch, R. M. Krauss and N. Rosenau 'Dissonance and Defensiveness' *Journal of Personality*, 30 (1962) 16–28, p. 17.

9. Festinger *Decision and Dissonance* p. 156 [7:5].

10. The problems associated with defining commitment will be examined in the next chapter.

11. Deutsch, *et al.* 'Dissonance and Defensiveness' p. 18 [7:8].

12. *Ibid.* p. 18.

13. Kiesler, *et al. Attitude Change* p. 159 [7:3].

14. P. Zimbardo and E. B. Ebbesen *Influencing Attitudes and Changing Behaviour* Reading, Addison–Wesley (1969) p. 83.

15. Deutsch and Krauss *Social Psychology* p. 73 [7:2].

16. R. P. Abelson 'Modes of Resolution of Belief Dilemmas' *Journal of Conflict Resolution*, 3 (1959) 343–52.

17. I. L. Janis 'Decisional Conflicts: A Theoretical Analysis' *Journal of Conflict Resolution*, 3 (1959) 6–27.

18. J. Galtung 'On the Effects of International Economic Sanctions With Examples from the Case of Rhodesia' *World Politics*, 19 (1967) 378–416.

19. E. Goffman 'On Cooling the Mark Out: Some Aspects of Adaptation to Failure' in A. M. Rose, ed. *Human Behaviour and Social Processes* London, Routledge (1962).

20. Abelson 'Belief Dilemmas' p. 346 [7:16].

21. 18.11.1823, *Journal of Mrs. Arbuthnot*, I, p. 275 [6:18].

22. 13.9.1826, Canning to A Court, FO/63/306.

23. 9.12.1826, *Journal of Mrs. Arbuthnot*, II, p. 62 [6:18].

24. 1.1.1827, *Correspondence of Canning*, II, p. 241 [3:63].

25. 9.12.1826, *Journal of Mrs. Arbuthnot*, II, p. 62 [6:18].

26. See Ch. 5.

27. 3.12.1826, A Court to Lamb, FO/63/310.

28. 2.12.1826, A Court to Canning, FO/63/310.

29. 8.12.1826, Canning to Granville, *Granville Papers*, PRO/30/29/8/12.

30. 7.11.1826, Canning to Granville, FO/27/347.

31. 11.12.1826, Canning to Granville, FO/27/347.

32. 1.12.1826, Canning to Granville, FO/27/347.

33. Stapleton, *Correspondence of Canning*, II, p. 164 [3:63].

34. 14.12.1826, Wellington to Canning, *WND*, III, p. 487 [2:43].

35. 21.12.1826, Wellington to Bathurst, *WND,* III, p. 500 [**2:43**].
36. 4.9.1827, Beresford to Wellington, *WND,* IV, p. 124 [**2:43**].
37. 13.12.1826, Wellington to Beresford, *WND,* III, pp. 485–7 [**2:43**].
38. 17.4.1862, Russell to Lyons, FO/5/818.
39. 6.3.1918, Balfour to Lockhart, FO/371/3285/W41335.
40. C. Lasch 'American Intervention in Siberia: A Reinterpretation' *Political Science Quarterly,* 77 (1962) 205–23.
41. 11.10.1918, FO/371/3344/W170806.
42. 23.7.1917, Lindley to FO, FO/371/2997/W159272.
43. 1.4.1918, Cecil to Cabinet, FO/371/3285/W58693.
44. 13.3.1918, Balfour to Lockhart, FO/371/3285/W43859.
45. 6.3.1918, FO/371/3285/W41335.
46. 6.3.1918, FO/371/3285/W41335.
47. Ullman *Intervention and the War* p. 88 [**2:24**].
48. 27.3.1918, FO/371/3285/W56595.
49. 27.3.1918, FO/371/3285/W56595.
50. 4.3.1918, FO to Lockhart, FO/371/3285/W40028.
51. W. A. Williams 'American Intervention in Russia' in D. Horowitz *Containment and Revolution* London, Blond (1967) p. 35.
52. 9.3.1918, FO/371/3285/W43859.
53. 18.3.1918, FO/371/3285/W50480.
54. Lockhart *Memoirs of a British Agent* p. 288 [**6:64**].
55. 18.3.1918, FO/371/3290/W51340.
56. 13.6.1918, FO/371/3333/W113345.
57. 22.3.1918, FO/371/3285/W53621.
58. Ullman *Intervention and the War* pp. 158–9 [**2:24**].
59. M. P. Price *My Three Revolutions* London, Allen & Unwin (1969) pp. 129–32.
60. 15.11.1918, FO/371/3344/W188386.
61. 26.9.1918, *Cabinet Papers,* WC/478.
62. 20.9.1918, *Cabinet Papers,* WC/475.
63. Price *My Three Revolutions* p. 127 [**7:59**].
64. S. R. Graubard *British Labour and the Russian Revolution* Cambridge, Harvard UP (1956) p. 62.
65. 19.8.1936, FO/371/20573/W9717.
66. 7.9.1936, FO/371/20575/W10779.
67. 8.2.1937, FO/371/21283/W2378.
68. 16.10.1936, FO/371/20580/W13680.
69. 17.10.1936, FO/371/20581/W13877.
70. 29.10.1936, A. Eden *Facing the Dictators* London, Cassell (1962) p. 412.
71. 18.11.1936, D. A. Puzzo *Spain and the Great Powers, 1936–41* New York, Columbia UP (1962) p. 101.
72. 23.11.1936, FO/371/20586/W16391.
73. 18.11.1936, FO/371/20585/W15880.
74. 8.7.1837, FO/371/21340/W12750.
75. Puzzo *Spain and the Great Powers* p. 101 [**7:71**].
76. 21.8.1936, FO/371/20578/W12363.
77. 21.8.1936, FO/371/20578/W12363.
78. 5.1.1937, FO/371/21318/W178.
79. 21.4.1937, FO/371/21332/W7951.
80. 19.11.1936, FO/371/20548/W16080.
81. 1.1.1937, FO/371/21317/W19.
82. 1.7.1937, FO/371/21340/W12962.
83. 6.7.1937, FO/371/21296/W13036.
84. 22.11.1936, *Cabinet Papers,* 24/265.
85. J. W. Brehm *A Theory of Psychological Reactance* New York, Academic (1966). It is argued that an individual experiences reactance when an option which was open to a decision-maker has been eliminated. Decision-makers endeavour to prevent options from being cut off.
86. 29.10.1936, Northedge *The Troubled Giant* p. 435 [**2:35**].

87. Eden *Facing the Dictators* p. 402 [**7:70**].
88. Ahlbrandt *The Policy of Simmering* p. 26 [**2:41**].
89. 18.11.1936, *Cabinet Papers*, 23/66.
90. 29.10.1936, Ahlbrandt *The Policy of Simmering* p. 25 [**2:41**].
91. 11.9.1936, *Ibid.* p. 16.

CHAPTER 8

1. For a discussion outside the social sciences see C. R. Roger 'Freedom and Commitment' *ETC.* 22 (1965) 133–51.
2. See D. H. Marlowe 'Commitment, Contract, Group Boundaries and Conflict' in J. H. Masserman, ed. *Violence and War* New York, Krune & Stratton (1963).
3. See H. S. Becker 'Notes on the Concept of Commitment' *American Journal of Sociology,* 66 (1960) 32–44; and E. Abramson, *et al.* 'Social Power and Commitment: A Theoretical Statement' *American Sociological Review,* 23 (1958) 15–22.
4. C. A. Kiesler 'Commitment' in R. P. Abelson *et al.* eds *Theories of Cognitive Consistency: A Source Book* Chicago, Rand McNally (1968).
5. T. C. Schelling *Arms and Influence* New Haven, Yale UP (1966).
6. Becker 'Commitment' p. 276 [**8:3**].
7. Deutsch and Krauss *Social Psychology* p. 73 [**7:2**].
8. J. W. Brehm and A. R. Cohen *Explorations in Cognitive Dissonance* New York, Wiley (1962) p. 9.
9. Festinger *Decision and Dissonance* p. 156 [**7:5**].
10. H. B. Gerard 'Basic Features of Commitment' in Abelson *Cognitive Consistency* p. 453 [**8:4**].
11. Zimbardo and Ebbesen *Changing Behaviour* [**7:14**].
12. Festinger *Decision and Dissonance* p. 9 [**7:5**].
13. Kiesler *Attitude Change* p. 200 [**7:3**].
14. Gerard 'Commitment' in Abelson *Cognitive Consistency* p. 457 [**8:4**].
15. Festinger *Decision and Dissonance* p. 156 [**7:5**].
16. Kiesler 'Commitment' p. 448 [**8:4**].
17. *Ibid.* p. 453.
18. Schelling *Arms and Influence* pp. 433–9 [**8:5**].
19. N. Miller 'As Time Goes By' in Abelson *Cognitive Consistency* p. 592 [**8:4**].
20. Becker 'Commitment' p. 38 [**8:3**].
21. G. A. Almond *The Appeals of Communism* Princeton, Princeton UP (1954) p. 297.
22. W. J. McGuire 'Inducing Resistance to Persuasion: Some Contemporary Approaches' in L. Berkowitz, ed. *Advances in Experimental Psychology* New York, Academic (1964).
23. K. Lewin 'Group Decision and Social Change' in E. E. Maccoby *et al.,* eds *Readings in Social Psychology* New York, Methuen (1959).
24. E. B. Bennett 'Discussion, Decision, Commitment and Consensus in "Group Decision" ', in Maccoby *Social Psychology* [**8:23**].
25. Kiesler 'Commitment' p. 453 [**8:4**].
26. J. D. Frank *Sanity and Survival: Psychological Aspects of War and Peace* London, Barrie (1968) p. 187.
27. A. Rapoport *Fights, Games and Debates* Ann Arbor, Michigan UP (1960) pp. 253–72.
28. F. Edmead 'Cutting Losses' Mimeo, London, Centre for the Analysis of Conflict (1968); and T. B. Roby 'Commitment' *Behavioural Science,* 5 (1960) 253–64.
29. S. S. Tomkins and C. E. Izard *Affect Cognition and Personality* New York, Springer (1965).
30. M. Deutsch and R. M. Krauss 'Studies of Interpersonal Bargaining' in M. Shubik, ed. *Game Theory and Related Approaches to Social Behavior* New York, Wiley (1964) p. 335.

31. L. Festinger, *et al. When Prophecy Fails* New York, Harper (1964).
32. W. Kornhauser 'Social Bases of Political Commitment' in Rose *Social Processes* [7:19].
33. 8.8.1826, A Court to Canning, FO/63/306; see also, 9.9.1826, Canning to A Court, FO/63/306.
34. 10.3.1826, A Court to Canning, FO/63/307.
35. 24.4.1826, A Court to Canning, FO/63/307.
36. 1.7.1826, A Court to Canning, FO/63/307.
37. 13.10.1826, A Court to Canning, FO/63/309.
38. 17.10.1826, A Court to Canning, FO/63/306.
39. 31.10.1826, Canning to A Court, FO/63/306.
40. 31.10.1826, Canning to A Court, FO/63/306.
41. 10.10.1826, Yonge *Earl of Liverpool*, III, p. 407 [**4:38**].
42. 27.10.1826, Stapleton *Canning and his Times* pp. 531–3 [**3:70**].
43. See Ch. 8.
44. 11.10.1826, Wellington to Liverpool, *WND*, III, pp. 417–8 [**2:43**].
45. 15.11.1826, Canning to A Court, FO/63/306. He indicated that the decision was partly dictated by economy and to assist the negotiations with France to remove the French troops from Spain, but it was also an effort to demonstrate confidence in the existing state of affairs in Portugal.
46. *Correspondence of Canning*, II, p. 171 [**3:63**].
47. 23.12.1826, Wellington to Bathurst, *WND*, III, pp. 503–4 [**2:43**].
48. 25.12.1826, Liverpool to Canning, *WND*, III, p. 505 [**2:43**].
49. 10.12.1826, Wellington to Bathurst, *WND*, III, p. 483 [**2:43**].
50. 28.12.1826, Bathurst to Wellington, *WND*, III, pp. 505–6 [**2:43**].
51. *Ibid.*
52. *Ibid.*
53. 10.12.1826, Wellington to Bathurst, *WND*, III, pp. 480–3 [**2:43**].
54. *Ibid.*
55. 1 and 3.1.1827, A Court to Canning, FO/63/319.
56. 20.1.1827, Yonge *Earl of Liverpool*, III, p. 419 [**4:38**].
57. *Ibid.*
58. 21.1.1827, Bathurst to Wellington, *WND*, III, pp. 555–7 [**2:43**].
59. Yonge, *Earl of Liverpool*, III, p. 425 [**4:38**].
60. 21.1.1827, Bathurst to Wellington, *WND*, III, pp. 555–7 [**2:43**].
61. 1.2.1827, Wellington to Bathurst, *WND*, III, pp. 580–1 [**2:43**].
62. 5.2.1827, Canning to Liverpool, Yonge *Earl of Liverpool* III, pp. 444–6 [**4:38**].
63. 6.2.1827, Liverpool to Canning *Ibid.* p. 449.
64. 18.5.1918, Ullman *Intervention and the War* pp. 169–70 [**2:24**].
65. 12.6.1918, Gregory memo, FO/371/3292/W104391.
66. 15.7.1918, FO to Lockhart, FO/371/3286/W122866.
67. 14.6.1918, Ullman *Intervention and the War* pp. 207–8 [**2:24**].
68. 24.6.1918, Fowler *British–American Relations* pp. 183–4 [**2:29**].
69. 28.6.1918, Ullman *Intervention and the War* p. 211 [**2:24**].
70. 17.5.1918, *Cabinet Papers*, WC/413.
71. 10.7.1918, Lloyd George to Reading, FO/371/3319
72. 9.7.1918, Fowler *British–American Relations* p. 190 [**2:29**].
73. *Ibid.* p. 190.
74. *Ibid.* p. 191.
75. *Ibid.* p. 191.
76. 18.8.1918, FO memo, FO/371/3324/W142775.
77. Fowler *British–American Relations* p. 193 [**2:29**].
78. 12.7.1918, Derby to FO, FO/371/3324/W122643.
79. 10.7.1918, FO to Reading, FO/371/3324/W120749.
80. Ullman *Intervention and the War* p. 224 [**2:24**].
81. 31.8.1918, Greene to FO, FO/371/3288/W150257.
82. Ullman *Intervention and the War* p. 259 [**2:24**].
83. Fowler *British–American Relations* p. 193 [**2:29**].
84. 5.8.1918, Balfour to Greene, FO/371/3324/W135964.

85. Ullman *Intervention and the War* p. 261 [**2:24**].
86. 1.7.1918, *Ibid.* p. 205.
87. 2.10.1918, *Cabinet Papers,* WC/481.
88. 7.8.1918, *Cabinet Papers,* WC/455.
89. 3.9.1918, Ullman *Britain and the Russian Civil War* p. 251 [**1:14**].
90. 10.9.1918, Barclay to FO, FO/371/3339/W154972.
91. 26.9.1918, Fowler *British–American Relations* p. 194 [**2:29**]
92. 21.8.1918, *Cabinet Papers,* WC/462.
93. 2.10.1918, Fowler *British–American Relations* p. 195 [**2:29**].
94. 2.10.1918, *Cabinet Papers,* WC/481.
95. 10.10.1918, Ullman *Intervention and the War* p. 253 [**2:24**].
96. 15.10.1918, FO/371/3344/W173318.
97. 6.6.1918, Ullman *Intervention and the War* p. 236 [**2:24**].
98. 18.10.1918, FO/371/3344/W174007.
99. 17.10.1918, Gregory memo, FO/371/3341/W172540.
100. 18.10.1918, Leaper memo, FO/371/3342/W174035.
101. 1.12.1919, Ullman *Britain and the Russian Civil War* p. 199 [**1:14**].
102. 4.7.1918, FO/371/3286/W117420.

CHAPTER 9

1. Roby 'Commitment' [**8:28**].
2. *Ibid.* p. 259.
3. Schelling *Arms and Influence* p. 65 [**8:5**]; Jervis *Logic of Images* pp. 155–65 [**3:4**].
4. F. B. Weinstein 'The Concept of Commitment in International Relations' *Journal of Conflict Resolution,* 13 (1969) 39–56, p. 40.
5. L. A. Coser 'The Termination of Conflict' in *Continuities in the Study of Social Conflict* New York, Free Press (1967) p. 42.
6. *Ibid.* p. 40.
7. F. C. Ikle *Every War Must End* New York, Columbia UP (1971) p. 16.
8. Dawson 'Forward Policy and Reaction' in Ward & Gooch *British Foreign Policy,* 3, p. 174 [**2:12**].
9. W. Millinship 'Nixon: No Pull-Out Until P.O.W.'s Are Free' *The Observer* 18.4.1971.
10. Festinger *Theory of Cognitive Dissonance* p. 130 [**7:7**]. For an analysis of the unfreezing of attitudes see K. Lewin 'Group Decision and Social Change' [**8:23**]. de Rivera looks at 'changing views of reality' in *Psychological Dimension of Foreign Policy* pp. 35–9 [**1:16**].
11. See J. K. Galbraith *The Affluent Society* Harmondsworth, Penguin (1958) pp. 138–40.
12. 11.3.1827, Lamb to Dudley, FO/72/327; and 16.3.1827, A Court to Dudley, FO/63/321.
13. 21.3.1827, *The Times.*
14. 14.5.1827, Dudley to A Court, FO/63/318.
15. 14.5.1827, *Ellenborough Papers,* PRO/30/12, 24/7.
16. 14.5.1827, Dudley to A Court, FO/63/318.
17. 29.5.1827, Dudley to Granville, FO/27/361.
18. 8.6.1827, *Parliamentary Debates,* XVII, pp. 1161–2.
19. pp. 1162–3.
20. 8.1.1827, A Court to Canning, FO/63/319.
21. 21.3.1827, *The Times.*
22. 19.3.1827, Dudley to Lamb, FO/63/318.
23. 20.2.1827, Canning to A Court, FO/63/318.
24. 8.6.1827, *Parliamentary Debates,* XVII, p. 1168.
25. 20.2.1827, Canning to A Court, FO/63/318.

26. 1.2.1827, Lamb to A Court, FO/63/320.
27. 5.7.1827, Dudley to A Court, FO/63/318.
28. 20.2.1827, Canning to A Court, FO/63/318.
29. 10.9.1827, A Court to Dudley, FO/72/329.
30. 1.6.1827, Lamb to Dudley, FO/72/328.
31. 16.8.1827, Dudley to A Court, FO/63/318.
32. 6.9.1827, Dudley to Wellesley, FO/7/196.
33. 5.10.1827, Granville to Dudley, FO/27/366.
34. 24.8.1827, E. Ashley *Life and Correspondence of Palmerston* 2 vols. London, Bentley (1879) I, p. 114.
35. 25.10.1827, Wellington to Bathurst *Report on the Manuscripts of Earl Bathurst* London, Historical Manuscripts Commission (No. 76) pp. 646–7.
36. 30.7.1827, Bathurst to Wellington, *WND,* IV, pp. 67–8 [**2:43**].
37. 14.5.1827, Dudley to A Court, FO/63/318.
38. 14.9.1827, Dudley to Granville, FO/27/362.
39. 21.11.1827, Dudley to Granville, FO/27/362.
40. 6.2.1828, Law *Earl of Ellenborough,* I, p. 20 [**2:44**] for a report of the French King's speech; see *Parliamentary Debates,* XVIII, p. 3 for the British King's speech.
41. 9.8.1827, Henry Unwin Addington wrote to Stratford Canning, 'It was Portugal that killed him, or rather, it was the double office of Premier and still Foreign Secretary.' He went on to say that the week before he died, 'Mr. Canning was then occupied in drawing up a minute for the Cabinet on Portuguese affairs, and, I am told by those who have seen it, a masterly one. For four days before his death, Mr. Canning had been in most singular state of half-wandering of mind. Every thought was evidently turned to one subject and that a public one [Portugal] and he was incessantly dictating something to Stapleton that showed perfect clearness of conception of mind, but inability of the physical powers to produce it in that shape.' Aspinall 'The Formation of Canning's Ministry' pp. 279–80 [**6:30**]. Croker also gives an account of Canning's last days and he mentions the long paper on Portugal, L. J. Jennings *The Croker Papers* [**4:67**].
42. 25.10.1827, Wellington to Bathurst *Report on Manuscripts of Earl of Bathurst* pp. 646–7 [**9:35**].
43. 2.11.1827, Huskisson to Clinton *Huskisson Papers* BM 38752, XIX.
44. 22.11.1827, Dudley to A Court, FO/63/318.
45. 3.12.1827, Granville to Dudley, FO/27/367.
46. 1.6.1827, Granville to Dudley, FO/27/364.
47. 1.1.1828, Dudley to Granville, FO/27/374.
48. 7.12.1827, Dudley to Granville, FO/27/362.
49. 1.3.1828, Lamb to Dudley, FO/63/332.
50. 23.1.1828, Huskisson to Clinton *Huskisson Papers,* BM 38754, XXI.
51. 8.3.1828, Lamb to Dudley, FO/63/332.
52. 12.3.1828, Lamb to Dudley, FO/63/332.
53. 25.1.1828, Huskisson to Seaford *Huskisson Papers,* BM 38754, XXI.
54. 18.3.1828, Law *Earl of Ellenborough,* I, pp. 61–2 [**2:44**].
55. 24.3.1828, *Ibid.* p. 67.
56. 18.3.1828, *Ibid.* pp. 62–3.
57. 18.3.1828, *Ibid.* pp. 62–3.
58. 16.7.1828, *Parliamentary Debates,* XIX, pp. 1735–6.
59. 19.3.1828, Dudley to Lamb, FO/63/331.
60. 14.11.1918, *Cabinet Papers,* WC/502.
61. 10.12.1918, *Cabinet Papers,* WC/511.
62. 14.11.1918, *Cabinet Papers,* WC/502.
63. 10.12.1918, *Cabinet Papers,* WC/511.
64. Ullman *Britain and the Russian Civil War* p. 27 [**1:14**].
65. 17.1.1919, Gregory minute, FO/371/3950/W11019.
66. 12.2.1919, *Cabinet Papers,* WC/531.
67. 12.2.1919, *Parliamentary Debates,* CXII, p. 165.
68. Ullman *Britain and the Russian Civil War* p. 83 [**1:14**].
69. Thompson *The Versailles Peace* p. 216 [**6:63**].

70. 20.6.1918, Ullman *Britain and the Russian Civil War* p. 211 [**1:14**].
71. *Ibid.* p. 182.
72. *Ibid.* p. 185.
73. James *Churchill: Study in Failure* p. 115 [**6:58**].
74. J. N. Rosenau 'Pre-Theories and Theories in Foreign Policy' in Farrell *Comparative and International Politics* [**Intro:3**], states that 'Idiosyncratic variables include all those aspects of a decision-maker – his values, talents, and prior experiences – which distinguish his foreign policy choices or behavior from those of every other decision-maker.' p. 43.
75. 3.2.1920, *DBFP*, 1st series, XII, p. 559 [**3:95**].
76. 9.2.1920, *Ibid.* p. 560.
77. *Ibid.* p. 560.
78. 21.1.1919, Thompson *The Versailles Peace* pp. 107–8 [**6:63**].
79. 22.9.1919, F. Owen *Tempestuous Journey: Lloyd George – His Life and Times* New York, McGraw–Hill (1955) pp. 519–20; and Riddell *Intimate Diary* p. 15 [**2:9**].
80. M. Hankey *The Supreme Control at the Paris Peace Conference* London, Allen & Unwin (1963) p. 70; Thompson *The Versailles Peace* p. 138 [**6:63**].
81. 23.12.1918, *Cabinet minutes*, WC45, in FO/371/3346/W213100.
82. 31.12.1918, *Cabinet minutes*, WC48, in FO/371/3954/W213100.
83. 25.9.1919, *Cabinet Papers*, 624/Appendix 2.
84. 5.10.1919, Churchill to Curzon, FO/371/3961/W137299.
85. 12.10.1919, FO/371/3979/W157024.
86. 14.7.1919, *Cabinet Papers*, 592.
87. *Ibid.*
88. 18.10.1918, FO memo, FO/371/3344/W174114.
89. 19.10.1918, FO memo, FO/371/3344/W175192.
90. 20.12.1918, FO/371/3346/W210041.
91. 31.12.1918, *Cabinet Papers*, WC/48.
92. 16.2.1919, Lloyd George to Kerr, FO/371/3956/W26048.
93. 16.1.1919, S. P. Tillman *Anglo–American Relations at the Paris Peace Conference* Princeton, Princeton UP (1961) p. 137.
94. 22.1.1919, Thompson *The Versailles Peace* p. 109 [**6:63**]
95. 15.5.1919, Colonel Wedgewood *Parliamentary Debates*, CXV, p. 1878.
96. 3.3.1919, *Parliamentary Debates*, CXIII, p. 84.
97. Bullitt, the American representative who went to Russia, claimed that Lloyd George lied in the House of Commons on the question of a conference with the Bolsheviks. See W. H. Wickham Steed *Through Thirty Years: A Personal Narrative* New York, Doubleday (1924).
98. 23.5.1919, *DBFP*, 1st series, III, p. 317 [**3:95**].
99. Thompson *The Versailles Peace* p. 148 [**6:63**].
100. 6.11.1918, FO memo, FO/371/3344/W184126.
101. 13.11.1918, Ullman *Britain and the Russian Civil War* p. 12 [**1:14**].
102. 23.7.1919, *Cabinet Papers*, WC/598.
103. 25.3.1919, Ullman *Britain and the Russian Civil War* p. 228 [**1:14**].
104. 6.7.1919, *DBFP*, 1st series, III, p. 419 [**3:95**].
105. 27.7.1919, *Ibid.* p. 530.
106. 9.8.1919, *Ibid.* p. 479.
107. 19.8.1919, *Ibid.* pp. 532–3.
108. 29.8.1919, *Ibid.* pp. 531–2.
109. 27.11.1919, *Ibid.* pp. 666–7.
110. 12.2.1919, *Parliamentary Debates*, CXII, p. 195.
111. 15.11.1919, *DBFP*, 1st series, III, pp. 647–8 [**3:95**].
112. 12.4.1861, Russell to Lyons, FO/5/754.
113. 28.7.1862, Russell to Lyons, FO/5/820.
114. 30.6.1862, *Parliamentary Debates*, CLXVII, p. 1214.
115. 18.7.1862, *Parliamentary Debates*, CLXVIII, p. 537.
116. 14.9.1862, Palmerston to Russell, *Russell Papers*, 30/22/14D.
117. 17.9.1862, Russell to Palmerston, *Russell Papers*, 30/22/14D.

118. 25.9.1862, Adams 'A Crisis in Downing Street' p. 401 **[6:96]**.
119. 30.9.1862, Palmerston to Russell, *Russell Papers*, 30/22/14D.
120. 23.9.1862, *Ibid.*
121. 22.9.1862, *Ibid.*
122. Duberman *Charles Francis Adams* p. 284 **[5:14]**.
123. 2.10.1862, Palmerston to Russell, *Russell Papers*, 30/22/14D.
124. 3.10.1862, *Ibid.*
125. 8.10.1862, *Ibid.*
126. Adams 'A Crisis in Downing Street' p. 424 **[6:96]**.
127. 20.6.1862, Adams 'A Crisis in Downing Street' p. 401 **[6:96]**.
128. 7.8.1862, Russell to Lyons, FO/5/820.
129. 21.10.1862, Palmerston to Russell, *Russell Papers,* 30/22/14D.
130. 2.11.1862, Palmerston to Russell, *Russell Papers,* 30/22/14D.
131. 2.2.1863, Lyons to Russell, FO/5/876.
132. 24.10.1862, Palmerston to Russell, Adams 'A Crisis in Downing Street' p. 402 **[6:96]**.
133. *Ibid.* p. 405.
134. 28.10.1862, Russell to Grey, G. P. Gooch *Later Correspondence of Lord John Russell* London, Longman, Green (1925) pp. 331–2.
135. 26.10.1862, Russell to Lewis, *Russell Papers*, 30/22/14D.
136. Adams 'A Crisis in Downing Street' p. 405 **[6:96]**.
137. 23.10.1862, Palmerston to Russell, *Russell Papers,* 30/22/14D.
138. Duberman, *Charles Francis Adams,* p. 482 **[5:14]**.
139. J. Morley *Life of Gladstone,* 2, pp. 81–3 **[6:86]**.
140. 15.6.1938, *Cabinet Papers,* 23/94.
141. 28.2.1938, FO/371/21638/W2799.
142. 1.3.1938, FO/371/21638/W2974.
143. 2.3.1938, *Cabinet Papers,* 23/92.
144. 19.7.1938, FO/371/22651/W10243.
145. 26.7.1938, FO/371/21335/W10558.
146. 15.3.1938, FO/371/21639/W3404.
147. 7.6.1937, FO/371/21335/W11004.
148. 30.9.1937, FO/371/21345/W17863.
149. 20.10.1937, *Cabinet Papers,* 23/89.
150. 8.1.1937, *Cabinet Papers,* 24/267.
151. 30.6.1937, FO/371/21296/W12187.
152. 14.12.1936, *Cabinet Papers,* 24/265.
153. 20.11.1937, FO/371/21384/W21389.
154. 17.12.1937, FO/371/21302/W22244.
155. 23.12.1937, FO/371/21302/W22043.
156. 20.2.1938, *Cabinet Papers,* 23/92.
157. 4.10.1938, FO/371/22654/W13067.
158. 11.3.1938, *Cabinet Papers,* 24/275.
159. 15.3.1938, FO/371/21639/W3404.
160. 23.3.1938, *Cabinet Papers,* 23/93.
161. 21.5.1938, FO/371/21645/W6590.
162. 16.4.1938, Ahlbrandt *Policy of Simmering* p. 122 **[2:41]**; see also, 4.10.1938, FO/371/22654/W13261.
163. 1.10.1938, FO/371/22654/W13025.
164. 4.10.1938, FO/371/22654/W13067.
165. 26.10.1938, *Cabinet Papers,* 23/96.
166. 12.11.1938, FO/371/21344/W15176.
167. 19.11.1938, FO/371/22656/W14998.
168. 25.1.1939, FO/371/24115/W1471.
169. Jones, for example noted: 'Every member of the Cabinet regards himself as an authority on the French Revolution', *Whitehall Diary,* 1, p. 59 **[3:76]**.
170. D. T. Campbell 'Ethnocentric and Altruistic Motives' in D. Levine *The Nebraska Symposium on Motivation,* 8 (1965) 283–311, p. 298.

CHAPTER 10

1. See Appendix 3 for a statement of the preliminary model and the reformulated model.
2. L. A. Coser *The Functions of Social Conflict* London, Routledge (1956) p. 129.
3. Devereux 'Parson's Sociological Theory' p. 57 [**5:8**].
4. See A. K. Cohen 'The Study of Social Disorganization and Deviant Behavior' in L. A. Coser and B. Rosenberg, eds *Sociological Theory* London, Macmillan (1969).
5. J. W. Burton *Conflict and Communication: The Use of Controlled Communication in International Relations* London, Macmillan (1969) p. x.
6. *Ibid.* p. xi.
7. *Ibid.* p. 122.
8. O. R. Holsti and R. C. North 'The History of Human Conflict' p. 156 [**1:21**].
9. S. Hoffmann 'Henkin and Falk: Mild Revolutionary and Mild Reformer' *Journal of International Affairs,* 24 (1970) 18–26, p. 122.
10. R. W. Tucker 'Review of Kaplan and Katzenbach' *Journal of Conflict Resolution,* 7 (1963) 69–95, p. 73.
11. R. J. Barnet 'Toward the Control of International Violence: The Limits and Possibilities of Law' in C. E. Black and R. A. Falk, eds *The Future of the International Legal Order* Princeton, Princeton UP (1971) p. 382.
12. E. W. Lefever *Uncertain Mandate: Politics of the U.N. Congo Operation* New York, John Hopkins UP (1967) p. 119.
13. *Ibid.* p. 125.
14. Scott *Revolution in Statecraft* p. 103 [**1:8**].
15. H. Cantril *The Human Dimension: Experience in Policy Research* New Brunswick, Rutgers UP (1967) pp. 1–5.
16. D. Horowitz *From Yalta to Vietnam* Harmondsworth, Penguin (1967) p. 158.
17. A. B. Bozeman *The Future of Law in a Multicultural World* Princeton, Princeton UP (1971) p. 192. The citation comes from *Pravda,* 25.9.1968.
18. J. S. Mill 'A Few Words on Non-intervention' in *Dissertations and Discussions* London, Longmans (1867) pp. 176–7.
19. R. Higgins 'Internal War and International Law' in Black and Falk *International Legal Order* p. 115 [**10:11**].
20. *Ibid.* p. 118.
21. L. P. Bloomfield and A. C. Leiss *Controlling Small Wars: A Strategy for the 1970's* London, Allen Lane (1970) p. 279.
22. A. L. Burns and N. Heathcote *Peace-Keeping by UN Forces* London, Pall Mall (1963) p. 18.
23. D. Howarth *The Observer,* 20.4.1969, p. 10.
24. Burton *Conflict and Communication* pp. 93–4 [**10:5**].
25. Temperley *Foreign Policy of Canning* p. 18 [**3:21**].
26. *Ibid.* p. 18.
27. Y. H. Ferguson 'Reflections on the Inter-American Principle of Non-intervention: A Search for Meaning in Ambiguity' *Journal of Politics,* 32 (1970) 628–54, p. 649.
28. N. G. Onuf 'The Principle of Nonintervention, the United Nations, and the International System' *International Organization,* 25 (1971) 209–27, pp. 225–6.

Name Index

Subject Index